BAMS:

The Essential Guide to

Becoming a Master Student

Doug Toft
Contributing Editor

Based on Dave Ellis'
Becoming a Master Student

WADSWORTH
CENGAGE Learning™

AUSTRALIA • BRAZIL • JAPAN • KOREA • MEXICO • SPAIN • UNITED KINGDOM • UNITED STATES

WADSWORTH
CENGAGE Learning™

BAMS: *The Essential Guide to Becoming a Master Student*

Editor in Chief: PJ Boardman

Senior Publisher: Lyn Uhl

Director of College Success: Annie Todd

Senior Sponsoring Editor: Shani Fisher

Senior Development Editor: Julia Giannotti

Assistant Editor: Daisuke Yasutake

Editorial Assistant: Cat Salerno

Marketing Manager: Kirsten Stoller

Marketing Communications Manager:
    Talia Wise

Project Manager, Editorial Production:
    Cathy L. Brooks

Creative Director: Rob Hugel

Art Director: Jill Haber

Print Buyer: Julio Esperas

Permissions Editor: Mary Dalton Hoffman

Text Designer: Susan Gilday

Art Editor: Karen Lindsay

Photo Researcher: Marcy Kagan

Copyeditor: Marianne L'Abbate

Cover Designer: Rokusek Design

Cover Image: ©Randy Faris/2007/Corbis

Compositor: Pre-PressPMG

For product information and technology assistance, contact us at
Cengage Learning Customer & Sales Support, 1-800-354-9706.
For permission to use material from this text or product,
submit all requests online at **www.cengage.com/permissions.**
Further permissions questions can be e-mailed to
permissionrequest@cengage.com.

Library of Congress Control Number: 2008934443

Student Edition:
ISBN-13: 978-0-547-19233-8
ISBN-10: 0-547-19233-9

Wadsworth
10 Davis Drive
Belmont, CA 94002-3098
USA

Cengage Learning is a leading provider of customized learning solutions with office locations around the globe, including Singapore, the United Kingdom, Australia, Mexico, Brazil, and Japan. Locate your local office at **international.cengage.com/region.**

Cengage Learning products are represented in Canada by Nelson Education, Ltd.

For your course and learning solutions, **visit academic.cengage.com.** Purchase any of our products at your local college store or at our preferred online store **www.ichapters.com.**

Printed in the United States of America
1 2 3 4 5 6 7 12 11 10 09 08

BAMS:
THE ESSENTIAL GUIDE TO BECOMING A MASTER STUDENT

"I really enjoyed reading this book. I think it is excellent. What I like most from this book is the realistic connection between the articles, experiments, and concepts. I think that most of my students would really connect and interact well with these chapters.
—OSCAR R. VELASQUEZ, EL PASO COMMUNITY COLLEGE

"From the TOC, I would say that this text covers the basic topics many first-year students need to help them be successful in college—both academically and personally. Encouraging students to reflect upon these topics and take them seriously will help them get the most out of their college experiences, and will lead to the acquisition of skills that will serve them well for their entire lives.
--SUSAN E. DUTCH, WESTFIELD STATE COLLEGE

Brief Table of Contents

www.cengage.com/success/masterstudent/BAMSEssentials

- Read the book online!
- Watch videos about students' struggles and successes with timely issues such as test taking, managing stress, staying healthy, managing money, and more!
- Manage your money and time with helpful templates.

Contents

Discover...
Commitment

Consider the possibility that you can create the life of your dreams. You can think new thoughts, say new things, and do what you never believed you could do. The possibilities are endless.

There are people who scoff at the suggestion that they can create the life of their dreams. These people have a perspective that is widely shared. If you share this perspective, set it aside.

You are about to start a journey that is so miraculous and full of wonder that your imagination at its most creative moment cannot encompass it. Paths are open to lead you to worlds beyond your wildest dreams.

If this sounds like a pitch for the latest recreational drug, it is. That drug is adrenaline, and it is automatically generated by your body when you are learning, growing, taking risks, and discovering new worlds inside and outside your skin.

If you use this book fully—if you actively read the contents, do the exercises, and apply the suggestions—you'll expand your possibilities. You'll learn new ways to set goals, plan your time, make your memory more effective, improve your reading skills, take useful notes, and raise your grades.

That's not all. You can also learn to think for yourself, resolve conflict, enjoy better relationships, live with vibrant health, and end money worries. All are steps on the path of becoming a master student.

That all sounds great, you might say. But how do I begin? Well, for starters, you can turn to the next page.

Create Master Students

power process

START WITH THE DISCOVERY WHEEL

The Discovery Wheel is an opportunity to tell the truth about the kind of person you are—and the kind of person you want to become.

This tool is based on a fundamental idea: Success in any area of life starts with telling the truth about what *is* working—and what *isn't* working—in our lives right now. When we acknowledge our strengths, we gain an accurate picture of what we can accomplish. When we admit that we have a problem, we free up energy to find a solution.

It's that simple. The Discovery Wheel gives you an opportunity to sit back for a few minutes and think about yourself. This is not a test. There are no trick questions. There are no grades. The answers you provide will have meaning only for you.

HOW THE DISCOVERY WHEEL WORKS

The purpose of the Discovery Wheel is to gain awareness of your current behaviors—especially the kind of behaviors that affect your success in school. With this knowledge, you can choose new behaviors and start to enjoy new results in your life.

During this exercise, you will fill in a circle similar to the one on this page. The closer the shading comes to the outer edge of the circle, the higher the evaluation of a specific skill. In the example below, the student has rated her reading skills low and her note-taking skills high.

The terms *high* and *low* are not positive or negative judgments. When doing the Discovery Wheel, you are just making observations about yourself. You're like a scientist running an experiment—just collecting data and recording the facts. You're not evaluating yourself as good or bad.

Also remember that the Discovery Wheel is not a permanent picture of who you are. It is a snapshot in time—a picture of what you're doing right now. You'll do this exercise again, near the end of this book and at the end of the course. That means you will have a chance to measure your progress. So be honest about where you are right now.

To succeed at this exercise, tell the truth about your strengths. This is no time for modesty! Also, lighten up and be willing to laugh at yourself. A little humor can make it easier to tell the truth about your areas for improvement.

To begin this exercise, read the following statements and give yourself points for each one. Use the point system described below. Then add up your point total for each category and shade the Discovery Wheel on page 3 to the appropriate level.

5 points
This statement is always or almost always true of me.

4 points
This statement is often true of me.

3 points
This statement is true of me about half the time.

2 points
This statement is seldom true of me.

1 point
This statement is never or almost never true of me.

1. _____ I can clearly state my overall purpose in life.

2. _____ I can explain how school relates to what I plan to do after I graduate.

3. _____ I can clearly describe what I want to experience in major areas of my life, including my career, relationships, financial well-being, and health.

4. _____ I consider different points of view and choose from alternative solutions.

5. _____ I use my knowledge of learning styles to support my success in school.

_____ Total score (1) *Purpose*

1. _____ I set goals and periodically review them.

2. _____ I plan each day and often accomplish what I plan.

3. _____ I have enough energy to study, attend classes, and enjoy other areas of my life.

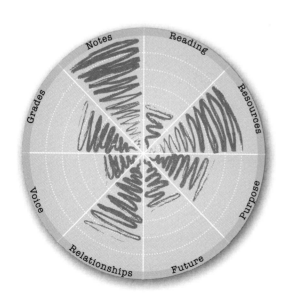

4. _____ I have a plan for making enough money to complete my education.

5. _____ I make regular deposits to a savings account.

_____ Total score (2) *Resources*

1. _____ When reading, I ask myself questions about the material.

2. _____ When I read, I am alert and awake.

3. _____ I relate what I read to my life.

4. _____ I select reading strategies to fit the type of material I'm reading.

5. _____ When I don't understand what I'm reading, I note my questions and find answers.

_____ Total score (3) *Reading*

1. _____ When I am in class, I focus my attention.

2. _____ I take notes in class.

3. _____ I can explain various methods for taking notes, and I choose those that work best for me.

4. _____ I distinguish key points from supporting examples.

5. _____ I put important concepts into my own words.

_____ Total score (4) *Notes*

1. _____ The way that I talk about my value as a person is independent of my grades.

2. _____ I often succeed at predicting test questions.

3. _____ I review for tests throughout the term.

4. _____ I manage my time during tests.

5. _____ I use techniques to remember key facts and ideas.

_____ Total score (5) *Grades*

1. _____ I plan for large writing assignments.

2. _____ When researching, I find relevant facts and properly credit their sources.

3. _____ I write brief, clear, and useful e-mail messages.

4. _____ I edit my writing for clarity, accuracy, and coherence.

5. _____ I prepare and deliver effective speeches.

_____ Total score (6) *Voice*

1. _____ Other people tell me that I am a good listener.

2. _____ I communicate my upsets without blaming others.

3. _____ I build rewarding relationships with people from other backgrounds.

4. _____ I effectively resolve conflict.

5. _____ I regularly take on a leadership role.

_____ Total score (7) *Relationships*

1. _____ I have a detailed list of my skills.

2. _____ I have a written career plan and update it regularly.

3. _____ I use the career-planning services offered by my school.

4. _____ I participate in internships, extracurricular activities, information interviews, and on-the-job experiences to test and refine my career plan.

5. _____ I have declared a major related to my interests, skills, and core values.

_____ Total score (8) *Future*

Using the total score from each category above, shade in each section of the blank Discovery Wheel on the next page. If you want, use different colors. For example, you could use green for areas you want to work on.

REFLECT ON YOUR DISCOVERY WHEEL

Now that you have completed your Discovery Wheel, spend a few minutes with it. Get a sense of its weight, shape, and balance. How would it sound if it rolled down a hill?

Next, complete the following sentences in the space below. Just write down whatever comes to mind. Remember, this is not a test.

The two areas in which I am strongest are . . .

_____

_____

The two areas in which I want to improve are . . .

_____

_____

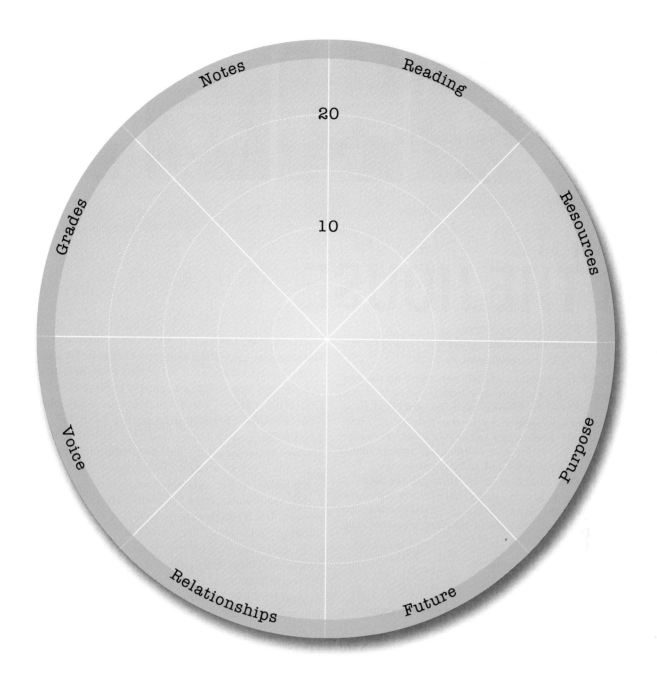

Finally, take about 15 minutes to do a "textbook reconnaissance." First, scan the table of contents for this book. Next, look at every page in the book. Move quickly. Skim the words in bold print. Glance at pictures. You'll see pages with ideas that might help you with the areas you want to improve. Find five such ideas that look especially interesting to you. Write the page number and a short description of each idea in the space below.

Page number   **Description**

_____

_____

_____

_____

_____

You're One Click Away . . .
from doing this exercise online.

MASTER STUDENT
IN THE HOUSE

In 1482, Leonardo da Vinci wrote a letter to a wealthy baron, applying for work. In excerpted form, he wrote,

"I can contrive various and endless means of offense and defense . . . . I have all sorts of extremely light and strong bridges adapted to be most easily carried . . . . I have methods for destroying every turret or fortress . . . . I will make covered chariots, safe and unassailable . . . . In case of need I will make big guns, mortars, and light ordnance of fine and useful forms out of the common type." And then he added, almost as an afterthought, *"In times of peace I believe I can give perfect satisfaction and to the equal of any other in architecture . . . can carry out sculpture . . . and also I can do in painting whatever may be done."*

The Mona Lisa, for example.

This book is about something that cannot be taught. It's about becoming a master student.

A *master* is a person who has attained a level of skill that goes beyond technique. For a master, methods and procedures are automatic responses to the task at hand. The master carpenter is so familiar with her tools, they are part of her. To a master chef, utensils are old friends. Because these masters don't have to think about the details of the process, their work seems to happen by itself.

Mastery can lead to flashy results—an incredible painting, for example, or a gem of a short story. In basketball, mastery might result in an unbelievable shot at the buzzer. For a musician, it might be the performance of a lifetime, the moment when everything comes together.

The master student is in all of us. By design, human beings are learning machines. We have an innate ability to learn, and all of us have room to grow and improve. The

unknown does not frighten the master student. In fact, she welcomes it—even the unknown in herself. The master student is open to changes in her environment and in herself.

One sign of mastery is a sense of profound satisfaction. Distractions fade. Time stops. Work becomes play. After hours of patient practice, after setting clear goals and getting precise feedback, the master has learned to be fully in control. At the same time, he lets go of control. Results happen without effort, struggle, or worry.

Of course, those statements make no sense. Mastery, in fact, doesn't make sense. It defies analysis. It cannot be explained. But it can be experienced. You could call it "flow" or being "in the zone." Or—*mastery*.

In each chapter of this book, you'll find a Power Process—a short article describing attitudes and actions that contribute to mastery. Look for them and try them out in your own life. Find out which of these articles work for you and adopt them or modify them to fit your own style.

Also look for the endless diversity of master students. They are old and young, male and female. They exist in every period of history. And they come from every culture, race, and ethnic group.

As you meet people, look for those who excel at learning. In fact, there's one living inside your skin. No matter what your past experiences, the master student within survives. The articles and exercises in this book offer one path to this discovery. Use them to discover the master student in you.

 You're One Click Away . . .
from 10 qualities of a master student.

Success essentials

Success is no mystery. Successful people have left clues—*many* clues, in fact. There are thousands of articles and books that give tools, tips, techniques, and strategies for **success.** Do a Google search on *success* and you'll get over 300 million results.

If that sounds overwhelming, don't worry. Success is simply the process of setting and achieving goals. And the essentials of that process can be described in 10 words or less.

Actually, three words: *Discovery. Intention. Action.*

Success is really that simple. It's not always easy, but there are no secrets about the process. If you did the Discovery Wheel on page 3, then you already got a taste of it.

Continue the process. Throughout this book are exercises labeled Commit to Action. These exercises are your chance to experience the essentials of success in three stages.

1. WRITE DISCOVERY STATEMENTS

The first stage is a Discovery Statement. These often begin with a prompt: "I discovered that ... ." Here is an opportunity to reflect on "where you are." Discovery Statements are about your current strengths and areas for improvement.

Discovery Statements can also be descriptions of your feelings, thoughts, and behavior. Whenever you get an "aha!" moment—a flash of insight or a sudden solution to a problem—put it in a Discovery Statement.

You'll find that your first year in higher education is a time that's especially rich with discoveries. Capture them. Build a habit of self-awareness that can last for the rest of your education and throughout your career.

To write effective Discovery Statements, remember the following.

Record specifics. If you spent 90 minutes chatting online with a friend instead of reading your anatomy text, write about it. Include the details, such as when you did it, where you did it, and how it felt. Record your observations quickly, as soon as you make them.

Suspend judgment. When you are discovering yourself, be gentle. Suspend self-judgment. If you continually judge your behaviors as "bad" or "stupid," your mind will quit making discoveries. For your own benefit, be kind.

Be truthful. Suspending judgment helps you tell the truth about yourself. "The truth will set you free" is a saying that endures for a reason. The closer you get to the truth, the more powerful your Discovery Statements will be. And if you notice that you are avoiding the truth, don't blame yourself. Just tell the truth about it.

2. WRITE INTENTION STATEMENTS

Intention Statements can be used to alter your course. They are statements of your commitment to do a specific task or achieve a longer-range goal. While Discovery Statements promote awareness, Intention Statements are blueprints for action. The two processes reinforce each other.

Make intentions positive. The purpose of writing intentions is to focus on what you want rather than what you don't want. Instead of writing "I will not fall asleep while studying accounting," write "I intend to stay awake when studying accounting."

Make intentions observable. Rather than writing "I intend to work harder on my history assignments," write "I intend to review my class notes and write summary sheets of my reading." Writing summary sheets is a visible, physical action. There's no fooling yourself about whether you get it done.

Make intentions achievable. Give yourself opportunities to succeed. Break large goals into small, specific tasks that can be accomplished quickly. Timelines can help. For example, if you are assigned to write a paper, break the assignment into small tasks and set a precise due date for each one. You might write: "I intend to select a topic for my paper by 9 a.m. Wednesday."

3. ACT NOW!

Carefully crafted Discovery Statements are a beauty to behold. Precise Intention Statements can inspire awe. But neither will be of much use until you put them into action.

Life responds to what you *do.* Successful people are those who consistently produce the results that they want. And results follow from specific, consistent behaviors. If you want new results in your life, then adopt new behaviors.

Even simple changes in behavior can produce results. If you feel like procrastinating, then tackle just one small, specific task related to your intention. Find something you can complete in five minutes or less and do it *now.* For example, access just one Website related to the topic of your next assigned paper. Spend just three minutes previewing a reading assignment. Taking "baby steps" like these can move you into action with grace and ease.

Changing your behavior might lead to feelings of discomfort. Instead of reverting back to your old behaviors, befriend the yucky feelings. Tell yourself you can handle the discomfort just a little bit longer. Act on your intention. You will be rewarded.

Values ... the invisible link to success

Values are the things in life that you want for their own sake. Values shape your attitudes, direct your goals, and guide your moment-by-moment choices. Success is about living a life that aligns with your values. This book is based on a particular value system, one that's behind the suggestions on every page. Each Power Process describes one of these values, based on the idea that a master student is:

• Intentional (see the Power Process: "Discover what you want," page 13).

• Courageous (see the Power Process: "Risk being a fool," page 25).

• Able to focus attention (see the Power Process: "Be here now," page 43).

• Open-minded (see the Power Process: "Ideas are tools," page 59).

• A problem-solver (see the Power Process: "Love your problems," page 77).

• Detached (see the Power Process: "Detach," page 93).

• Contributing (see the Power Process: "Find a bigger problem," page 109).

• Aware of the power of language (see the Power Process: "Choose your conversations," page 125).

• In control (see the Power Process: "I create it all," page 145).

Values are the essence of a liberal education. Courses in the humanities, arts, and sciences give you a chance to think critically and creatively about values. In creeds, scriptures, philosophies, myths, and sacred stories, the human race has left a vast and varied record of what's worth living for. Examine them. Based on what you learn, write Discovery Statements that put *your* values into words. Follow up with Intention Statements about how you'll act on your values today.

 You're One Click Away . . .

from more information about the value of higher education.

REPEAT THE CYCLE

The process of discovery, intention, and action is a cycle. First, you write Discovery Statements about where you are now. Next, you write Intention Statements about where you want to be, and the specific steps you will take to get there. Follow up with action—the sooner, the better.

Then start the cycle again. Write Discovery Statements about whether you act on your Intention Statements— and what you learn in the process. Follow up with more Intention Statements about what you will do differently in the future. Then move into action and describe what happens next.

This process never ends. Each time you repeat the cycle, you get new results. It's all about getting what you want and becoming more effective in everything you do. This is the path of mastery, a path that you can travel for the rest of your life.

 You're One Click Away . . .

from more suggestions for Discovery, Intention, and Action Statements.

Commit to thinking

Every day we get opportunities to stretch and strengthen our thinking muscles. Advertisers want us to spend money on their products. Political candidates want us to "buy" their stands on the issues. Teachers want us to agree that their classes are vital to our success. Parents want us to accept their values. Broadcasters want us to spend our time in front of the radio or television, consuming their programs and not those of the competition. Authors want us to read their books, and almost everyone wants us to check out their Website.

All these people are making claims. Accepting any of them at face value might not be in your best interest.

During a 1954 interview, Ernest Hemingway told a writer for the *Atlantic* magazine that every writer needs a "built in, automatic crap detector."[1] If only he'd lived to see the Internet. All information is not created equal, and the sheer quantity of it means that we must become vigilant to avoid getting fooled.

In addition, technology sometimes fails. What happens if you depend on the GPS system on your car and you come to a road closure that the computer does not register? You'll need to think critically about alternate routes—and fast—to stay on course.

Protect yourself from misinformation and technical glitches with a lifelong commitment to thorough thinking. This is a skill with two major elements: critical thinking and creative thinking.

ESSENTIALS OF CRITICAL THINKING

How can you apply critical thinking to your everyday life? Start by testing logic and examining evidence about the information that you receive.

Test logic. Logic is a set of principles for sound reasoning—the process of arriving at conclusions and choosing among alternatives. When you find yourself drowning in the seas of nonsense, knowledge about logic can serve as your lifeboat. Be on the lookout for errors in logic such as the following:

- *Jumping to conclusions.* Jumping to conclusions is the only exercise that some lazy thinkers get. This fallacy involves drawing conclusions without sufficient evidence. Take the bank officer who hears about a student failing to pay back an education loan. After that, the officer turns down all loan applications from students. This person has jumped to a conclusion about all students based on one negative example.

- *Attacking the person.* This mistake is common at election time. An example is the candidate who claims that her opponent has failed to attend church regularly during the campaign. This may be true—and it can also be irrelevant to the true issues in the campaign.

- *Pointing to a false cause.* The fact that one event follows another does not mean that the two events have a cause-effect relationship. All we can really say is that the events may be correlated. As children's vocabularies improve, for example, they can get more cavities. This does not mean that increasing your vocabulary causes cavities. Instead, the increase in cavities is due to other factors, such as physical maturation and changes in diet.

- *Thinking in "all-or-nothing" terms.* Consider these statements: *Doctors are greedy . . . . You can't trust politicians . . . . Students these days are just in school to get high-paying jobs; they lack ideals . . . . Homeless people don't want to work.* Such opinions ignore individual differences, claiming that all members of a group are exactly alike. They also ignore key facts—for instance, that some doctors volunteer their time at free medical clinics, and that many homeless people are children who cannot support themselves.

Examine evidence. Responsible writers and speakers back up their main points with evidence—facts, examples, and expert opinions. Examine each point by asking the following questions:

- Are all or most of the relevant facts presented?
- Are the facts consistent with each other?
- Are facts presented accurately—or in a misleading way?
- Are enough examples included to make a solid case for the point?
- Do the examples truly support the main point?
- Are the examples typical or unusual?
- If an expert is quoted, is this person credible—truly knowledgeable about the topic?
- Is the expert biased? For example, is the expert paid to represent the views of a corporation that is promoting a product or service?
- Is the expert quoted accurately?

ESSENTIALS OF CREATIVE THINKING

Most of us think of creativity as a skill possessed only by poets, novelists, painters, or musicians. But creativity is also practiced by the accountant who finds a new tax deduction for a client, the doctor who diagnoses a rare illness, and the mechanic who diagnoses an intermittent noise in your car engine. Use the following suggestions to unleash creative thinking in any area of your life.

Collect ideas. We all have ideas. People who treat their ideas with care are often labeled "creative." They recognize ideas, record them, and then refine them.

To create good ideas, collect ideas—*lots* of them. Carry index cards and a small pen in your pocket, purse, or bag.

Use these simple tools to capture ideas for your courses, your career plan, your relationships, your next semester or next vacation. You can also stockpile ideas in a personal journal that you maintain on paper or on a computer. Review it regularly for key discoveries and intentions.

Alex Osborn introduced the concept of brainstorming in his 1953 book *Applied Imagination*.[2] This is still a popular technique for creative thinking. The purpose of brainstorming is simply to generate as many ideas as possible. To brainstorm, state a question that you want to answer. Then set a time limit and then write down every answer that pops into your head. Accept every idea. Quantity, not quality, is the goal. This is a powerful technique to use in groups.

Refine ideas. After a brainstorming session or creative frenzy of writing in your journal, take a break to clear your head. Then come back to your newfound and unrefined ideas. Sift, review, evaluate, and edit. Toss out any truly nutty ideas, but not before you give them a chance.

This step involves molding and shaping a rough-cut idea into a polished creation. The necessary skills include the ability to spot assumptions, apply the rules of logic, weigh evidence, separate fact from opinion, organize thoughts, and avoid careless errors. Write about your ideas in more detail and ask other people for input. All this can be challenging. It can also be energizing and fun.

 You're One Click Away . . .

from more strategies for critical and creative thinking.

Attitudes of a critical thinker

The American Philosophical Association invited a panel of 46 scholars from the United States and Canada to come up with answers to the following two questions: "What is college-level critical thinking?" and "What leads us to conclude that a person is an effective critical thinker?" After two years of work, this panel concluded that critical thinkers share seven core attitudes:

Critical thinkers are **truth-seeking**: "Let's follow this idea and see where it leads, even if we feel uncomfortable with what we find out."

Critical thinkers are **open-minded**: "I have a point of view on this subject, and I'm anxious to hear yours as well."

Critical thinkers are **analytical**: "Taking this stand on the issue commits me to take some new actions."

Critical thinkers are **systematic**: "The speaker made several interesting points, and I'd like to hear some more evidence to support each one."

Critical thinkers are **self-confident**: "After reading this book for the first time, I was confused. I'll be able to understand it after studying the book some more."

Critical thinkers are **inquisitive**: "When I saw that painting for the first time, I wanted to know what was going on in the artist's life when she painted it."

Critical thinkers are **mature**: "I'll wait to reach a conclusion on this issue until I gather some more facts."[3]

y r u @ school?

IN EACH CHAPTER of this book is at least one Critical Thinking Experiment. These exercises offer you a chance to actually apply one or more of the strategies presented in "Commit to thinking" on page 7:

- Test logic

- Examine evidence

- Collect ideas

- Refine ideas

This first experiment in thinking has two parts. The first involves collecting ideas, while the second calls for refining them.

Part 1

Select a time and place when you know you will not be disturbed for at least 20 minutes. Relax for two or three minutes, clearing your mind. Then complete the following sentences with any ideas that enter your mind. Continue on additional paper as needed.

What I want from my education is ...

When I complete my education, I want to be able to . . .

I also want . . .

Part 2

After completing Part 1, take a short break. Reward yourself by doing something that you enjoy. Then review the above list of things that you want from your education. See if you can summarize them in a one-sentence, polished statement. This will become a statement of your purpose for taking part in higher education.

Write several drafts of this mission statement, and review it periodically as you continue your education. With each draft, see if you can capture the essence of

what you want from higher education—and from your life. Make it one that you can easily memorize, one that sparks your enthusiasm and makes you want to get up in the morning.

You might find it difficult to express your purpose statement in one sentence. If so, write a paragraph or more. Then look for the sentence that seems most charged with energy for you.

Following are some sample purpose statements:

- My purpose for being in school is to gain skills that I can use to contribute to others.

- My purpose for being in school is to live an abundant life that is filled with happiness, health, love, and wealth.

- My purpose for being in school is to enjoy myself by making lasting friendships and following the lead of my interests.

Write at least one draft of your purpose statement below:

 You're One Click Away . . .
from more sample purpose statements.

MASTER STUDENTS
IN ACTION

The master student is not a vague or remote ideal. Master students move freely among us. Consider the following examples of people who have found success in their own way.

Jennifer Jarding

College: Kilian Community College, Sioux Falls, SD

Major: Chemical Dependency Counseling

Goals: My goals in life today are simple really; I want to be the best me I can be. I have set an educational goal to finish my associate's degree in chemical dependency counseling. I have a financial goal to become debt-free. I have set personal goals to have better relationships with my family. I aspire to be a more spiritually grateful and giving person as well.

Advice: My advice to new college students is to follow your dreams and don't underestimate yourself. Be aware of the reality of the study time that goes along with the classes you take. Sit in the front row. Ask questions. Participate often. Remember that you are paying for this so you want to get as much out of it as possible. Not every class you take will be fun, but the satisfaction that comes from achieving definitely is.

Jennie Long

College: Seminole Community College, Sanford, FL

Major: Nursing

Goals: My goals are to become a registered nurse, to be a mentor to other adult learners, and to strive to learn something new every day. Every day I wake up determined to stay on track toward my goals. I am attending classes and studying to obtain my nursing degree and I keep abreast of new medical discoveries. Also, I try to encourage someone else each day to pursue their goals.

Advice: It is important to keep a positive attitude and have an open mind while in college. Be willing to learn about new ideas and concepts and then apply this knowledge every day.

Alex Denizard

College: Technical Career Institute—College of Technology, New York, NY

Major: Networking Technology

View of Success: The feeling of accomplishment is a feeling like no other. To know what it is like to finish what you started and what it took to get there . . . I believe that success is not about what you have gained, but what you have gone through to achieve success.

Advice: Look ahead and never give up on yourself. Know that you are worth something and that no one can tell you any different. Think about all you have been through. Think about what it took to get you thus far in your life. Don't think of being in college as a burden; on the contrary, think of it as just one more step toward your many other goals. It's not the getting there, it's the getting there.

Liz Murray

Liz Murray's life is about setting outrageous goals and meeting them. This is true even though she grew up in a household where both parents were addicted to cocaine and money was scarce. By age 16, Liz was living on the streets of New York City and had lost her mother to AIDS. Liz sensed that her life was now in her own hands. She vowed that she would create a new future for herself.

Though she had poor grades, Liz entered the Humanities Preparatory Academy in Manhattan at age 17. Because she was homeless, she spent long hours studying in a stairwell at school. The hard work paid off: She graduated in just two years.

After hearing about a college scholarship offered by the *New York Times* to needy students, Liz decided to apply. It worked. The *Times* awarded her a scholarship, and with that financial support, Liz set a goal to attend Harvard University. She succeeded, enrolling there in the fall of 2000. After taking time off to care for her father, she transferred to Columbia University and today works as an inspirational speaker.

Cesar Chavez

Cesar Chavez dedicated his life to improving conditions for migrant workers in the United States. Chavez knew those conditions well. He, along with his four siblings and parents, entered the ranks of migrant workers during the Great Depression after the family lost their farm.

When Chavez was 12, his father and uncle joined a union, part of the Congress of Industrial Organizations, that was organizing fruit workers. Chavez learned firsthand about strikes, boycotts, fasts, and other nonviolent means of creating social change.

He never forgot those lessons. After serving in the United States Navy, Chavez returned to the fields as a community organizer. Despite the fact that he'd attended 65 elementary schools and never graduated from high school, Chavez cofounded and led the United Farm Workers (UFW) until his death in 1993. The UFW gained a national profile in 1968 after organizing a successful grape boycott that led to new contracts for migrant workers. Today the UFW is the largest union of its kind, with members in ten states.

Sampson Davis

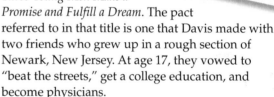

"Determination is simply fixing your mind on a desired outcome, and I believe it is the first step to a successful end in practically any situation," wrote Sampson Davis, coauthor of *The Pact: Three Young Men Make a Promise and Fulfill a Dream*. The pact referred to in that title is one that Davis made with two friends who grew up in a rough section of Newark, New Jersey. At age 17, they vowed to "beat the streets," get a college education, and become physicians.

To become a physician, Sampson had to take a state board exam. The first time he took the exam, Sampson failed it. Instead of giving up, he got help. He started seeing a counselor. He also asked for support from George Jenkins and Rameck Hunt, the friends with whom he'd made "the pact." He took the exam again and passed.

Today Davis is a board-certified emergency physician at St. Michael's Medical Center in Newark. Along with Jenkins and Hunt, he directs The Three Doctors Foundation, which offers mentoring, educational programs, and health services to kids from inner-city communities.

 You're One Click Away . . .
from more personal profiles in the Master Student Hall of Fame.

Commit to Action

Earn back the price of this book—and more

THIS BOOK IS WORTHLESS—*if* you just read it. On the other hand, if you read and reread this book, mark it up, argue with it, and actively experiment with its suggestions, you can create benefits that go way beyond the cover price.

This is not a sales pitch. You already bought this book. Now get the most from it. You can do this through the cycle of discovery, intention, and action.

Discovery Statement

Begin with the power of commitment—specifically, your commitment to using this book. In the interest of saving your valuable time and energy, take the time now to declare your level of involvement up front.

From the numbered choices below, choose the sentence that best describes your commitment to using this book. Write the number in the space provided at the end of the list.

1 "Well, I'm reading this book right now, aren't I?"

2 "I will read the book, think about it, and do the exercises that look interesting."

3 "I will read the book, do most of the Critical Thinking Experiments and Commit to Action exercises, and use some of the techniques."

4 "I will study this book, do most of the Critical Thinking Experiments and Commit to Action exercises, and experiment with many of the techniques in order to discover what works best for me."

5 "I will use this book as if the quality of my education depends on it—doing all the Critical Thinking Experiments and Commit to Action exercises, experimenting with most of the techniques, inventing techniques of my own, and planning to reread this book in the future."

Enter your commitment level and today's date here:

Commitment level _____ Date _____

If you selected commitment level 1, consider passing this book on to a friend. If your commitment level is 2 or 3, then continue to approach this book with an open mind and experiment with its suggestions. If your commitment level is 4 or 5, you've demonstrated an attitude that promotes success.

Intention Statement

Now, raise the stakes. Scan the entire text and look for suggestions that could help you save money or increase income in significant ways. For example:

- Use "Commit to Action: Give your goals some teeth" on page 27 to create a detailed plan for getting a job—or gaining a skill that will make it easier for you to get a higher-paying job.

- See "Campus resources—you paid for 'em, now use 'em" on page 42 to discover a free campus service that you'd have to pay for if you were not a student.

- See "Commit to Action: Plan your career now" on page 138 to begin creating your dream job.

In the space below, write your ideas. Use additional paper as needed.

To create real financial value from my experience of this book, I intend to . . .

Next, make a note on your calendar to return to this exercise.

Action Statement

After you've had some time to test it out, review the Intention Statement that you wrote in the space above. Did you turn your intention into action? If so, then describe exactly what you did and the results that you achieved. If not, then write a new intention in the space below and declare your level of commitment to getting it done.

To create real financial value from my experience of this book, I intend to . . .

 You're One Click Away . . .

from another look at the cash value of your classes—"Education by the hour"

Discover
what you want

KNOWING WHERE WE WANT to go increases the probability that we will arrive at our destination. Discovering what we want makes it more likely that we'll attain it. Once our goals are defined precisely, our brains reorient our thinking and behavior. We're well on the way to actually *getting* what we want.

Suppose that you ask someone what she wants from her education and you get this answer: "I plan to get a degree in journalism with double minors in earth science and Portuguese so that I can work as a reporter covering the environment in Brazil." Chances are you've found a master student. The details of a person's vision offer a clue to her mastery.

Discovering what you want greatly enhances your odds of succeeding in higher education. Many students quit school simply because they are unsure of their goals. If you know what you want, you can constantly look for connections between your passions and your coursework. The more connections you discover, the more likely you'll stay in school—and succeed.

To move into action, use this book. It's filled with places—including the Discovery Wheel and Commit to Action exercises—that encourage you to discover what you want to have, do, and be. Fill up those pages. Then turn your discoveries into immediate action. Every day, do one thing—no matter how simple or small—that takes you one step closer to your goals. Watch your dreams evolve from fuzzy ideals into everyday realities.

 You're One Click Away . . .
from more ideas about discovering what you want.

1 Discover...
Your Style

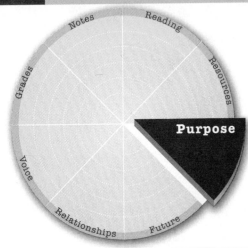

The Discovery Wheel on page 1 includes a section titled Purpose. If you did the Discovery Wheel exercise, you'll recall that one of the items in this section is: "I use my knowledge of learning styles to support my success in school." That's what this chapter is all about.

Before you read the rest of this chapter, take a few minutes to go beyond your initial responses to the Discovery Wheel. Reflect on the Skills Snapshot below to take a closer look at your skills. Complete these statements honestly, then flip to the articles or exercises highlighted in this chapter for strategies that will promote your success.

Skills SNAPSHOT

If someone asked me, "What do you mean by learning styles, and can you give me an example?" I'd say . . . *

check out:
"Discover the natural learner in you," page 15

check out:
"Seeing the cycle of learning in action," page 17

To discover my preferred styles of learning, I . . . *

check out:
Commit to Action: "Explore your learning styles," page 18

When I get confused about something I'm supposed to learn, I usually . . . *

check out:
"45 ways to get smart," page 20

check out:
Critical Thinking Experiment #2: "Discover the joy of bafflement," page 19

*I apply my knowledge of learning styles by using certain strategies, such as . . . *
*When I study or work with people whose styles differ from mine, I usually respond by . . .

check out:
Commit to Action: "Create value from learning styles," page 22

check out:
" 'It's just who I am' — resolving differences in style," page 23

To overcome any fear of exploring new learning styles, I . . . *

check out:
Power Process: "Risk being a fool," page 25

DISCOVER THE
NATURAL LEARNER IN YOU

As an infant, you learned to walk. As a toddler, you learned to talk. By the time you reached age 5, you'd mastered many of the skills needed to thrive in a world filled with adults. Never in your life will you again learn so much in so short a time. And you learned it all without formal instruction, without lectures, without books, without conscious effort, and without fear.

Shortly after we start school, however, something happens to us. Somehow we start forgetting about the master student inside us. Even under the best teachers, we experience the discomfort that sometimes accompanies learning. We start avoiding situations that might lead to embarrassment. We turn away from experiences that could lead to mistakes. Slowly we restrict our possibilities and potentials.

As people grow older, they sometimes accumulate a growing list of ideas to defend, a catalog of familiar experiences that discourages them from learning anything new. Some people even "learn" that they are slow learners. If they learn it well enough, their behavior comes to match such labels.

However, the story doesn't end there. You can open a new chapter in your life, starting today. You can rediscover the natural learner within you.

WHAT HAPPENS WHEN WE LEARN

When we learn well, says psychologist David Kolb, two things initially happen.[1] First, we notice new information. We *perceive* the steady stream of events in our world. Second, we make sense of the information. We *process* it in a way that helps us understand what's going on and makes the information our own.

Some people like to absorb information through their five senses. These people perceive through **concrete experience** meaning they learn by getting directly involved in new experiences. When solving problems, they rely on their intuition as much as intellect. These people typically function well in unstructured learning classes that allow them to take the initiative.

Other people take in information best when they can analyze, intellectualize, and create theories. These people perceive by **abstract conceptualization**. Often these people take a scientific approach to problem solving and excel in traditional classrooms.

There are also differences in the way that people process experiences. Some people favor processing information by jumping in and doing things immediately, also known as **active experimentation**. These people do not mind taking risks as they attempt to make sense of things

because this helps them learn. They are results-oriented and look for practical ways to apply what they have learned.

Then there are people who prefer to stand back, watch what is going on, and think about it. These people process information by **reflective observation**. Often they consider several points of view as they attempt to make sense of things and can generate many ideas about how something happens. They value patience, good judgment, and a thorough approach to understanding information.

FOUR KEY QUESTIONS THAT REVEAL YOUR STYLE

All this psychological theory can get a little heady. However, you can make it practical simply by remembering four questions that apply to learning anything:

1. Why? Some of us question why we are learning things. We seek a purpose for information and a personal connection with the content. We want to know why the course content matters and how it challenges or fits in with what we already know.

2. What? Some of us crave information. When learning something, we want to know critical facts. We seek a theory to explain what's happening and see what experts have to say on the topic. We break a subject down into its key components or steps and master each one.

3. How? Some of us hunger for an opportunity to try out what we're studying. We ask ourselves: "Does this idea make sense? Will it work, and, if so, *how* does it work? How can we use this information?" We want to apply and test theories. We excel at taking the parts or key steps of a subject and assembling them into a meaningful sequence.

4. What if? Some of us get excited about going beyond classroom assignments. We aim to adapt what we're learning to another course or to a situation at work or at home. By applying our knowledge, we want to make a difference in some area that we care about. We ask ourselves: "What if we tried . . . ?" or "What if we combined . . . ?"

Each of these questions is based on a unique set of preferences relating to concrete experience, reflective observation, abstract conceptualization, and active experimentation. You might find yourself asking one of these key questions more often than the others. This is a clue to your favorite *learning style*, or preferred ways of perceiving and processing.

To get the most value from knowing your learning style, look for ways to apply this knowledge in school and at work. Remember that the term *favorite learning style* refers to the way you've typically approached learning in the past. It does not describe the way you have to learn in the future. No matter what aspects of learning you've tended to prefer, you can develop the ability to use different styles of learning. Doing so offers many potential benefits. For example, you can excel in different types of courses, seize more opportunities for learning outside the classroom, and expand your options for declaring a major and choosing a career.

ASSOCIATE WITH STUDENTS WHO HAVE DIFFERENT LEARNING STYLE PROFILES

If your instructor asks your class to form groups to complete an assignment, avoid joining a group in which everyone shares your preferred styles of learning. Get together with people who both complement and challenge you. This is one way you can develop skills in all learning styles and become a more well-rounded student.

RECOVERING YOUR GENIUS

Your preferred style represents the way you've typically approached learning in the past. However, it does *not* describe the way you have to learn in the future. Starting today, you can ask all four questions when you learn—and engage in a full range of activities that lead to answers.

Think of the benefits. By developing several styles of learning, you can excel in many types of courses. You can seize more opportunities for learning inside and outside the classroom. You can expand your options for declaring a major and choosing a career. You can more fully understand people who learn differently from you, opening new dimensions of your professional and personal relationships.

Above all, you can recover your natural gift for learning. You can rediscover a world where the boundaries between learning and fun, between work and play, all disappear. While immersing yourself in new experiences, you can blend the sophistication of an adult with the wonder of a child. This is the path that you can travel for the rest of your life, and any of the articles and exercises in this chapter can lead to your next step.

 You're One Click Away . . .

from more information on Kolb's ideas, the VAK system, and multiple intelligence.

More views of learning styles

There are many theories of learning styles, and any of them can support your success in school. In addition to David Kolb's ideas about experiential learning, for example, you might hear about the VAK system.[2] This theory focuses on preferences related to:

- Seeing, or *visual* learning
- Hearing, or *auditory* learning
- Movement, or *kinesthetic* learning

In addition, Howard Gardner of Harvard University believes that no single measure of intelligence can tell us how smart we are. In his theory of multiple intelligences, Gardner describes:[3]

Verbal/linguistic intelligence—learning through speaking, writing, reading, and listening.

Mathematical/logical intelligence—skill at working with numbers, logic, problem solving, patterns, relationships, and categories.

Visual/spatial intelligence—a preference for learning through images, including charts, graphs, maps, mazes, tables, illustrations, art, models, puzzles, and costumes.

Bodily/kinesthetic intelligence—learning through physical activity such as role playing, games, and model building.

Musical/rhythmic intelligence—a preference for expression through songs and rhythms.

Intrapersonal intelligence—self-motivation combined with a deep awareness of personal feelings and values.

Interpersonal intelligence—skill at cooperative learning and awareness of the feelings of others.

Naturalist intelligence—a love of the outdoors and skill at observing nature.

SEEING THE CYCLE OF LEARNING IN ACTION

Asking the four questions discussed in "Discover the natural learner in you" on page 15 will take you through a cycle of learning. To see how it works, consider how this cycle applies to note taking.

ASKING *WHY?*

Answers to this question help you discover a *purpose* for what you're learning. This involves *planning*—the ability to choose from alternative behaviors, predict their consequences, and monitor your progress in meeting your goals.

Example: When reading about note-taking strategies in Chapter Four, consider the positive differences that more effective notes could make. These might include better retention of key concepts, more efficient review for tests, and higher grades.

ASKING *WHAT?*

Answers to this question help you master the *content*—key ideas, information, and skills. This involves *analysis*, the ability to separate a whole subject into its parts.

Example: Review the strategies in Chapter Four and list five that interest you. From this list, choose one that you'd be willing to start in the next 24 hours and use consistently for at least one week. Choose a strategy with the potential to make an immediate and positive difference in your academic success.

ASKING *HOW?*

Answers to this question help you find ways to *practice* what you learn. This involves *synthesis*, the ability to combine parts to form a meaningful whole.

Example: Think of a specific time and place to use your chosen strategy for note taking, or schedule a time in your calendar to do it. Be sure to build in opportunities for feedback on your performance. For instance, ask one of your instructors or another student to review your notes and evaluate them for clarity and accuracy. The key is to get feedback promptly—but not so soon that it interferes with your practice.

ASKING *WHAT IF?*

Answers to this question help you find ways to *apply* new ideas and skills in several areas of your life.

Example: At the end of the week, evaluate how well the strategy for note taking worked for you. If it worked well, consider making it a habit. If the suggestion did not work well, ask why. Perhaps you can modify the suggestion so that it becomes a better fit for you.

Note: The above questions imply a cycle of activities that you can repeat to learn any skill: Choose a suggestion to practice—a strategy that's aligned with your goals. Plan where and when you will act on that suggestion. Then evaluate how well the suggestion worked for you. Repeating this cycle of choosing, applying, and evaluating suggestions can quickly increase your success in higher education—and in any career that you choose.

 You're One Click Away . . .
from more suggestions for using learning styles to succeed in school.

You're using the cycle of learning right now

Just by using this book, you are actively experimenting with the "big four" questions that relate to learning styles:

- At the beginning of each chapter, you complete a Skills Snapshot designed to connect the chapter to your current life experience and help you find benefits from this book (answers to Question 1: Why?).

- Next, you read articles that are filled with ideas, information, and suggestions that can help you experience success (answers to Question 2: What?).

- You practice new skills by doing the Critical Thinking Experiments and Commit to Action exercises (answers to Question 3: How?).

- Finally, at the end of each chapter, you reflect on a Power Process that puts the chapter content in a bigger context and suggests further applications (answers to Question 4: What if?).

Commit to Action
Explore your learning styles

RECALL A RECENT LEARNING experience—inside *or* outside the classroom—that you enjoyed. Then read through the following list and circle the number of any statements that apply to you. (Remember that this is not a formal assessment of learning styles. Instead, it offers a way to start thinking about the ways that you prefer to learn.)

1. I enjoy learning in ways that involve all my senses.
2. When solving problems, I often rely on intuition as much as logical reasoning.
3. I function well in unstructured learning situations where I can take the initiative.
4. Before taking action, I prefer to watch and ponder what's going on.
5. I like to consider different points of view and generate many ideas about how things happen.
6. When trying to understand information, I value patience, good judgment, and being thorough.
7. I enjoy intellectual analysis and like to view information from many perspectives.
8. I value the scientific approach—using theories to make sense of experiences, creating predictions based on those theories, and testing those predictions.
9. I usually excel in learning situations that are well-defined and highly structured.
10. Activity helps me learn, so I like to jump in and start doing things immediately.
11. I like to use learning to produce new results in my life.
12. I look for practical ways to apply what I learn.

In the above list, items 1–3 describe a preference for learning through concrete experience. Items 4–6 illustrate learning through reflective observation. Items 7–9 describe conceptualization, and items 10–12 refer to active experimentation.

After reflecting on your responses to these items, review "Discover the natural learner in you" on page 15. After you finish, complete the following sentences.

Discovery Statement

When reflecting on the ways I prefer to learn, I discovered that I . . .

Intention Statement

To take advantage of the ways I prefer to learn, I will apply this discovery to the way that I approach one of my current courses. Specifically, I intend to . . .

Action Statement

To act on my intention within the next 24 hours, I will . . .

You're One Click Away . . .

from more suggestions for exploring your learning styles.

Discover the joy of bafflement

THE POET WENDELL BERRY wrote about confusion as an opportunity to learn: "When we no longer know what to do, we have come to our real work, and when we no longer know which way to go, we have begun our real journey. The mind that is not baffled is not employed. The impeded stream is the one that sings."[4] We're all going to experience periods of confusion. You can start preparing for them now—and even learn to welcome confusion as a path to thinking.

This three-step exercise is about becoming confused on purpose—and seeing what possibilities open up as a result. In the process you will generate and collect new ideas—one of the core thinking skills presented in "Commit to thinking" on page 7.

1 In the space below, write something that you're sure is true about yourself (for instance: "I'm sure that I will never take a philosophy course").

2 Next, take the same statement and put a question mark after it (for example: "I would never take a philosophy course?"). You might need to rephrase the question for grammatical sense.

3 Are you feeling confused? If so, great. Go a little deeper. Brainstorm some questions related to the one you just wrote. ("In what ways would taking a philosophy course serve my success in school?"

"Could taking a philosophy course help me with designing software?")

Write your questions in the space below.

4 Finally, circle one of the questions you wrote in step 3. For 10 minutes, brainstorm answers to this question. Write down all your ideas. Don't worry about whether they're logical or practical. Just see if you can get into a zone of pure creative thinking.

You're One Click Away . . .
from more strategies for creative thinking.

45 WAYS TO GET SMART

There's a saying: "Experience is the best teacher." However, 20 years of experience might include just one year of learning—followed by 19 years of rote repetition.

One path to a lifetime of continuous learning is to seek out experiences that match your preferred learning style. Another is to develop additional styles, which increases your flexibility as a learner.

Following is a list of 45 strategies for achieving both of those goals. Any of them can help you answer the four questions presented in "Discover the natural learner in you" on page 15. In addition, these strategies draw on multiple intelligences along with visual, auditory, and kinesthetic learning.

Don't feel pressured to use all of the strategies listed below or to tackle them in order. As you read, note the strategies you think will be helpful. Pick one and start using it today. When it becomes a habit, come back to this article and select another one. Repeat this cycle and enjoy the results as they unfold in your life.

1. Engage your emotions by reading a novel or seeing a film related to your courses.

2. Interview an expert in the subject you're learning or a master practitioner of a skill you want to gain.

3. Conduct role plays, exercises, or games based on your courses.

4. Conduct an information interview with someone in your chosen career or shadow that person for a day on the job.

5. Look for a part-time job, internship, or volunteer experience that complements what you do in class.

6. Deepen your understanding of another culture and extend your language skills by studying abroad.

7. Keep a personal journal and write about connections between your courses.

8. Form a study group to discuss and debate topics related to your courses.

9. Set up a Website, computer bulletin board, e-mail listserv, or online chat room related to your major.

10. Create analogies to make sense of concepts; for instance, see if you can find similarities between career planning and putting together a puzzle.

11. Visit your course instructor during office hours to ask questions.

12. During social events with friends and relatives, briefly explain what your courses are about.

13. Take notes on your reading in outline form; consider using word processing software with an outlining feature.

14. Take ideas presented in your textbooks or lectures and translate them into visual form—tables, charts, diagrams, and maps (see Chapter Four).

15. Take hand-drawn visuals and use computer software to re-create them with more complex graphics and animation.

16. Make predictions based on theories you learn and see if events in your daily life confirm your predictions.

17. Highlight, underline, and write notes in your textbooks.

18. Code your notes by using different colors to highlight main topics, major points, and key details.

19. Before you try a new task, visualize yourself doing it well.

20. Be active in ways that support concentration; for example, pace as you recite, read while standing up, and create flash cards.

21. Carry course materials with you and practice studying in several different locations.

22. During a study break, play music or dance to restore energy.

23. Put on background music that enhances your concentration while studying.

24. Relate key concepts to songs you know.

25. Write original songs based on course content.

26. Connect readings and lectures to a strong feeling or significant past experience.

27. Keep a journal that relates your course work to events in your daily life.

28. Create flash cards and use them to quiz study partners.

29. Volunteer to give a speech or lead group presentations on course topics.

30. Teach the topic you're studying to someone else.

31. During study breaks, take walks outside.

32. Post pictures of outdoor scenes where you study and play recordings of outdoor sounds while you read.

33. Invite classmates to discuss course work while taking a hike or going on a camping trip.

34. Preview reading assignments by looking for elements that are highlighted visually—bold headlines, charts, graphs, illustrations, and photographs.

35. When taking notes in class, leave plenty of room to add your own charts, diagrams, tables, and other visuals later.

36. Transfer your handwritten notes to your computer. Use word processing software that allows you to format your notes in lists, add headings in different fonts, and create visuals in color.

37. Before you begin an exam, quickly sketch a diagram on scratch paper. Use this diagram to summarize the key formulas or facts you want to remember.

38. During tests, see if you can visualize pages from your handwritten notes or images from your computer-based notes.

39. Reinforce memory of your notes and readings by talking about them. When studying, stop often to recite key points and examples in your own words.

40. After doing several verbal summaries of your notes, record your favorite version or write it out.

41. Read difficult passages in your textbooks slowly and out loud.

42. Look for ways to translate course content into three-dimensional models that you can build. While studying biology, for example, create a model of a human cell using different colors of clay.

43. Supplement lectures with trips to museums, field observations, lab sessions, tutorials, and other hands-on activities.

44. Recite key concepts from your courses while you walk or exercise.

45. Create a practice test and write out the answers in the room where you will actually take the exam.

 You're One Click Away . . .
from more learning styles strategies.

When learning styles conflict, you have options

When they experience difficulty in school, some students say: "The classroom is not conducive to the way I learn" or "This teacher creates tests that are too hard for me" or "In class, we never have time for questions" or "The instructor doesn't teach to my learning style."

Such statements can become mental crutches—a set of beliefs that prevent you from taking responsibility for your education. To stay in charge of your learning, consider adopting attitudes such as the following:

• I will discover the value in learning this information.

• I will find out more details and facts about this information.

• I will discover how I can experiment with this information.

• I will discover new ways to use this information in my life.

• I will study this information with modes of learning that are not my preferred style.

Remember that you can base your behaviors on such statements even if you don't fully agree with them. One way to change your attitudes is to adopt new behaviors and watch for new results in your life.

Commit to Action
Create value from learning styles

REFLECT ON THE CONTENT of this chapter, including "45 ways to get smart" on page 20. In the space below, reflect on the insights into your learning preferences. Create a comprehensive list of strategies that you will use to build on your current preferences—and to explore other learning styles.

Realize that discomfort is a natural part of the discovering and the learning process. As you participate in styles of learning that do not energize you, allow yourself to notice your struggle with a task or your lack of interest in completing it. Realize that you are balancing your learning preferences. By tolerating discomfort and using all of the different styles of learning, you increase your chances for success.

Discovery Statement

Regarding my preferences for learning, I discovered that . . .

I will also experiment with five strategies for exploring other learning styles. Specifically, I intend to . . .

Intention Statement

I will experiment with at least five strategies that draw on my preferred learning styles. Specifically, I intend to . . .

Action Statement

The first thing that I will do to act on the above intentions is . . .

"IT'S JUST WHO I AM"
RESOLVING DIFFERENCES IN STYLE

As higher education and the workplace become more diverse and technology creates a global marketplace, you'll meet people who differ from you in profound ways. Your fellow students and coworkers will behave in ways that express a variety of preferences for perceiving information, processing ideas, and acting on what they learn. For example:

- A roommate who's moving while studying—reciting facts out loud, pacing, and gesturing—probably prefers concrete experience and learning by taking action.

- A coworker who talks continually on the phone about a project may prefer to learn by listening, talking, and forging key relationships.

- A supervisor who excels at abstract conceptualization may want to see detailed project plans and budgets submitted in writing, well before a project swings into high gear.

When different learning styles intersect, there is the potential for conflict—and an opening for creativity. Succeeding with peers often means seeing the classroom and workplace as a laboratory for learning from experience. Resolving conflict and learning from mistakes are all part of the learning cycle.

DISCOVER THE STYLES OF PEOPLE AROUND YOU

You can learn a lot about other people's styles simply by observing them during the workday. Look for clues such as the following.

Approaches to a task that requires learning. Some people process new information by sitting quietly and reading or writing. When learning to use a piece of equipment, such as a new computer, they'll read the instruction manual first. Others will skip the manual, unpack all the boxes, and start setting up equipment. And others might ask a more experienced colleague to guide them in person, step by step.

Word choice. Some people like to process information visually. You might hear them say, "I'll look into that" or "Give me the big picture first." Others like to solve problems verbally: "Let's talk though this problem" or "I hear you!" In contrast, some people focus on body sensations ("This product feels great") or action ("Let's run with this idea and see what happens.")

Body language. Notice how often coworkers or classmates make eye contact with you and how close they sit or stand next to you. Observe their gestures as well as the volume and tone of their voice.

Content preferences. Notice what subjects they openly discuss and which topics that they avoid. Some people talk freely about their feelings, their families, and even their personal finances. Others choose to remain silent on such topics and stick to work-related matters.

Process preferences. Look for patterns in the way that your coworkers and classmates meet goals. When attending meetings, for example, some might stick closely to the agenda and keep an eye on the clock. Other people might prefer to "go with the flow," even if it means working an extra hour or scrapping the agenda.

ACCOMMODATE DIFFERING STYLES

Once you've discovered differences in styles, look for ways to accommodate them. As you collaborate on projects with other students or coworkers, keep the following suggestions in mind.

Remember that some people want to reflect on the "big picture" first. When introducing a project plan, you might say, "This process has four major steps." Before explaining the plan in detail, talk about the purpose of the project and the benefits of completing each step.

Allow for abstract conceptualization. When leading a study group or conducting a training session, provide handouts that include plenty of visuals and step-by-step instructions. Visual learners and people who like to think abstractly will appreciate it. Also schedule periods for questions and answers.

When designing a project, encourage people to answer key questions. Remember the four essential questions that guide learning. Answering *Why*? means defining the purpose and desired outcomes of the project. Answering *What*? means assigning major tasks, setting due dates for each task, and generating commitment to action. Answering *How*? means carrying out assigned tasks and meeting regularly to discuss what's working well and ways to improve the project. And answering *What if*? means discussing what the team has learned from the project and ways to apply that learning to the whole class or larger organization.

When working on teams, look for ways to complement each other's strengths. If you're skilled at planning, find someone who excels at doing. Also seek people who can reflect on and

interpret the team's experience. Pooling different styles allows you to draw on everyone's strengths.

RESOLVE CONFLICT WITH RESPECT FOR STYLES

When people's styles clash in educational or work settings, we have several options. One is to throw up our hands and resign ourselves to personality conflicts. Another option is to recognize differences, accept them, and respect them as complementary ways to meet common goals. From that perspective, you can do the following.

Resolve conflict within yourself. You might have mental pictures about classrooms and workplaces as settings where people are all "supposed" to have the same style. Notice those pictures and gently let them go. If you *expect* to find differences in styles, you can respect those differences more easily.

Let people take on tasks that fit their learning styles. As you do, remember that style is both stable and dynamic. People gravitate toward the kinds of tasks they've succeeded at in the past. They can also broaden their styles by tackling new tasks to reinforce the different questions of learning (*Why? What? How? What if?*).

Rephrase complaints as requests. "This class is a waste of my time" can be recast as "Please tell me what I'll gain if I participate actively in class." "The instructor talks too fast" can become "What strategies can I use for taking notes when the instructor covers the material rapidly?"

GEAR PRESENTATIONS TO DIFFERENT LEARNING STYLES

When you want classmates or coworkers to adopt a new idea, use a new procedure, or promote a new product, you might make a speech or give a presentation. To persuade more people, gear your presentation to several learning styles.

For example, some people want to see the overall picture first. You can start by saying, "This product has four major features." Then explain the benefits of each feature in order.

Also allow time for verbally oriented people to ask questions and make comments. For those who prefer a hands-on approach, offer a chance to try out the new product for themselves—to literally "get the feel of it."

Finish with a handout that includes plenty of illustrations, charts, and step-by-step instructions. Visual learners and people who like to think abstractly will appreciate it.

BRING A CONVERSATION ABOUT STYLES TO YOUR WORKPLACE

The whole concept of learning styles has gained a lot of attention in higher education. Once you enter a workplace, however, you might find the conversation about learning styles to be less common. To extend your understanding of styles, attend a workshop or course on this topic and share what you learn with coworkers. You can also take the initiative to bring such training to your workplace.

 You're One Click Away . . .
from more strategies for building effective relationships at work.

Risk being a fool

ALL OF US ARE FOOLS at one time or another. There are no exceptions. If you doubt it, think back to that stupid thing you did just a few days ago. You know the one. Yes . . . *that* one. It was embarrassing and you tried to hide it. You pretended you weren't a fool. This happens to everyone.

We are all fallible human beings. Most of us, however, spend too much time and energy trying to hide our foolhood. No one is really tricked by this—not even ourselves. And whenever we pretend to be something we're not, we miss part of life.

This Power Process comes with a warning label: Taking risks does *not* mean escaping responsibility for our actions. "Risk being a fool" is not a suggestion to get drunk at a party and make a fool of yourself. It is not a suggestion to act the fool by disrupting class. It is not a suggestion to be foolhardy or to "fool around."

"Risk being a fool" means that foolishness—along with courage and cowardice, grace and clumsiness—is a human characteristic. We all share it. You might as well risk being a fool because you already are one, and nothing in the world can change that. Why not enjoy it once in a while?

There's one sure-fire way to avoid any risk of being a fool, and that's to avoid life. The writer who never finishes a book will never have to worry about getting negative reviews. The center fielder who sits out every game is safe from making any errors. And the comedian who never performs in front of an audience is certain to avoid telling jokes that fall flat.

For a student, the willingness to take risks means releasing your pictures about how you're "supposed" to learn. Be willing to appear the fool as you experiment with new learning styles. The rewards can include more creativity, more self-expression, and more joy.

 You're One Click Away . . .

from more suggestions for creative foolhood.

The Discovery Wheel on page 1 includes a section titled Resources. This section is based on the idea that three key resources for succeeding at anything you do are time, health, and money.

Before you read the rest of this chapter, take a few minutes to go beyond your initial responses to the Discovery Wheel. Reflect on the skills snapshot below to take a closer look at your skills. Complete these statements honestly, then flip to the article or exercise highlighted for strategies that will promote your success.

Skills SNAPSHOT

If someone asked about my success with setting and achieving goals, ✳ ········►
check out:
Commit to Action: "Give your goals some teeth," page 27

My ability to stay on task and stay productive can be described as ... ✳ ········►
check out:
"Seven ways to take back your time," page 28

The five activities that take up most of my time each week are ... ✳ ········
check out:
Commit to Action: "Discover where your time goes," page 30

check out:
"Procrastination unplugged," page 33

········✳ My effectiveness at overcoming procrastination is ...

········✳ I would describe my current state of health as ...
check out:
"Put an end to money worries," page 39
Critical Thinking Experiment #3: "Release money myths," page 41

check out:
"Health matters," page 35
Commit to Action: "Take a fearless look at your health," page 38

Right now my skills at managing money can be described as ... ✳

I take advantage of campus and community services, including ... ✳ ········►
check out:
"Campus resources— you paid for 'em, so use 'em," page 42

········✳ When distracted, I refocus my attention by ...

check out:
Power Process: "Be here now," page 43

Give your goals some teeth

MANY OF US HAVE NOTIONS about what we want out of life. They are warm, fuzzy ideals such as "I want to be a good person," "I want to be financially secure," or "I want to be happy." Left in such vague terms, however, these notions will seldom lead to any results.

Another option is to translate your ideals into goals. Find out what a goal looks like. Listen to what it sounds like. Pick it up and feel it. Make your goal as real as the teeth on a chain saw.

The key is to state your goals as observable actions and measurable results. Think in detail about how things will be different once your goals are attained. List the changes in what you'll see, feel, touch, hear, do, or have.

Suppose that one of your goals is to become a better student by studying harder. You're headed in a powerful direction; now go for the specifics. Translate that goal into a behavior, such as "I will study two hours for every hour I'm in class."

Perhaps one of your desires is to get a good education and graduate on time. Translate that into: "I will graduate with a B.S. degree in engineering, with honors, by 2013."

Using a process of brainstorming and evaluation, you can break even the longest-term goal into short-term actions. When you analyze a goal down to this level, you're well on the way to meeting it.

You're about to experience the process of setting goals for yourself. Gather a pen, extra paper, and a watch with a second hand. To get the most benefit, follow the stated time limits. The entire exercise takes about 30 minutes.

Discovery Statement

Use a separate sheet of paper for this part of the exercise. For 10 minutes write down everything that you want in your life. Write as fast as you can and write whatever comes into your head. Leave no thought out. Don't worry about accuracy. The object of a brainstorm is to generate as many ideas as possible. To begin, simply brainstorm as many answers as possible to the following sentence:

I discover that I want . . .

Intention Statement

After you have finished brainstorming, spend the next five minutes looking over your list. Analyze what you wrote. Read the list out loud. If something is missing, add it.

Then look for one thing on the list that's most important to you right now, even if it's something that might take many years and many steps to achieve. State this as a goal—a specific result to achieve by a specific date.

Write your goal in the following space.

I intend to . . .

Action Statement

Now spend 10 minutes writing a list of specific actions that can lead to the accomplishment of your goal. Be specific. Create your list in the space below and use separate paper as needed.

For five minutes, review your brainstormed list of actions. Are they specific? Can you see yourself actually *doing* each of them? If anything on your list is vague or fuzzy, go back and revise it. Remember: The idea is to list actions that you could include on a daily to-do list or write down on a calendar.

Congratulations! Take one more minute to savor the feeling that comes with getting clarity about your deepest values and heartfelt desires. You can take the process you just used and apply it to getting *anything* you want in life. The essential steps are the same in each case: State your desire as a specific goal. Then translate the goal into a list of concrete actions.

 You're One Click Away . . .
from an online goal-setting exercise.

Discover Your Resources

2

CHAPTER 2 27

SEVEN WAYS TO
TAKE BACK YOUR TIME

The truth about time management is that it doesn't exist. Think about it: Time cannot be managed. Every human being gets exactly the same allotment of hours: 24 per day, 168 per week.

However, we can manage our *behavior* so that we become more productive during the fixed number of hours that we all have.

You might know people who seem efficient and yet relaxed. These people do not have more time than you do. They simply manage their behavior in productive ways.

Experiment with the following behaviors. Each of them is a strategy for using the time of your life in the way that you choose. Select one strategy to apply right away. When it becomes a habit, come back to this article and choose another one. Repeat this process as often as you like and reap the rewards.

1. DO IT NOW

Postponing decisions and procrastinating are major sources of stress. An alternative is to handle the task or decision immediately. Answer that letter now. Make that phone call as soon as it occurs to you.

Also use waiting time. Five minutes waiting for a subway, 20 minutes waiting for the dentist, 10 minutes between classes—waiting time adds up fast. Have short study tasks ready to do during these periods. For example, you can carry index cards with facts, formulas, or definitions and pull them out anywhere.

2. DELEGATE

Asking for help can free up extra hours you need for studying. Instead of doing all the housework or cooking yourself, assign some of the tasks to family members or roommates. Instead of driving across town to deliver a package, hire a delivery service to do it.

It's not practical to delegate certain study tasks, such as writing term papers or completing reading assignments. However, you can still draw on the ideas of other people in completing such tasks. For instance, form a writing group to edit and critique papers, brainstorm topics or titles, and develop lists of sources.

3. SAY NO

Suppose that someone asks you to volunteer for a project and you realize immediately that you don't want to do it. Save time by graciously telling the truth up front. Saying "I'll think about it and get back to you" just postpones the conversation until later, when it will take more time.

Saying no graciously and up front can be a huge time-saver. Many people think that it is rude to refuse a request. But saying no can be done effectively and courteously. When you tell people that you're saying no to a new commitment

because you are busy educating yourself, most of them will understand.

Saying no includes logging off e-mail and instant messaging when appropriate. The Internet is the ultimate interrupter. In today's world, responses to e-mails or instant messages are expected almost immediately. Set an "away" message for instant messages and set specific times during the day to check your e-mail.

Also experiment with doing less. Planning is as much about dropping worthless activities as about adding new ones. See if you can reduce or eliminate activities that contribute little to your values or goals.

4. USE A CALENDAR

Use a calendar to remind yourself about commitments that will take place at a certain date and time—classes, meetings, appointments, and the like. You can also schedule due dates for assignments, review sessions for tests, and any other events you want to remember.

Many students use a paper-based calendar that they can carry along with their textbooks and class notes. Other people favor online calendars such as those offered by Google and Yahoo! Experiment with both and see what works best for you.

When using any kind of calendar, schedule fixed blocks of time first. Start with class time and work time, for instance. These time periods are usually determined in advance. Other activities must be scheduled around them. As an alternative to entering class times in your calendar each week, you can simply print out your class schedule and consult it as needed. As a general guideline, schedule about two hours of study time each week for every hour that you spend in class.

Tasks often expand to fill the time we allot for them, so use your calendar to set clear starting and stopping times. Plan a certain amount of time for that reading assignment, set a timer, and stick to it. Feeling rushed or sacrificing quality is not the aim here. The point is to push yourself a little and discover what your time requirements really are.

Avoid scheduling marathon study sessions, however. When possible, study in shorter sessions. Three three-hour sessions are usually far more productive than one nine-hour session.

Recognize that unexpected things will happen, and leave some holes in your schedule. Build in blocks of unplanned time, and mark these in your calendar as "flex time" or "open time."

5. WRITE REMINDERS

Almost every book about personal productivity mentions a to-do list. This is a list of specific actions—phone calls to make, errands to run, assignments to complete. Also include actions that are directly related to your goals. (See Commit to Action: "Give your goals some teeth" on page 27.)

Save your to-do list for actions that do not have to be completed on a certain date or at a certain time. Complete your to-do items at times between the scheduled events in your day. Delete items on your list when you complete them, and add new items as you think of them.

You can record your to-do items on sheets of paper. Another option is to put each to-do item on its own index card. This allows for easy sorting into categories. Also, you'll never have to recopy your to-do list. Whenever you complete a to-do item, simply throw away or recycle the card.

Computers offer similar flexibility. Just open up a file and key in all your to-do items. In a single window on your screen, you'll be able to see at least a dozen to-do items at a glance. As with index cards, you can delete and rearrange to your heart's content.

6. DISCOVER YOUR PERSONAL RHYTHMS

Many people learn best during daylight hours. If this is true for you, then schedule study time for your most difficult subjects when the sun is up.

When you're in a time crunch, get up a little early or stay up later. Experiment with getting up 15 minutes early or going to bed 15 minutes later each day on a more permanent basis. Over the course of one year, either choice will yield 91 extra hours of waking activity.

7. GO FOR THE LONG TERM

Experiment with longer-term planning. Thinking beyond today and the current week can help you see how your daily activities relate to longer-range goals. On your calendar, include *any* key dates for the upcoming quarter, semester, or year. These can relate to any area of life—academic, career, or family events. Examples are:

- Test dates
- Lab sessions
- Due dates for assignments
- Days when classes will be canceled
- Interim due dates, such as when you plan to complete the first draft of a term paper
- Birthdays, anniversaries, and other special occasions
- Medical and dental checkups
- Application due dates for internships
- Concerts and plays
- Due dates for major bills—insurance, taxes, car registration, credit card and installment loan payments, medical expenses, interest charges, and charitable contributions
- Trips, vacations, and holidays

 You're One Click Away . . .
from additional ways to become more productive.

Forget about time management—*just get things done*

David Allen, author of *Getting Things Done: The Art of Stress-Free Productivity*, says that a lack of time is not the real issue for the people he coaches. Instead, the problem is "a lack of clarity and definition about what a project really is, and what the associated next-action steps required are."[1] Allen translates this idea into the following suggestions.

1. Collect. To begin, gather notes about every unfinished project, incomplete task, misplaced object—or anything else that's nagging you—and dump it into an in-basket.

2. Process. Pick up each note in your in-basket, one at a time, and ask: "Do I truly want to or need to do something about this?" If the answer is no, then calmly dispose of the item. If the answer is yes, then choose immediately how to respond. The overall goal is to *empty* your in-basket at least once each week.

3. Organize. Now group your reminders into appropriate categories. Allen recommends using a calendar for scheduled events, a list of current projects, and a list of next actions.

4. Review. Every week, update your reminders. Ask yourself: What are all my current projects? And what is the *very next physical action* (such as a phone call or errand) that I can take to move each project forward?

5. Do. Every day, review your calendar and lists. Based on this information and on your intuition, make moment-to-moment choices about how to spend your time.

Commit to Action
Discover where your time goes

DO YOU EVER HEAR YOURSELF saying "Where did my morning go?" Many people have little idea where their time really goes. But with some heightened awareness and minimal record keeping, you can discover exactly how you spend your time. With this knowledge you can diagnose productivity problems with pinpoint accuracy. You can delete the time-killers and the life-drainers—activities that consume hours yet deliver the least in results or satisfaction. This frees up more time for the activities that you truly value.

If you think you already have a good idea of how you spend time, then predict how many hours you devote each week to sleeping, studying, working, attending classes, and socializing. Use this exercise to monitor your time for one week. Then notice how accurate your predictions were. You'll quickly see the value of collecting accurate data about the way you use time.

Following is a series of steps for monitoring your use of time. To get the most benefit from this exercise, proceed like a scientist. Adopt the hypothesis that you can manage your time in more optimal ways. Then see if you can confirm or refute that hypothesis by collecting precise data in the laboratory—the laboratory in this case being your life.

❶ Choose a specific period to monitor

To get the most benefit from monitoring your time, do it for at least one day. You can extend this practice over several days, a week, or even a month. Monitoring your time over greater intervals can reveal broader patterns in your behavior. You'll get more insight into the way that you spend your most precious resource—you.

❷ Plan how to record your data

The key to this exercise is to record the times that you start and stop each activity over a period of 24 hours: sleeping, eating, studying, traveling to and from class, working, watching television, listening to music, sitting in lectures, taking care of the kids, running errands. To promote accuracy and accumulate useful data, track your activity in 30-minute intervals. Tracking 15-minute intervals can be even more useful.

You can record this data in any way that works. Consider these options:

- **Carry an index card** with you each day for recording your activities. Every time that you start a new activity, describe it in a word or two and write down the time you started.

- **Use a daily calendar** that includes slots for scheduling appointments at each hour of the day. Instead of scheduling events ahead of time, simply note how you actually spend each hour.

- **Use time-tracking software.** For the latest products, key the words *time tracking* into a search engine.

- **Create your own form** for time monitoring. Before you go to bed, review your day and write down your activities along with starting and stopping times. (See the illustration on this page.)

SAMPLE TIME MONITOR		
Activity	Start	Stop
Sleeping	11:00 pm	6:00 am
Jog/Stretch	6:00 am	7:00 am
Shower/Dress	7:00 am	7:30 am
Breakfast	7:30 am	8:00 am
Travel to Campus	8:30 am	9:00 am
History	9:00 am	10:20 am
Check Email	10:30 am	11:00 am
English Lit	11:00 am	12:00 pm
Lunch/Review for Psych test	12:00 pm	1:00 pm
Work-Study Job	1:00 pm	4:00 pm
Run Errands	4:00 pm	5:00 pm
Travel Home	5:00 pm	5:30 pm
Watch TV/Relax	5:30 pm	6:30 pm
Dinner/Socialize	6:30 pm	8:00 pm
Read Chapter 4/English	8:00 pm	9:00 pm
Make Flashcards for Psych test	9:00 pm	10:00 pm
Review notes from today's History/English Lectures	10:00 pm	11:00 pm

Note: Keep this exercise in perspective. No one says that you have to keep track of the rest of your life in 15-minute intervals. Eventually you can monitor selected activities in your life and keep track of them only for as long as you choose.

3 **Record your data**

Now put your plan into action. For a minimum of one day, collect data about how much time you spend on each activity.

4 **List how much time you spent on each activity**

At the end of the day or week, compute the total hours you devoted to each activity. Examples might include eight hours for sleeping, two hours for watching a movie, three hours of class, and six hours for studying. Make sure the grand total of all activities is 24 hours per day or 168 hours per week. Using the data that you collected, add up how much time you spent in each of your activities.

5 **Group your activities into major categories**

After you've monitored your time for at least one week, group your activities together into broader categories. Examples are *sleep, class, study,* and *meals.* Another category, *grooming,* might include showering, putting on makeup, brushing your teeth, and getting dressed. *Travel* can include walking, driving, taking the bus, and riding your bike. Other categories might be *exercise, entertainment, work, television, domestic,* and *children.* Use categories that make sense for you.

6 **Summarize your data**

Use the blank two-column chart on this page to summarize the results of the previous steps. Include each category of activity and the number of hours for each category. First, look at the sample chart below. Then, using the blank chart provided, fill in your own information.

CATEGORIES OF ACTIVITY	HOURS SPENT ON EACH ACTIVITY
Class	15 hrs.
Study/Reading for Classes	45 hrs.
Meals (including cooking)	21 hrs.
Free Time	10 hrs.
Exercise	4 hrs.
Clean Apartment	3 hrs.
Laundry	2 hrs.
Call Family	2 hrs.
Work	10 hrs.
Personal Maintenance	7 hrs.
Sleep	49 hrs.
Total	168 hrs.

CATEGORIES OF ACTIVITY	HOURS SPENT ON EACH ACTIVITY

Total _____

Using a pie chart to track your time is powerful for two reasons. First, a circle is a fixed shape, reinforcing the idea that you have only a fixed amount of time to work with: 24 hours a day, 168 hours per week. Second, seeing your life represented on a pie chart tempts you to adjust the sizes of the slices—each slice being a category of activity. You make this adjustment by consciously choosing to devote more or less time to each category. Look at the sample chart below and then fill in your own pie chart using the information from your chart on page 31.

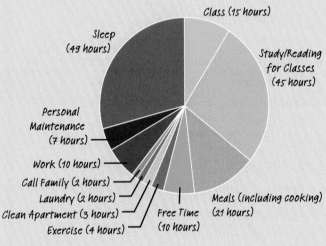

Class (15 hours)
Sleep (49 hours)
Study/Reading for Classes (45 hours)
Personal Maintenance (7 hours)
Work (10 hours)
Call Family (2 hours)
Laundry (2 hours)
Clean Apartment (3 hours)
Exercise (4 hours)
Free Time (10 hours)
Meals (including cooking) (21 hours)

7 Reflect on your time monitor

Complete the following sentences.

After monitoring my time, I discovered that . . .

I was surprised that I spent so much time on . . .

I was surprised that I spent so little time on . . .

I intend to spend more time on . . .

I intend to spend less time on . . .

 You're One Click Away . . .

from an online version of this exercise.

PROCRASTINATION UNPLUGGED

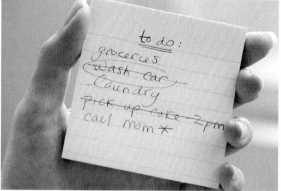

The terms *self-discipline, willpower,* and *motivation* are often used to describe something missing in ourselves. Time after time, we invoke these words to explain another person's success—or our own shortcomings: "If I were more motivated, I'd get more involved in school." "Of course she got an A. She has self-discipline." "If I had more willpower, I'd lose weight."

It seems that certain people are born with lots of motivation, while others miss out on it.

An alternative way of thinking is to stop assuming that motivation is mysterious, determined at birth, or hard to come by. In fact, perhaps the whole concept of motivation is just a myth. Maybe what we call motivation is something that you already possess—the ability to do a task even when you don't feel like it.

We don't need the concept of motivation to change our behavior. Rather, immediate action can flow from genuine commitment. With that idea in mind, test the following suggestions.

CHECK FOR ATTITUDES THAT PROMOTE PROCRASTINATION

Certain attitudes fuel procrastination and keep you from experiencing the rewards in life that you deserve. In their book, *Procrastination: Why You Do It and What to Do About It,* psychologists Jane Burka and Lenora Yuen list these examples:

> I must be perfect.
>
> Everything I do should go easily and without effort.
>
> It's safer to do nothing than to take a risk and fail.
>
> If it's not done right, it's not worth doing at all.
>
> If I do well this time, I must always do well.
>
> If I succeed, someone will get hurt.[2]

If you find such beliefs running through your mind, write them down. Getting a belief out of your head and on to paper can rob that belief of its power. Also write a more effective belief that you want to adopt. For example: "Even if I don't complete this task perfectly, it's good enough for now and I can still learn from my mistakes."

ACCEPT YOUR FEELINGS OF RESISTANCE—THEN TAKE ACTION

If you wait to exercise until you feel energetic, you might wait for months. Instead, get moving now and watch your feelings change. After five minutes of brisk walking, you might be in the mood for a 20-minute run. Don't wait to feel "motivated" before you take action. Instead, apply the principle that action *creates* motivation.

This principle can be applied to any task you've been putting off. You can move into action no matter how you feel about a task. Simply notice your feelings of resistance, accept them, and then do one small task related to your goal. Then do one more task, and another. Keep at it, one task at a time, and watch procrastination disappear.

 You're One Click Away . . .

from five more ways to get past procrastination.

10 things you can do in 10 minutes (or less)

- Preview a textbook chapter.
- Write a Discovery or an Intention Statement.
- Reread an article in this book.
- Do an exercise (or part of an exercise) in this book.
- Create your weekly budget.
- Take a brisk walk or climb several flights of stairs for exercise.
- Do a spiritual practice, such as meditation or prayer.
- Write and use an affirmation.
- Write a goal or action plan. Review your calendar or to-do list. (Refer to Commit to Action: "Give your goals some teeth.")
- Nothing. Just chill. Stare out the window. Breathe deeply and notice how good it feels.

PLANNING
SETS YOU FREE

An effective plan is flexible, not carved in stone. You can change your plans frequently and still preserve the advantages of planning—choosing your overall direction and taking charge of your life. And even when other people set the goal, you can choose how to achieve it.

Planning is a self-creative venture that lasts for a lifetime. Following are eight ways to get the most from this process. The first four are suggestions about goal setting. The rest are about the details of scheduling activities based on your goals.

1. Back up to a bigger picture. When choosing activities for the day or week, take some time to lift your eyes to the horizon. Step back for a few minutes and consider your longer-range goals—what you want to accomplish in the next six months, the next year, the next five years, and beyond.

Ask whether the activities you're about to schedule actually contribute to those goals. If they do, great. If not, ask whether you can delete some items from your calendar or to-do list to make room for goal-related activities. See if you can free up at least one hour each day for doing something you love instead of putting it off to a more "reasonable" or "convenient" time.

2. Look boldly for things to change. It's fascinating to note the areas that are off-limits when people set goals. Money, sex, career, marriage, and other topics can easily fall into the category "I'll just have to live with this."

When creating your future, open up your thinking about what aspects of your life can be changed and what cannot. Be willing to put every facet of your life on the table. Staying open-minded can lead to a future you never dreamed was possible.

3. Look for what's missing—and what to maintain. Goals often arise from a sense of what's missing in our lives. Goal setting is fueled by unresolved problems, incomplete projects, relationships we want to develop, and careers we still want to pursue.

However, not all planning has to spring from a sense of need. You can set goals to maintain things that you already have, or to keep doing the effective things that you already do. If you exercise vigorously three times each week, you can set a goal to keep exercising. If you already have a loving relationship with your spouse, you can set a goal to nurture that relationship for the rest of your life.

4. Think even further into the future. To have fun and unleash your creativity, set goals as far in the future as you can. The specific length of time doesn't matter. For some people, long-range planning might mean 10, 20, or even 50 years from now. For others, planning 3 years ahead feels right. Do whatever works for you.

Once you've stated your longest-range goals, work backward until you can define a next step to take. Suppose your 30-year goal is to retire and maintain your present standard of living. Ask yourself: "In order to do that, what financial goals do I need to achieve in 20 years? In 10 years? In one year? In one month? In one week?" Put the answers to these questions in writing.

5. Schedule fixed blocks of time first. When planning your week, start with class time and work time. These time periods are usually determined in advance. Other activities must be scheduled around them. Then schedule essential daily activities such as sleeping and eating. In addition, schedule some time each week for actions that lead directly to one of your written goals.

6. Set clear starting and stopping times. Tasks often expand to fill the time we allot for them.

Try scheduling a certain amount of time for a reading assignment—set a timer, and stick to it. Students often find that they can decrease study time by forcing themselves to read faster. This can usually be done without sacrificing comprehension.

The same principle can apply to other tasks. Some people find they can get up 15 minutes earlier in the morning and still feel alert throughout the day. Plan 45 minutes for a trip to the grocery store instead of one hour. Over the course of a year, those extra minutes can add up to hours.

7. Schedule for flexibility and fun. Recognize that unexpected things will happen and allow for them. Leave some holes in your schedule. Build in blocks of unplanned time. Consider setting aside time each week marked "flex time" or "open time." Use these hours for emergencies, spontaneous activities, catching up, or seizing new opportunities.

Include time for errands. The time we spend buying toothpaste, paying bills, and doing laundry is easy to overlook. These little errands can destroy a tight schedule and make us feel rushed and harried all week. Remember to allow for travel time between locations. Also make room for fun. Take time to browse aimlessly through the library, stroll with no destination, ride a bike, or do other things you enjoy.

8. Involve others when appropriate. Sometimes the activities we schedule depend on gaining information, assistance, or direct participation from other people. If we neglect to inform them of our plans or forget to ask for their cooperation at the outset—surprise! Our schedules can crash.

 You're One Click Away . . .
from an online goal-setting exercise.

HEALTH MATTERS

No resource is more important than your own mind and body. There is some basic confusion about what the word *health* means. Ask 20 different people for a definition. You'll probably get 20 different answers—10 of them variations on "I don't know." That's amazing, given the fact that bookstores stock hundreds of titles about health, and popular magazines feature the topic every month. Through moment-to-moment choices, you either build up or deplete the reserves of physical and mental energy that you can use to succeed in school. This is especially true for choices about eating, exercise, stress management, drugs, and sex.

EAT FOR HEALTH *AND* PLEASURE

Nutrition can get complicated. Michael Pollan, a reporter, spent several years sorting out the scientific literature.[3] He boiled the key guidelines down to seven words in three phrases:

- "Eat food." In other words, choose whole, fresh foods over processed products with a lot of ingredients.

- "Not too much." If you want to manage your weight, then control how much you eat. Notice portion sizes. Pass on snacks, seconds, and desserts, or indulge just occasionally.

- "Mostly plants." Fruits, vegetables, and grains are loaded with vitamins, minerals, and antioxidants that help to prevent disease. Plant-based foods, on the whole, are also lower in calories than foods from animals (meat and dairy products).

Remember that you can get complete proteins from low-fat dairy products, occasional lean meats, and soy foods. Enjoy fats and sweets in moderation. Also, your body is mostly water, so drink plenty.

Pollan's guidelines are consistent with recommendations from the U.S. Department of Agriculture. To find out more, go online to **http://www.mypyramid.gov**.

Fast foods can be tempting, especially if you're pressed for time. When eaten consistently, these foods can also expand your waistline and drain your budget. A medium soda, large order of fries, and double cheeseburger can pack over 1,500 calories and 60 grams of fat. To save money and promote health, prepare meals at home and center them on whole grains, legumes, fruits, and vegetables.

When you do eat out, reduce portions. Restaurant portions—especially at fast-food places—have swelled in recent decades. Splitting a meal with someone reduces both cost and calories.

Eating can be one of life's greatest pleasures. If you eat slowly and savor each bite, you can be satisfied with smaller portions. Use meal times as a chance to relax, reduce stress, and connect with people.

DO EXERCISE YOU ENJOY

Regular exercise can improve your alertness and ability to learn. Exercise is also a way to dissipate the tension that you build up while hunched over a keyboard hammering out a term paper.

Do something you enjoy. Start by walking briskly for at least 15 minutes every day. Increase that time gradually and add a little running. Once you're in reasonable shape, stay in shape by doing aerobic activity on most days of the week. An hour of daily activity is ideal, but do whatever you can. Remember that this hour can include activity that burns calories—such as cleaning and gardening—that you might not officially label as "exercise." Look for exercise facilities on campus. Classes may also be offered in aerobics, swimming, yoga, basketball, and more. School can be a great place to get in shape.

MANAGE STRESS

Stress, at appropriate times and at manageable levels, is normal and useful. It can sharpen our awareness and boost our energy just when we need it the most. When stress persists or becomes excessive, it is harmful.

To reduce stress, exercise. Vigorous movement is good for your heart. It's also good for your mood.

Also get sound sleep. As a student, you might be tempted to cut back drastically on your sleep once in a while for an all-night study session. If you indulge in them often, use the strategies in this chapter for some time-management ideas. Depriving yourself of sleep is a choice you can avoid. If you have problems sleeping, avoid naps during the daytime. Monitor your caffeine intake, especially in the afternoon and evening.

Beyond these suggestions, see "Relax—it's just a test" in Chapter Five. The techniques included there can work for managing all kinds of stress. If those suggestions don't work within a few weeks, then see a counselor at the student health service on your campus.

GET HELP FOR ALCOHOL OR OTHER DRUG ABUSE

According to the National Institute on Alcohol Abuse and Alcoholism, 31 percent of college students met the criteria for a diagnosis of alcohol abuse.[4] When people continue to use alcohol or other drugs despite negative consequences, they're abusing chemicals. If they find it impossible to stop using on their own, they may be addicted.

Be willing to admit the truth about your relationship to alcohol and other drugs. If you have any concerns, go to the student health service on your campus and ask about treatment options. Taking charge of your relationship to alcohol and other drugs can remove one of the greatest obstacles to success in higher education.

MOVE FROM ADDICTION TO RECOVERY

Most addictions share some key features, such as:

- *Loss of control*—continued substance use or activity in spite of adverse consequences.
- *Pattern of relapse*—vowing to quit or limit the activity or substance use and continually failing to do so.

- *Tolerance*—the need to take increasing amounts of a substance to produce the desired effect.
- *Withdrawal*—signs and symptoms of physical and mental discomfort or illness when the substance is taken away.[5]

This list can help you determine if addiction is a barrier for you right now. The items above can apply to anything from cocaine use to compulsive gambling.

If you have a problem with addiction in any form, then get help. Consider the following suggestions.

- **Use responsibly.** Show people that you can have a good time without alcohol or other drugs. If you do choose to drink, consume alcohol with food. Pace yourself and take time between drinks. Avoid promotions that encourage excess drinking. "Ladies Drink Free" nights are especially dangerous; women are affected more quickly by alcohol, making them targets for rape. Also stay out of games that encourage people to guzzle. And avoid people who make fun of you for choosing not to drink.

- **Look at the costs.** There is always a tradeoff to addiction. Drinking six beers might result in a temporary high, and you will probably remember that feeling. You might feel terrible the morning after consuming six beers, but some people find it easier to forget *that* pain. Stay aware of how addiction makes you feel. Before going out to a restaurant or bar, set a limit for the number of drinks you will consume. If you consistently break this promise to yourself and experience negative consequences afterward, then you have a problem.

- **Take responsibility for recovery.** Nobody plans to become an addict. If you have pneumonia, you seek treatment and recover without guilt or shame. Approach an addiction in the same way. You can take responsibility for your recovery without blame, shame, or guilt.

Prevent and treat eating disorders

Eating disorders affect many students. These disorders involve serious disturbances in eating behavior. Examples are overeating or extreme reduction of food intake, as well as irrational concern about body shape or weight. Women are much more likely to develop these disorders than are men.

Bulimia involves cycles of excessive eating and forced purges. A person with this disorder might gorge on a pizza, donuts, and ice cream and then force herself to vomit. Or she might compensate for overeating with excessive use of laxatives,

enemas, or diuretics. *Anorexia nervosa* is a potentially fatal illness marked by self-starvation, either through extended fasts or by eating only one food for weeks at a time.

These disorders are not due to a failure of willpower. Instead, these are real illnesses in which harmful patterns of eating take on a life of their own.

Eating disorders can lead to many complications, including life-threatening heart conditions and kidney failure. Many people with eating disorders also struggle with depression, substance abuse, and anxiety.

These disorders require immediate treatment to stabilize health. This is usually followed by continuing medical care, counseling, and medication to promote a full recovery.

If you're worried about having an eating disorder, visit a doctor, campus health service, or local public health clinic. If you see signs of an eating disorder in someone else, express your concern with "I" messages as explained in Chapter Seven: Discovering Your Relationships. For more information, contact the National Eating Disorders Association at 1-800-931-2237 and online at **http://www. nationaleatingdisorders.org.**

MAKE SANE CHOICES ABOUT SEX

Sex is a basic human drive, and it can be wonderful. In certain conditions, sex can also be hazardous to your health.

Sexually transmitted diseases (STDs) are often spread through body fluids that are exchanged during sex—semen, vaginal secretions, and blood. Some STDs, such as herpes and genital warts, are spread by direct contact with infected skin. Human immunodeficiency virus (HIV) can be spread in other ways as well.

Technically, anyone who has sex is at risk of getting an STD. Without treatment, some of these diseases can lead to blindness, infertility, cancer, heart disease, or even death. Sometimes there are no signs or symptoms of an STD. The only way to tell if you're infected is a medical test.

For the latest news about preventing and treating STDs, go online to the U.S. Centers for Disease Control and Prevention at **http://www.cdc.gov/std/default.htm**.

Also think about preventing unwanted pregnancy. Of course, abstinence is 100 percent effective in preventing pregnancy when practiced faithfully. Use of condoms and methods that deliver extra hormones to a woman—through pills, injections, or implants—can also be effective.

However, effectiveness rates can only be estimated. Results depend on the health of the people using them, the number of sex partners, frequency of sex, and how carefully and consistently the methods are used.

Get the latest information about contraception from your campus health clinic.

 You're One Click Away . . .

from more strategies for taking charge of your health.

10 ways to stay healthy in (almost) no time

The best intentions to stay healthy can go out the window when you have only 20 minutes to eat between classes, or when you don't get home from classes until 10 p.m. The more hurried you become, the more important it becomes to take care of yourself. Following are 10 little things you can do to experience maximum health benefits in minimum time.

1. When you're in a hurry, eat vegetarian. There's no meat to thaw or cook. In the time it takes to cook a pot of pasta, you can cut and steam some fresh vegetables.

2. For a quick, nutritious meal, choose cereal. Buy whole grain cereal and add skim milk.

3. Make healthier choices from vending machines. Instead of soda, choose bottled waters. Also choose packages of nuts or whole grain crackers instead of candy.

4. Eat more fruit. It's still the world's most portable, nutritious food. For a meal that takes almost no time to prepare, combine fresh fruit with some nuts and whole grain crackers.

5. Switch to whole grain bread. Choosing whole grain over wheat takes no extra time from your schedule. And the whole grain comes packed with more nutrients than white bread.

6. Park farther away from your destination. You'll build some exercise time into your day without having to join a gym.

7. Whenever possible, walk. Walk between classes or while taking a study break. Instead of meeting a friend for a restaurant meal or a movie, go for a walk instead.

8. Keep dumbbells by your desk. Instead of reaching for another cup of coffee or a sugary snack, restore alertness with a quick set of repetitions with weights.

9. Take the stairs. Skip the elevator, especially if you're going up just one or two flights. Stair climbing is a highly aerobic form of exercise.

10. Drink water. Keep a bottle of water close by during the school day and while studying. Staying hydrated can help you stay alert.

From *Student's Guide to Succeeding at Community College*, First Edition. Copyright 2007 Wadsworth, a part of Cengage Learning, Inc. Reproduced by permission. **www.cengage.com/permissions**

Take a fearless look at your health

THIS EXERCISE ALLOWS YOU TO look closely at your health. As with the Discovery Wheel exercise in the Introduction, the usefulness of this exercise will be determined by your honesty and courage.

To begin, draw a simple outline of your body on a separate sheet of paper. You might have positive and negative feelings about various internal and external parts of your body. Label the parts and include a short description of the attributes you like or dislike, for example, straight teeth, fat thighs, clear lungs, double chin, straight posture, etc.

The body you drew substantially reflects your past health practices. To discover how well you take care of your body, complete the following sentences on a separate sheet of paper.

Eating

1. What I know about the way I eat is . . .

2. What I would most like to change about my diet is . . .

3. My eating habits lead me to be . . .

Exercise

1. The way I usually exercise is . . .

2. The last time I did 20 minutes or more of heart/lung (aerobic) exercise was . . .

3. As a result of my physical conditioning, I feel . . .

4. And I look . . .

5. It would be easier for me to work out regularly if I . . .

6. The most important benefit for me in exercising more is . . .

Substances

1. My history of cigarette smoking is . . .

2. An objective observer would say that my use of alcohol is . . .

3. In the last 10 days, the number of alcoholic drinks I have had is . . .

4. I would describe my use of coffee, colas, and other caffeinated drinks as . . .

5. I have used the following illegal drugs in the past week:

6. I take the following prescription drugs:

7. When it comes to drugs, what I am sometimes concerned about is . . .

Relationships

1. Someone who knows me fairly well would say I am emotionally . . .

2. The way I look and feel has affected my relationships by . . .

3. My use of drugs or alcohol has been an issue with . . .

4. The best thing I could do for myself and my relationships would be to . . .

Sleep

1. The number of hours I sleep each night is . . .

2. On weekends I normally sleep . . .

3. I have trouble sleeping when . . .

4. Last night I . . .

5. The quality of my sleep is usually . . .

Following up

1. In doing this exercise, I discovered that my main concern about my health is . . .

2. I could make a big difference in my health by changing one of my behaviors. Specifically, I intend to . . .

3. I will act on my intention today by . . .

Discover Your Resources

2

PUT AN END TO MONEY WORRIES

"I can't afford it" is a common reason that students give for dropping out of school. "I don't know how to pay for it" or "I don't think it's worth it" are probably more accurate ways to state the problem.

No matter what the money problem, the solution usually includes two elements:

- Discover the facts about how much money you have and how much you spend.

- Commit to live within your means—that is, spend no more than you have.

DISCOVER THE FACTS

Money likes to escape when no one is looking. And usually no one *is* looking. That's why the simple act of noticing the details about money can be so useful—even if this is the only idea from this chapter that you ever apply.

To discover the facts, record all the money you receive and spend over the course of each month. This sounds like a big task. But if you use a simple system, you can quickly turn it into a habit.

One option is to carry index cards. Every time you receive money, write the date, the source of income, and the amount on a card. Be sure to use a separate card for each amount.

Do the same for money that you spend. On separate cards, list the date, the amount you spent, and what you paid for.

At the end of the month, sort your cards into income and expense categories and then total the amounts for each category. There's a payoff for this action. When you know how much money you really earn, you'll know how much you really have to spend. And if you know what your biggest expenses are, you'll know where to start cutting back if you overspend.

Of course, index cards are not the only tool for tracking your income and expenses. You can also use computer software and online banking services. Or carefully file all your receipts and paycheck stubs and use them to tally up your monthly income and expenses. Whatever tools you choose, start using them today.

LIVE WITHIN YOUR MEANS

There are three broad strategies for living within your means: increase your income, decrease your expenses, or do both.

Increase income. If you work while you're in school, you can earn more than money. You'll gain experience, establish references, and expand your contacts for getting a new job or making a career change. And regular income in any amount can make a difference in your monthly cash flow.

On most campuses, there is a person in the financial aid office whose job is to help students find work while they're in school. See that person. In addition, check into career-planning services. Using these resources can greatly multiply your job options.

Once you graduate and land a job in your chosen field, continue your education. Look for ways to gain additional skills or certifications that lead to higher earnings and more fulfilling work assignments.

Once you get a job, make it your intention to excel as an employee. Be as productive as possible. Look for ways to boost sales, increase quality, or accomplish tasks in less time. These achievements can help you earn a raise. A positive work experience can pay off for years by leading to other jobs, recommendations, and contacts.

Decrease expenses. When you look for places to cut expenses, start with the items that cost the most. Choices about where to live, for example, can save you thousands of dollars. Sometimes a place a little farther from campus, or a smaller house or apartment, will be much less expensive. You can also keep your housing costs down by finding a roommate.

Another high-ticket item is a car. Take the cost of buying or leasing and then add expenses for parking, insurance, repairs, gas, maintenance, and tires. You might find that it makes more sense to use public transportation. Or find a friend with a car and chip in for gas.

Decreasing the money you spend on low-cost purchases can make the difference between a balanced budget and rising debt. For example, three dollars spent at the coffee shop every day adds up to $1,095 over a year. That kind of spending can give anyone the jitters.

Cook for yourself. This single suggestion could save many a sinking budget.

Do comparison shopping. Prices vary dramatically. Shop around, wait for off-season sales, and use coupons. Check out second-hand stores, thrift stores, and garage sales. Before plunking down the full retail price for a new

2

item, also consider whether you could buy it used. You can find "pre-owned" clothes, CDs, furniture, sports equipment, audio equipment, and computer hardware in retail stores and on the Internet.

Conserve energy. To save money on utility bills, turn out the lights. Keep windows and doors closed in the winter. Avoid loss of cool air in summer. In cool weather, dress warmly and keep the house at 68 degrees or less. In hot weather, take cool showers and baths. Leave air conditioning at 72 degrees or above. Explore budget plans for monthly payments that fluctuate, such as those for heating your home. These plans average your yearly expenses so you pay the same amount each month.

When you spend money on entertainment, ask yourself what the benefits will be and whether you could get the same benefits for less money. You can read magazines for free at the library or online. Most libraries also loan CDs and DVDs for free. Meeting your friends at a bar can be less fun than meeting at a friend's house, where there is no cover charge.

START SAVING NOW

You can being saving now even if you are in debt and living in a dorm on a diet of macaroni. Saving now helps you establish a habit that will really pay off in the future.

Take some percentage of every paycheck you receive and immediately deposit that amount in a savings account. To build money for the future, start saving 10 percent of your income. Then see if you can increase that amount over time.

The first purpose of this savings account is to have money on hand for surprises and emergencies—anything from a big repair bill to a sudden job loss. For peace of mind, have an emergency fund equal to three to six months of living expenses.

Next, save for longer-term goals. Examples are a new car, a child's education, and your own retirement.

 You're One Click Away . . .
from 10 ways to pay for school.

Use credit cards with care

Scrutinize credit card offers. Beware of cards offering low interest rates. These rates are often only temporary. After a few months, they could double or triple. Also look for annual fees, late fees, and other charges buried in the fine print.

Be especially wary of credit card offers made to students. Remember that the companies who willingly dispense cards on campus are not there to offer an educational service. They are in business to make money by charging you interest.

Avoid cash advances. Due to their high interest rates and fees, credit cards are not a great source of spare cash. Even when you get cash advances on these cards from an ATM, it's still borrowed money. As an alternative, get a debit card tied to a checking account and use that card when you need cash on the go.

Pay off the balance each month. An unpaid balance is a sure sign that you are spending more money than you have. To avoid this outcome, keep track of how much you spend with credit cards each month. Then save an equal amount in cash. That way, you can pay off the card balance each month and avoid interest charges. *Following this suggestion alone might transform your financial life.*

If you do accumulate a large credit card balance, go to your bank and ask about ways to get a loan with a lower interest rate. Use this loan to pay off your credit cards. Then promise yourself never to accumulate credit card debt again.

Check statements against your records. File your credit card receipts each month. When you get the bill for each card, check it against your receipts for accuracy. Mistakes in billing are rare, but they can happen. In addition, checking your statement reveals the interest rate and fees that are being applied to your account.

Use just one credit card. To simplify your financial life and take charge of your credit, consider using only one card. Choose one with no annual fee and the lowest interest rate. Don't be swayed by offers of free T-shirts or coffee mugs. Consider the bottom line and be selective.

Release money myths

WHEN IT COMES TO conversations about money, you can profit from questioning the most obvious "truths." Through your thinking, you might discover a path to a lifetime of financial sanity. The purpose of this exercise is to think creatively by brainstorming some alternatives to your current beliefs about money. Before you do, consider the following examples.

Belief: To get an education, you have to go heavily into debt.

Alternative: The surest way to manage debt is to avoid it altogether. If you do take out loans, then *borrow only the amount that you cannot get from other sources*—scholarships, grants, employment, work-study assignments, paid internships, gifts from relatives, and personal savings. Shop around for loans with fixed interest rates that are guaranteed by the federal government. Avoid loans with prepayment penalties (extra charges for paying off the loan before the final due date).

Belief: To have fun, you have to spend money.

Alternative: Look for free entertainment on campus. Also remember that donating your time to community organizations can be a way to contribute to society—and have fun at the same time.

Belief: Money management is complicated.

Alternative: Most money problems result from spending more than is available. It's that simple, even though often we do everything we can to make the problem much more complicated. The solution also is simple: Don't spend more than you have. This idea has never won a Nobel Prize in economics, but you won't go broke applying it.

In the space below, list one of your own current beliefs about money:

Now, brainstorm some alternatives to that belief. One creative technique is to state the *opposite* of your belief—and then see if you can find evidence for it. Write your ideas below and continue on separate paper as needed.

 You're One Click Away . . .
from more creative ways to think about money.

Discover Your Resources

2

CAMPUS RESOURCES
YOU PAID FOR 'EM, SO USE 'EM

Think about all the services and resources that your tuition money buys: academic advising to help you choose classes and select a major; access to the student health center and counseling services; a career planning office that you can visit even after you graduate; athletic, arts, and entertainment events at a central location; and much more.

If you live on campus, you also get a place to stay with meals provided, all for less than the cost of an average hotel room.

And, by the way, you get to attend classes.

Following are a few examples of services available on many campuses. Check your school's catalog for even more.

Academic advisors can help you with selecting courses, choosing majors, career planning, and adjusting in general to the culture of higher education.

Alumni organizations can be good sources of information about the pitfalls and benefits of being a student at your school.

Arts organizations can include concert halls, museums, art galleries, observatories, and special libraries.

Athletic centers and gymnasiums often open weight rooms, swimming pools, indoor tracks, and athletic courts for students.

Chapels are usually open to students of many religions.

Childcare is sometimes provided at a reasonable cost through the early-childhood education department.

Computer labs, where students can go 24 hours a day to work on projects and use the Internet, are often free.

Counseling centers help students deal with the emotional pressures of school life, usually for free or at low cost.

Financial aid offices help students with loans, scholarships, grants, and work-study programs.

Job placement and career-planning offices can help you find part-time employment while you are in school and a job after you graduate.

Libraries are a treasure on campus and employ people who are happy to help you locate information.

Newspapers published on campus list events and services that are free or inexpensive.

Registrars handle information about transcripts, grades, changing majors, transferring credits, and dropping or adding classes.

School media—including campus newspapers, radio stations, Websites, and instructional television services—provide information about school policies and activities.

School security employees provide information about parking, bicycle regulations, and traffic rules. Some school security agencies provide safe escort at night for students.

Student government can assist you in developing skills in leadership and teamwork. Many employers value this kind of experience.

Student health clinics often provide free or inexpensive treatment of minor problems. Many counseling and student health centers target certain services to people with disabilities.

Student organizations offer you an opportunity to explore fraternities, sororities, service clubs, veterans' organizations, religious groups, sports clubs, political groups, and programs for special populations. The latter include women's centers, multicultural student centers, and organizations for international students, disabled students, and gay and lesbian students.

Student unions are hubs for social activities, special programs, and free entertainment.

Tutoring programs can help even if you think you are hopelessly stuck in a course—usually for free. Student athletes and those who speak English as a second language can often get help here.

Note: Community resources—those located off-campus—can range from credit counseling and chemical dependency treatment to public health clinics and churches. Check the city Website.

 You're One Click Away . . .

from more resources that can save you time and money.

Be here now

TO "BE HERE NOW" means to do what you're doing when you're doing it and to be where you are when you're there.

We all have a voice in our head that rarely shuts up. If you don't believe it, try this: Close your eyes for 10 seconds and pay attention to what is going on in your head. Do this right now.

Notice something? Perhaps your voice was saying, "Forget it. I'm in a hurry." Another might have said, "I wonder when 10 seconds is up." Another could have been saying, "What little voice? I don't hear any little voice."

That's the voice.

Instead of trying to force the voice out of your head—a futile enterprise—simply notice it. Accept it. Tell yourself, "There's that thought again." Then gently return your attention to the task at hand. That thought, or another, will come back. Your mind will drift. Simply notice again where your thoughts take you and gently bring yourself back to the here and now.

Another way to return to the here and now is to notice your physical sensations. Notice the way the room looks or smells. Notice the temperature and how the chair feels. Once you've regained control of your attention by becoming aware of your physical surroundings, you can more easily take the next step and bring your full attention back to your present task.

The idea behind this Power Process is simple. When you plan for the future, plan for the future. When you listen to a lecture, listen to a lecture. When you read this book, read this book. And when you choose to daydream, daydream.

Do what you're doing when you're doing it.

Be where you are when you're there.

Be here now . . . and now . . . and now.

 You're One Click Away . . .
from more ways to be here now.

2

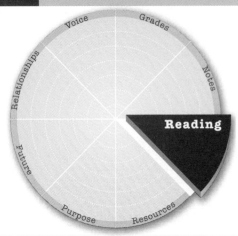

The Discovery Wheel on page 1 includes a section titled Reading. Before you read the rest of this chapter, take a few minutes to go beyond your initial responses to the Discovery Wheel. Reflect on the Skills Snapshot below to take a closer look at your skills. Complete these statements honestly, then flip to the articles or exercises highlighted for strategies that will promote your success.

Skills SNAPSHOT

When faced with a long reading assignment, I prepare for it by ... * ⟶

check out:
Question your text, page 45

* To make sure that I understand what I'm reading, I ...

check out:
Read for answers, page 47

I would rate my ability to remember what I read as ... * ⟶

check out:
Review the answers, page 49

When asked to evaluate what I read, I usually respond by ... * ⟶

check out:
Critical Thinking Experiment #4: "Dear author—I don't necessarily agree," page 51

check out:
Decoding the deadly textbook: Three key strategies, page 52

When faced with an especially difficult reading assignment, I respond by ... *

To succeed in courses with a heavy reading load, I ... * ⟶

check out:
Commit to Action: Five ways to make time for reading, page 55

check out:
Read across the curriculum, page 56

I use different strategies to read a novel or short story than I use for a science or math textbook. For example ... *

check out:
Commit to Action: Experiment with active reading, page 58

If asked to rate the growth in my reading skills over the last year, I would say ... * ⟶

When someone writes or says something that I disagree with, I respond by ... * ⟶

check out:
Power Process: Ideas are tools, page 59

QUESTION YOUR TEXT

When faced with reading assignments, use this three-phase technique to extract the ideas and information you want:

Question your text

Read for answers

Review for answers

The type of reading process that's described in the next several pages may take a little time to learn. At first you might feel like it's slowing you down. That's natural when you're learning a new skill. Mastery comes with time and practice.

Powerful reading starts with powerful questions. Questions open up inquiries. Questions focus your attention and prompt you to become an active learner. Questions help you get your money's worth from your textbooks.

To frame questions about your reading, first do a preview. Also create an informal outline to discover how the material is organized.

PREVIEW

Previewing can significantly increase your comprehension of reading material. It's also an easy way to get started when an assignment looks too big to handle. When you preview, look for the following:

- Book front matter such as the copyright page, preface, dedication, introduction, and contents; also look for sectional or chapter contents, chapter previews, and abstracts.

- Graphically highlighted material—anything underlined or printed in large, bold, italic, or color type.

- Visuals, including boxes, charts, tables, diagrams, illustrations, and photographs.

- Book back matter such as a glossary, bibliography, list of references or works cited, and index; in books, look for chapter summaries and lists of review questions.

Keep the preview short. If the entire reading assignment will take less than an hour, your preview might take five minutes.

When previewing, look for familiar concepts, facts, or ideas. Read all chapter headings and subheadings. Like the headlines in a newspaper, these are usually printed in large, bold type. Often headings are brief summaries in themselves. These items can help link new information to previously learned material. Also look for ideas that spark your imagination or curiosity. Ask yourself how the material can relate to your long-term goals. Are you reading just to get to the main points? Key supporting details? Additional

details? All of the above? Your answers will guide what you do with each phase of the reading process.

Note: When you face a long reading assignment, break it into manageable chunks and preview each one. Textbooks are usually divided into chapters—a logical chunk. However, if the chapter is long or difficult, feel free to tackle it in smaller sections with study breaks between each section.

OUTLINE

With complex material, take time to understand the structure of what you are about to read. Outlining actively organizes your thoughts about the assignment, and it can make complex information easier to understand. If your textbook provides chapter outlines, spend some time studying them.

To get started, stick with a simple, informal outline. Capture each topic in a single word or phrase. List topics in the order that they're mentioned in the text. You can create this outline in pencil in the margins of a book or article. For added precision, copy your outline on separate paper and edit it after reading. Or open a computer file and create your outline there.

The amount of time you spend on this step will vary. For some assignments (fiction and poetry, for example), skip it. For other assignments, a 10-second mental outline is all you need.

LIST QUESTIONS

Before you begin a careful reading, determine what you want from an assignment. Write a list of questions.

Have fun with this technique. Make the questions playful or creative. You don't need an answer to every question that you ask. The purpose of making up questions is to get your brain involved in the assignment.

Questions can come from the previous steps—previewing and outlining. For example:

- Brainstorm a list of topics covered in a chapter. Then write a question about each topic.

- Turn chapter headings and subheadings into questions. For example, if a heading is Transference and Suggestion, ask yourself: "What are transference and suggestion? How does transference relate to suggestion?" Make up a quiz as if you were teaching this subject to your classmates.

- Have an imaginary dialogue with your teacher, or with the author of the book. List the questions you would ask.

- If you do not understand a concept, write specific questions about it. The more detailed your questions, the more powerful this technique becomes.

Another option is to use the six journalist questions: Who? What? When? Where? Why? How? Reporters ask these questions when researching a story. You can use the same strategy to dig out the news from your reading assignments. For example:

- Ask, "Who?" Who wrote this, and what qualifications or special experience does this author bring to bear on the subject? Who is the publisher, and has this organization published other useful texts on the same subject?

- Ask, "What?" What are the key terms in this material, and what is the definition for each one? What are the major topics covered in this text? What do I already know about these topics? What are the main points the author makes about each topic? Can I give an example of each major concept? What points will the author make next?

- Ask, "When?" When was this material published, and does it matter? (For scientific and technical topics, you may want the most current information that's available.)

- Ask, "Where?" Where can I use the ideas and information contained in this text? Where can I find out more about the topics covered?

- Ask, "Why?" Why did my teacher assign this reading? Why does this material matter to me?

- Ask, "How?" How can I explain this material to someone else? How can I organize or visualize this information to make it more vivid? How can I remember these ideas? How can I relate this material to something I already know? How will I be tested or otherwise evaluated on this material? How can learning this material benefit me in this course, in another course, or in my life outside the classroom?

Note: These six kinds of questions will lead you to common test items.

Keep track of your questions. Write them on index cards, one question per card. Or open a word processing file on your computer and key in your questions. Take your unanswered questions to class, where they can be springboards for class discussion.

 You're One Click Away . . .
from more strategies for powerful previewing.

Create outlines from headings

Headings in a chapter or article can serve as major and minor entries in your outline. For added clarity, distinguish major headings from minor headings.
Using the headings from the previous articles in this chapter, you can create the following outline:

DISCOVER . . . YOUR READING (major heading on page 44)
  QUESTION YOUR TEXT (major heading on page 45)
    Preview (minor heading on page 45)
    Outline (minor heading on page 45)
    List questions (minor heading on page 46)

Note: Feel free to rewrite headings so that they are more meaningful to you. Substitute complete sentences for headings that consist of just a single word or phrase. In addition, you can write a sentence or two after each heading to include some more details about the topic.

READ FOR ANSWERS

Previewing, outlining, and questioning set the stage for incoming information by warming up a space in your mental storage area. Now you're ready to inspect the text in greater detail.

READ WITH FOCUSED ATTENTION

Create an image of an active reader in your mind. This is a person who:

- Stays alert, poses questions about what she reads, and searches for the answers.

- Recognizes levels of information within the text, separating the main points and general principles from supporting details.

- Quizzes herself about the material, makes written notes, and lists unanswered questions.

- Instantly spots key terms and takes the time to find the definitions of unfamiliar words.

- Thinks critically about the ideas in the text and looks for ways to apply them.

Before you dive into the first paragraph, take a few moments to reflect on what you already know about the subject. Do this even if you think you know nothing. This technique prepares your brain to accept the information that follows.

It's easy to fool yourself about reading. Just having an open book in your hand and moving your eyes across a page doesn't mean you are reading effectively. Reading textbooks takes energy, even if you do it sitting down.

As you read, be conscious of where you are and what you are doing. When you notice your attention wandering, gently bring it back to the present.

One way to stay focused is to avoid marathon reading sessions. Schedule breaks and set a reasonable goal for the entire session. Then reward yourself with an enjoyable activity for five or 10 minutes every hour or two.

For difficult reading, set shorter goals. Read for a half-hour and then take a break. Most students find that shorter periods of reading distributed throughout the day and week can be more effective than long reading sessions.

You can use the following techniques to stay focused during these sessions:

- Visualize the material. Form mental pictures of the concepts as they are presented. Get a "feel" for the subject. If you read that a voucher system can help control cash disbursements, picture a voucher handing out dollar bills. If you are reading about the microorganism called a paramecium, imagine what it would feel like to run your finger around the long, cigar-shaped body of the organism.

- Read it out loud. This is especially useful for complicated material. Some of us remember better and understand more quickly when we hear an idea.

- Get off the couch. Read at a desk or table and sit up, on the edge of your chair, with your feet flat on the floor. If you're feeling adventurous, read standing up.

- Get moving. Make reading a physical as well as an intellectual experience. As you read out loud, get up and pace around the room. Read important passages slowly and emphatically, and add appropriate gestures.

MAKE MULTIPLE PASSES THROUGH THE TEXT

Somehow, students get the idea that reading means opening a book and dutifully slogging through the text—line by line, page by page—moving in a straight line from the first word until the last. Actually, this can be an inflexible and ineffective way to interact with published material.

Feel free to shake up your routine. Make several passes through any reading material. During a preview, for example, just scan the text to look for key words and highlighted material.

Next, skim the entire chapter or article again, spending a little more time and taking in more than you did during your preview.

Finally, read in more depth, proceeding word by word through some or all of the text. Save this type of close reading for the most important material—usually the sections that directly answer the questions you raised while previewing.

ANSWER YOUR QUESTIONS

From the text, get the answers to the questions you raised earlier and write those answers down. Note when you don't get the answers you wanted to find, and write down new questions. Bring these questions to class, or see your instructor personally.

If you listed your questions on index cards, write an answer on the back of each card. If you entered your questions in a computer file, then open the file again and add answers. Either way, you'll instantly have useful review materials on hand.

When you read, create an image of yourself as a person in search of the answers. You are a detective, watching for every clue, sitting erect in your straight-back chair, demanding that your textbook give you what you want—the answers.

 You're One Click Away . . .

from more strategies for powerful reading.

Eight ways to overcome confusion

Active readers monitor their understanding of a text. When they get confused, they use strategies such as the following.

Collect data about your confusion. When you feel stuck, stop reading for a moment and diagnose what's happening. At these stop points, mark your place in the margin of the page with a penciled S for "stuck." Seeing a pattern to your marks over several pages might indicate a question you want to answer before reading further. Or you might discover a reading habit you'd like to change.

Look for essential words. If you are stuck on a paragraph, mentally cross out all the adjectives and adverbs and read the sentence without them. Find the important words. These will usually be verbs and nouns.

Read it again. Difficult material—such as the technical writing in science—is often easier the second or third time around.

Skip around. Jump immediately to the end of the article or chapter. You may have lost the big picture, and sometimes simply seeing the conclusion or summary is all you need to put the details in context. Retrace the steps in a chain of ideas and look for examples. Absorb facts and ideas in whatever order works for you—which may be different than the author's presentation.

Summarize. Pause briefly to summarize what you've read so far, verbally or in writing. Stop at the end of a paragraph and recite, in your own words, what you have read. Jot down some notes or create a short outline.

Ask for help. Admit when you are stuck and make an appointment with your instructor. Most teachers welcome the opportunity to work individually with students. Be specific about your confusion. Point out the paragraph that you found toughest to understand. Find a tutor. Many schools provide free tutoring services. If tutoring services are not provided by your school, then other students who have completed the course can assist you.

Pretend you understand, then explain it. We often understand more than we think we do. Pretend that the topic is clear as a bell and explain it to another person. Write your explanation down. You might be amazed by what you know. To go even further, volunteer to teach the topic to a study group.

Stop reading. When none of the above suggestions work, do not despair. Admit your confusion and then take a break. Catch a movie, go for a walk, study another subject, or sleep on it. The concepts you've already absorbed may come together at a subconscious level while you pursue other activities. Allow some time for that process. When you return to the reading material, see it with fresh eyes.

REVIEW
THE ANSWERS

This stage of reading completes the process that you begin when previewing and posing questions. After digging into the text to uncover answers, take your understanding of them to a deeper level.

REFLECT ON THE ANSWERS

Reading has been defined as borrowing the thoughts of others just long enough to stimulate your own thinking. To get lasting pleasure and benefit from reading, use it as fuel for insights and aha! moments of your own. Review the answers you uncovered by reading. Mull them over, ponder them, wonder about them, question them, modify them, make them your own.

Begin by testing your understanding of the author's ideas. See if you can think of your own examples to illustrate the main points. Convert text into visual forms, such as charts, diagrams, and maps.

Also review the outline you created while previewing and review it for accuracy. Ask yourself how each chapter or section of the material relates to the rest. Aim to see how the whole book, chapter, or article is organized. Understanding the overall organization gives you a context for the details, making individual facts easier to remember.

RECITE THE ANSWERS

To understand the reasons for reciting, briefly review the way that your memory works:

- The process starts with sense perception, such as words and images printed on a page or displayed on a screen.

- Your brain translates these perceptions into ideas and places them in your short-term memory.

- However, the content of short-term memory quickly fades—unless you actively rehearse it.

Five ways to read with children underfoot

It is possible to combine effective study time and quality time with children by following these tips:

1. Attend to your children first. Spend 10 minutes with your children before you settle in to study.

2. Use "pockets" of time. Look for an extra 15 minutes in your day that you could spend on your reading assignments. You may find extra time at the doctor's office, waiting for the bus, or while your children are warming up for soccer or dance.

3. Plan special activities for your child while you're studying. Find a regular playmate for your child when you need to get schoolwork done.

4. Find community activities and services. Ask if your school provides a day care service or look into community agencies such as the YMCA.

5. When you can't read everything, just read something. It's OK to realize that you can't get all the reading done in one sitting. Just get something done with the time you have. (Caution: Supplement this strategy with others so you can stay on top of your work.)

Reciting offers one means of rehearsal. The benefits are enormous. Reciting helps to move information into your long-term memory. What's more, reciting instantly focuses your attention and turns you into an active learner. If you recite the key points from a chapter by explaining them to someone, you engage your sense of hearing as well as seeing. If you recite by writing a summary of what you've read, you move your fingers and engage all your kinesthetic senses. In each way, your reading experience becomes more vivid.

When you recite, you get important feedback about your learning. If there are any gaps in your understanding of the material, they'll become obvious as you speak or write. Also, reciting forces you to put ideas in your own words and avoid the pitfalls of rote memorization.

Besides being useful, reciting can be fun. Experiment with any of the following options.

Just speak. Talk informally about what you've read. Stop after reading a chapter or section and just speak off the cuff.

If you underlined or highlighted any main points in the text, use these as cues to recite. Note what you marked, then put the book down and start talking out loud. Explain as much as you can about that particular point.

Pretend that you've been asked to give an impromptu speech about the book or article. Talk about what you found significant or surprising in the material. Talk about what you intend to remember. Also talk about how you felt about the reading, and whether you agree or disagree with the author.

Just write. Stop at any point in your reading and write freely. Don't worry about following a particular format or creating a complete summary. Just note the points that emerge with the most clarity and force from your reading, along with your responses to them.

Structure your reciting. Find a chapter title or heading in the text. Then close your book and summarize the text that follows that heading. When you're done, go back to the text and check your recitation for accuracy. Go on to the next heading and do the same. Or choose a passage that you've underlined and explain as much as you can about that particular point.

Another option is to summarize the material in topic-point format. To practice this skill, pick one chapter (or one section of one chapter) from any of your textbooks. State the main topic covered in this chapter (or section of the chapter). Then state the main points that the author makes about this topic.

For even more structure, put your recitation in writing by using one of the note-taking formats explained in Chapter Four.

Recite alone. To make this technique more effective, recite aloud in front of a mirror. It may seem silly, but the benefits can be enormous. Reap them at exam time.

Recite in the presence of people. Friends are even better than mirrors. Form a group and practice teaching each other what you have read. One of the best ways to learn anything is to teach it to someone else, so talk about your reading whenever you can. Tell friends and family members what you're learning from your textbooks.

REVIEW REGULARLY

Plan to do your first complete review within 24 hours of reading the material. Sound the trumpets! This point is critical: A review within 24 hours moves information from your short-term memory to your long-term memory.

The final step is the weekly or monthly review. This step can be very short—perhaps only four or five minutes per assignment. Simply go over your notes. Read the highlighted parts of your text. Recite one or two of the more complicated points. These short reviews will pay off when it is time to recall what you've read.

 You're One Click Away . . .
from more strategies for powerful reviewing.

Deface your book

Something magical happens when you annotate a book—that is, touch it with a pencil or pen. When you make notes in the margin, you can hear yourself talking with the author. When you doodle and underline, you can see the author's ideas take shape. You can even argue with an author or create your own ideas.

Of course, you can only annotate books that you own, and that means you must buy them. The payoff is that you get to mark up the material in a way that truly makes it your own. For example:

Underline the main points—phrases or sentences that answer your questions about the text.

Place asterisks (*) in the margin next to an especially important sentence or term.

Circle key terms and words to look up later in a dictionary.

Write short definitions of key terms in the margin.

Write a Q in the margin to highlight possible test questions, or questions to ask in class.

Write personal comments in the margin—points of agreement or disagreement with the author.

Write mini-indexes in the margin—the numbers of other pages in the book where the same topic is discussed.

Draw diagrams, pictures, tables, and maps to translate straight text into visual forms.

Number each step in a series of related points.

Note: Avoid annotating too soon. Wait until you complete a chapter or section to make sure you know what is important. Then annotate.

Also, underline sparingly, usually less than 10 percent of the text. If you mark up too much on a page, you defeat the purpose—to flag the most important material for review.

"Dear author — I don't necessarily agree"

TWO CORNERSTONES OF CRITICAL thinking are the abilities to test logic and examine evidence. Some strategies for doing both are explained in "Commit to thinking" on page 7. In addition to looking for logical fallacies, you can test logic with the following questions about what you read:

- Does the author define her key terms?
- Do any of the author's main points contradict each other?
- Has the author clearly stated her assumptions (the points that she simply accepts as true without trying to prove them)?
- Is the author's material free of logical fallacies?

Choose a current reading assignment—a nonfiction piece rather than a novel, short story, or poem. Focus on a particular chapter or section of this assignment and test it by asking the above questions. If you answered no to any of the above questions, then explain your reasons for doing so in the space below:

points. Did she present enough facts, examples, or expert testimony to support each one? If you answered no to this question, then explain your reasons for doing so in the space below:

Now review the same chapter or section and examine evidence. In the space below, list the author's main

You're One Click Away . . .
from more ways to think critically about your reading.

DECODING THE DEADLY TEXTBOOK
THREE KEY STRATEGIES

It's no secret: Some textbooks are deadly—dry, disorganized, and long. Skilled readers actually create benefit from such books by using them to practice high-level reading skills. Three of the most important strategies about reading difficult material are to make choices about what to read, adjust your reading pace, and build your vocabulary.

MAKE CHOICES ABOUT WHAT TO READ

Flexible readers constantly make choices about what to read—and what *not* to read. They realize that some texts are more valuable for their purposes than others, and that some passages within a single text are more crucial than the rest. When reading, they instantly ask: What's most important here?

The answer to this question varies from assignment to assignment, and even from page to page within a single assignment. Pose this question each time that you read, and look for clues to the answers. Pay special attention to:

- Parts of the text that directly answer the questions you generated while previewing.
- Any part of the text that's emphasized graphically—for example, headings, subheadings, lists, charts, graphs, and passages printed in bold or italic.
- Summary paragraphs (usually found at the beginning or end of a chapter or section).
- Any passage that provokes a strong response from you or raises a question that you cannot answer.

Use the 80/20 principle. Books about time management often mention the 80/20 principle. The idea is that 80 percent of the value created by any group derives from only 20 percent of its members. If you have a to-do list of ten items, for example, you'll get 80 percent of your desired results by doing only the two most important items on the list. If you go to an hour-long meeting, you might find that the most valuable information gets imparted in the first 12 minutes (20 percent of the meeting time).

The point is not to take these figures literally but to remember the underlying principle: *Focus on what creates the most value.* The most important items may be only a fraction of the total content or of the options available to you in any situation.

You can apply the 80/20 principle to reading. For example:

- In a 10-paragraph newspaper article, you might find 80 percent of the crucial facts in the headline and first paragraph. (In fact, journalists are *taught* to write this way.)
- If you have a 100-page assignment, you may find that the most important facts and ideas could be summarized in 20 pages.

A caution. The 80/20 principle is not an invitation to attend only 20 percent of your classes. Nor is it a license to complete only 20 percent of your reading assignments. Making such choices will undermine your education.

Also remember that to find the top 20 items in any group, you must attend to 100 percent of the items. Likewise, to find the most important parts of anything you read, you first need to get familiar with the whole. Only then can you make sound choices about what you want to remember and apply.

Read it again. Somehow, students get the idea that reading means opening a book and dutifully slogging through the text—line by line, page by page—moving in a straight line from the first word until the last. Actually, this can be an ineffective way to read much of the published material you'll encounter in college.

Feel free to shake up your routine. Make several "passes" through any reading material. During a preview, for example, just scan the text to look for key words and highlighted material.

Next, skim the entire chapter or article again, spending a little more time and taking in more than you did during your preview. Finally, read in more depth, proceeding word by word through some or all of the text.

Difficult material—such as the technical writing in science texts—is often easier the second time around. Isolate difficult passages and read them again, slowly.

If you read an assignment and are completely lost, do not despair. Sleep on it. When you return to the assignment the next day, see it with fresh eyes.

Ask: "What's going on here?" When you feel stuck, stop reading for a moment and diagnose what's happening. At these stop points, mark your place in the margin of the page with a penciled "S" for "Stuck." A pattern to your marks over several pages might indicate a question you want to answer before going further. Or you might discover a reading habit you'd like to change.

ADJUST YOUR READING PACE

Another key aspect of flexible reading is choosing your pace. Most people can read faster simply by making a conscious effort to do so. In fact, you probably can read faster without any loss in comprehension. Your comprehension might even improve.

Experiment with this idea right now. Read the rest of this chapter as fast as you can. After you finish, come back and reread the material at your usual rate. Notice how much you remembered from your first sprint through. You might be surprised to find how well you comprehend material even at dramatically increased speeds.

Following are more strategies for adjusting your reading pace.

Set a time limit. When you read, use a clock or a digital watch with a built-in stopwatch to time yourself. The objective is not to set speed records, so be realistic.

For example, set a goal to read a chapter in an hour. If that works, set a goal of 50 minutes to read a similar chapter. Test your limits. The idea is to give yourself a gentle push, increasing your reading speed without sacrificing comprehension.

Notice and release tension. It's not only possible to read fast when you're relaxed, it's easier. Relaxation promotes concentration. And remember, relaxation is not the same thing as sleep. You can be relaxed and alert at the same time.

Before you read, take a minute to close your eyes, notice your breathing, and clear your mind. Let go of all concerns other than the reading material that's in front of you. Then slowly open your eyes and ease into the text.

Get your body ready. Gear up for reading faster. Get off the couch. Sit up straight at a desk or table, on the edge of your chair, with your feet flat on the floor. If you're feeling adventurous, read standing up.

Notice and release regressions. Ineffective readers and beginning readers make many regressions. That is, they back up and reread words.

You can reduce the number of regressions by paying attention to them. Use an index card to cover words and lines you have read. This can reveal how often you stop and move the card back.

Don't be discouraged if you stop often at first. Being aware of it helps you naturally begin to regress less frequently.

Notice and release vocalizing. Obviously, you're more likely to read faster if you don't read aloud or move your lips. You can also increase your speed if you don't subvocalize—that is, if you don't mentally "hear" the words as you read them. To stop doing it, just be aware of it.

Practice with simpler materials. When you first attempt to release regression and vocalizing, read simpler material. That way, you can pay closer attention to your reading habits. Gradually work your way up to more complex material.

If you're pressed for time, skim. When you're in a hurry, experiment by skimming the assignment instead of reading the whole thing. Read the headings, subheadings, lists, charts, graphs, and summary paragraphs. Summaries are especially important. They are usually found at the beginning or end of a chapter or section.

Remember that speed isn't everything. Skillful readers vary their reading rate according to their purpose and the nature of the material. An advanced text in analytic geometry usually calls for a different reading rate than the Sunday comics.

You also can use different reading rates on the same material. For example, you might sprint through an assignment for the key words and ideas, then return to the difficult parts for a slower and more thorough reading.

BUILD YOUR VOCABULARY

As a skilled reader, you will build your vocabulary. The benefits are many. A large vocabulary makes reading more enjoyable and increases the range of materials you can read. In addition, increasing your vocabulary gives you more options for self-expression when speaking or writing. When you can choose from a larger pool of words, you increase the precision and power of your thinking.

Strengthen your vocabulary by taking delight in words. Look up unfamiliar words. Pay special attention to words that arouse your curiosity.

Keep a dictionary handy. Students regularly use two kinds of dictionaries: the desk dictionary and the unabridged dictionary. A desk dictionary is an easy-to-handle abridged dictionary that you normally use several times in the course of a day. Keep this book within easy reach (maybe in your lap) so you can look up unfamiliar words while reading. You can find a large, unabridged dictionary in a library or bookstore. It provides more complete information about words and definitions not included in your desk dictionary, as well as synonyms, usage notes, and word histories. Both kinds of dictionaries are available on CDs for personal computers.

Computer software such as Microsoft Word comes with a built-in dictionary. Also look for dictionary sites on the World Wide Web. To find them, go to any search engine and use the key words *dictionary* or *reference*.

Put your dictionaries to active use. When you find an unfamiliar word, write it down on an index card. Copy the sentence in which it occurred below the word. You can look up each word immediately or accumulate a stack of these cards and look them up later. Write the definition on the back of the card and add the diacritical marks that tell you how to pronounce the word. You can find a list of these marks in the front of many dictionaries.

Distinguish among word parts. Words consist of discrete elements that can be combined in limitless ways. These parts include roots, prefixes, and suffixes:

- *Roots* are "home base," a word's core meaning. A single word can have more than one root. *Bibliophile*, for example, has two roots: *biblio* (book) and *phile* (love). A *bibliophile* is a book lover.

- *Prefixes* come at the beginning of a word and often modify the meaning of the word root. In English, a common prefix is the single letter *a-*, which often means *not*. Added to *typical*, for example, this prefix results in the word *atypical*, which means "not typical."

- *Suffixes* come at the end of a word. Like prefixes, they can alter or expand the meaning of the root. For instance, the suffix *-ant* means "one who." Thus, an *assistant* is "one who assists."

One strategy for expanding your vocabulary is to learn common roots, prefixes, and suffixes. See an unabridged dictionary for examples.

Look for context clues. You can often deduce the meaning of an unfamiliar word simply by paying attention to context—the surrounding words or images. Later you can confirm your trial definition of the word by consulting a dictionary.

Practice looking for context clues such as:

- *Definitions.* A key word may be defined right in the text. Look for phrases such as *the definition is* or *in other words*.

- *Examples.* Authors often provide examples to clarify a word meaning. If the word is not explicitly defined, then study the examples. They're often preceded by the phrases *for example*, *for instance*, or *such as*.

- *Lists.* When a word is listed in a series, pay attention to the other items in the series. They may, in effect, define the unfamiliar word.

- *Comparisons.* You may find a new word surrounded by synonyms—words with a similar meaning. Look for synonyms after words such as *like* and *as*.

- *Contrasts.* A writer may juxtapose a word with its antonym—a word or phrase with the opposite meaning. Look for phrases such as *on the contrary* and *on the other hand*.

 You're One Click Away . . .

from more ways to master challenging reading material.

English as a second language

If you grew up reading and speaking a language other than English, you're probably called a student of English as a Second Language (ESL) or English Language Learner (ELL). Experiment with the following suggestions to learn English with success.

- **Build confidence.** Make it your intention to speak up in class. List several questions and plan to ask them. Also, schedule a time to meet with your instructors during office hours. These strategies can help you build relationships while developing English skills.

- **Learn by speaking and listening.** To gain greater fluency and improve your pronunciation, make it your goal to *hear* and *speak* English. For example, listen to

radio talk shows. Imitate the speaker's pronunciation by repeating phrases and sentences that you hear. During conversations, also notice the facial expressions and gestures that accompany certain English words and phrases.

- **Gain skills in note taking and test taking.** When taking notes, listen for key words, main points, and important examples. You may also find that certain kinds of test questions—such as multiple choice items—are more common in the United States than in your native country. Chapter 5: Discover Your Grades can help you master these and other types of tests.

- **Create a community of English learners.** Learning as part of a community can increase your

mastery. For example, when completing a writing assignment in English, get together with other people who are learning the language. Read each other's papers and suggest revisions. Plan on revising your paper a number of times based on feedback from your peers.

- **Celebrate your gains.** Every time you analyze and correct an error in English, you make a small gain. Celebrate those gains. Taken together over time, they add up to major progress in mastering English as a second language.

Five ways to make time for reading

TO STAY ON TOP OF YOUR SCHEDULE, create a reading plan for the semester. Planning dispels panic *(I've got 100 pages to read by tomorrow morning!)* and helps you finish off your entire reading load for a term.

You can create a reading plan in less than an hour, and the benefits are beyond calculation. Even if your estimates are off, you'll still go beyond blind guessing or leaving the whole thing to chance. Your reading matters too much for that.

Creating a reading plan is relatively simple. Experience this for yourself by applying the following five steps to your reading assignments for one of your current courses. Steps 1 through 3 add up to a Discovery Statement about the amount of reading assigned for one of your current courses. In step 4, you'll create a specific intention for completing all that reading. And in step 5, you'll evaluate the results you experienced by acting on your intention.

Remember that you can create value from this exercise even if your estimates are not 100 percent accurate.

1 Estimate the total number of pages that you're assigned to read

To arrive at this figure, check your course syllabus. In your estimate, include textbook pages and other materials, such as handouts and Web pages.

Write your total number of assigned pages here:

2 Estimate how many pages you can read during one hour

Remember that your reading speed will differ for various materials, depending on the layout of the pages and the difficulty of the text. To give your estimate some credibility, base it on actual experience. Spend an hour reading several types of assigned materials and see how many pages you complete.

Write your total number of pages per hour here:

3 Estimate the total number of hours you'll need for reading

Take your total number of pages from step 1 and divide it by your pages-per-hour total from step 2.

Consider giving yourself some "wiggle room": Take the figure you just wrote and boost it by 10 percent. This builds in extra time for rereading some assignments and completing any additional assignments that are not listed on the syllabus.

Write your estimated total hours here:

4 Schedule reading time

Take your total number of hours from step 3 and divide it by the number of weeks in your current term. This is the number of hours to set aside for reading each week.

Write that figure here:

Next, pull out your calendar and see if you can schedule that number of hours each week for the next month. Remember to look for pockets of time in your schedule—for example, while you're between classes or riding a bus.

5 Evaluate and repeat

Mark your calendar to return to this exercise and reflect on your reading plan. Are you completing your reading assignments? Do you find that you need more or less time than you originally planned? Consider adjusting the number of hours that you schedule for reading each week.

If this method of planning your reading works for you, also consider using it to plan the reading for all your courses.

 You're One Click Away . . .

from more ways to finish your reading assignments on time.

Discover Your Reading

3

READ ACROSS THE CURRICULUM

The humanities, the sciences, the arts, and other academic subjects did not arise out of a void. Rather, these subjects sprang from human curiosity. People asked questions about the nature of the world and about human nature. The subjects we study today began with those questions—and the vast range of answers that have been created.

A liberal education calls for a lot of reading in different subjects. That creates a challenge: A textbook in differential calculus demands to be read in a different way than *Things Fall Apart*, the novel by Chinua Achebe. Getting the most from either work means tailoring your approach to the subject matter.

If you understand the specific questions behind any subject matter, then you're well on the way to finding answers. Following are two different sets of questions for two different types of reading material.

READ TO SOLVE PROBLEMS

The purpose of some books and articles is to tackle specific problems and propose solutions. Their subjects range from the abstract problems of pure mathematics to the practical problems of engineering or computer science.

As a reader in these subjects, therefore, your purpose is to understand clearly the nature of various problems and the techniques for solving those problems. Ask questions such as these:

- What is the purpose of solving this problem, or what benefits will come from having a solution?
- What are the key features of this problem—the elements that are already known and the elements that have to be discovered?
- If the problem is a technical one, can I restate it in plain English?
- Can I take a problem stated in plain English and restate it in mathematical or other technical terms?
- Have I encountered similar problems before, and if so, how did I solve them?
- Is there a standard formula or process that I can use to solve this problem?
- What are alternative methods that can I use to solve this problem?
- If I had to estimate or guess the best solution to this problem right now, what would it be?

- Can I solve this problem using a single operation, or does it call for several steps? What will each step accomplish?
- Will solving this problem call on me to collect data or do any other research?
- Can I derive a formula from my solution or generalize the solution I reached to similar kinds of problems?

PREPARE FOR READING AT WORK

In the workplace, your purpose for reading is probably to produce a specific outcome—to gain a skill or gather information needed to complete a task. The key to successfully reading for work is to make several passes through the material. Remember that you don't have to "get it all" the first time or even read sections in order.

Another strategy is to create a "to read" folder. Much of the paper that crosses your field of attention at work will probably consist of basic background material—items that are important but not urgent. Place these documents in a folder, label it "to read," and pull it out the next time you have a few minutes to spare.

READ FOR INTERPRETATION AND INSIGHT

Courses in literature, drama, and film do not propose carefully reasoned theories about the world or human nature. Nor do they focus on solving problems. Instead, they teach through *vicarious experience*.

When you read a novel, see a play, or watch a film, you see the world through another human being's eyes. You get a window into that person's thoughts and feelings as the events of her life unfold. Just as you gain insight from your own experiences, you can gain insights from the experiences of others.

Works of fiction call for a substantial shift in your reading approach. Some points to remember include the following.

One of your purposes is pure enjoyment. People love a good story. This is something that's easy to forget when you're dissecting a poem or analyzing a play in one of your literature classes.

Another purpose is interpretation. When encountering literature, your concern is not only with what is being said but how it is being said. You respond not only to content (the artist's essential message) but to technique (the way that the artist gets her message across). For a literary artist, technique includes the challenges of creating characters, crafting plot lines, and writing dialogue. When you can notice these elements and explain how they affect you, you've done the job of interpretation.

Interpretation calls for more than one reading. Read a poem, novel or play once through simply for enjoyment. Then allow time for several more readings so that you can pick up the details of the plot and the nuances of the character's personalities.

Interpretation often means going beyond the page. To get the full effect of a poem, for example, read it out loud. Also remember that a play is ultimately meant to be observed rather than simply read. Whenever possible, see a live or recorded performance of the work.

With these points in mind, you can ask useful questions to guide interpretation and promote insight:

- Who are the major characters in this work?
- What does each character want, and what obstacles stand in his or her way?
- How does each character change throughout the course of the story?

- What is the key complication in the story—the early event that sets a major character in pursuit of what he or she wants?
- What are the major events in the story—the points at which the action takes a significant turn?
- Is the story told in chronological order? If not, why not?
- When and where does the story take place, and are these details important?
- Who tells the story—a character or a narrator? How does this point of view shape the story?
- What is the theme of the story—the major topic it deals with or the fundamental point of view behind it?

 You're One Click Away . . .
from more strategies for reading across the curriculum.

Critical thinking for online reading

Anyone can post a Website. This means that digital content is highly democratic—and sometimes highly questionable. Don't get bamboozled.

Examine the features of the Website in general. Notice the effectiveness of the text and visuals as a whole. Also note how well the site is organized and whether you can navigate the site's features with ease. Look for the date that crucial information was posted, and determine how often the site is updated.

Take a detailed look at the site's content. Examine several of the site's pages and look for consistency of facts, quality of information, and competency with grammar and spelling. Are the links easy to follow?

Evaluate the site's links to related Web pages. Look for links to pages of reputable organizations. Click on a few of those links. If they lead you to dead ends, this might indicate a site that's not updated often—one that's not a reliable source for late-breaking information.

Consider the source. Think about the credibility of the person or organization that posts a Website. Look for a list of author credentials and publications. Perhaps the site's sponsoring organization wants you to buy a service, a product, or a point of view. If so, determine whether this fact colors the ideas and information posted on the Website.

Look for contact information. Reputable sites usually include a way for you to contact the author or sponsoring organization outside the Internet, including a mailing address and phone number. If you question a site, ask a librarian or your professor for help in evaluating it.

 You're One Click Away . . .
from more strategies for avoiding misinformation on the Internet.

Commit to Action

Experiment with active reading

RECALL A TIME WHEN YOU encountered problems with reading, such as words you didn't understand or paragraphs you paused to reread more than once. Perhaps you remember a time when you were totally confused by a reading assignment and had no idea how to overcome that confusion.

In either case, sum up the experience and how you felt about it by completing the following statement.

Discovery Statement

I discovered that I . . .

Next, list the three most useful suggestions for reading that you gained from this chapter.

Intention Statement

Describe how you will apply a suggestion from this chapter to a current reading assignment.

I intend to . . .

Action Statement

After acting on your intention, consider how you might adapt or modify the suggestion to make it more useful to you.

I intend to . . .

You're One Click Away . . .
from more reading strategies.

Ideas are tools

THERE ARE MANY IDEAS in this book. When you first encounter them, don't believe any of them. Instead, think of them as tools.

For example, you use a hammer for a purpose—to drive a nail. When you use a new hammer, you might notice its shape, its weight, and its balance. You don't try to figure out whether the hammer is "right." You just use it. If it works, you use it again. If it doesn't work, you get a different hammer.

This is not the attitude most people adopt when they encounter new ideas. The first thing most people do with new ideas is to measure them against old ones. If a new idea conflicts with an old one, the new one is likely to be rejected.

People have plenty of room in their lives for different kinds of hammers, but they tend to limit their capacity for different kinds of ideas. A new idea, at some level, is a threat to their very being—unlike a new hammer, which is simply a new hammer.

This book is a toolbox, and tools are meant to be used. If you read about a tool in this book that doesn't sound "right" or one that sounds a little goofy, remember that the ideas here are for using, not necessarily for believing. Suspend your judgment. Test the idea for yourself. If it works, use it. If it doesn't, don't.

A word of caution: A master mechanic carries a variety of tools because no single tool works for all jobs. If you throw a tool away because it doesn't work in one situation, you won't be able to pull it out later when it's just what you need. So if an idea doesn't work for you and you are satisfied that you gave it a fair chance, don't throw it away. File it away. The idea might come in handy sooner than you think.

 You're One Click Away . . .
from more ways to see ideas as tools.

4 Discover...
Your Notes

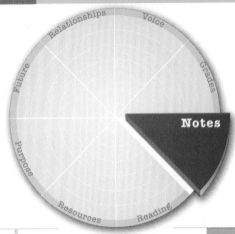

The Discovery Wheel on page 1 includes a section titled Notes. Before you read the rest of this chapter, take a few minutes to go beyond your initial responses to the Discovery Wheel. Reflect on the Skills Snapshot below to take a closer look at your skills. Complete these statements honestly, then flip to the articles or exercises highlighted for strategies that will promote your success.

Skills SNAPSHOT

I would describe my overall note-taking skills as . . . *

check out:
"Notes that rock,"
page 61

To prepare for taking effective notes, I . . . *

check out:
"Notes that rock: Set the stage," page 62

During class, I find that I take better notes when . . . *

check out:
"Notes that rock: Show up for class," page 64

check out:
Critical Thinking
Experiment #5: "Listen for key points," page 66

* To distinguish between the key points in a lecture and the supporting details, I . . .

check out:
"Notes that rock: Predict test questions," page 69

* If I find myself trying to write down everything an instructor says, I . . .

As tools for predicting test questions, my notes are . . . *

check out:
"Notes that rock: Capture key words," page 67

If asked to rate my flexibility as a note taker (the ability to take notes in various formats), I would say that . . . *

check out:
"Notes that rock: Play with formats," page 70

If I looked back at notes that I took last term or last year, I would describe them as . . . *

check out:
"Notes that rock: Mine your notes for more value," page 74

* To improve my skills at note taking, I intend to . . .

check out:
Commit to Action:
"Transform your note taking," page 76

When faced with a tough problem, my usual response is to . . .

*

check out:
Power Process: "Love your problems," page 77

Notes that Rock

> INTRO TO PHILOSOPHY, 1/10/09   1
>
> <u>Philosophy</u>—from the Greek <u>philosophia</u>—"lover of wisdom"
> Philosophers have different views of their main task:
> —reflect on the nature of ultimate reality
> —create a framework to unite all fields of knowledge
> —critically evaluate all claims to knowledge
> Traditional topics on philosophy = 5 areas:
> 1. Determine when a series of assertions is coherent and
>   consistent (logic)
> 2. Determine what is ultimately real (ontology)
> 3. Determine what constitutes real knowledge
>   (epistemology)
> 4. Determine what is truly valuable (axiology and
>   aesthetics)
> 5. Determine what forms of behavior best sustain human
>   society (ethics and politics)

You enter a lecture hall filled with dozens of students. A lone person stands at the front of the room behind a lectern. For the next hour, he will do most of the talking. Everyone else in the room is seated and silent, taking notes. One person—the lecturer—seems to be doing all the work.

Don't be deceived. Look more closely and you'll see some people taking notes in a way that radiates energy. They're awake and alert, poised on the edge of their seats. They're writing, a physical activity that expresses mental engagement—the ability to listen for levels of ideas and information, make choices about what to record, and create effective materials to review later.

While you participate in higher education, you may spend hundreds of hours taking notes. Experimenting with ways to make those notes more effective is a direct investment in your success. Think of your notes as a textbook that *you* create—one that's more current and more in tune with your learning preferences than any textbook you could buy.

Legible and speedy handwriting is useful in taking notes. Knowledge about outlining is handy, too. A nifty pen, a new notebook, and a laptop computer are all great note-taking devices. And they're all worthless—unless you take notes in a way that helps you *think* about what you're reading and experiencing in class.

One way to understand note taking is to realize that taking notes is just one part of the process. Effective note taking consists of a series of activities. For example, you observe an "event"—a statement by an instructor, a lab experiment, a slide show of an artist's works, or a chapter of required reading. Then you record your observations of that event, that is, you "take notes." Then you review what you have recorded and reflect on it more deeply.

Each phase of note taking is essential, and each depends on the others. Your observations determine what you record. What you record determines what you review. And the quality of your review can determine how effective your next observations will be.

Use the suggestions in this chapter to complete each phase of note taking more effectively. The main strategies are to:

- Set the stage.
- Show up for class.
- Listen for key points.
- Capture key ideas.
- Predict test questions.
- Play with formats.
- Mine your notes for more value.

If you put these ideas into practice, you can turn even the most disorganized chicken scratches into tools for learning.

 You're One Click Away . . .

from more perspectives on the power of note taking.

NOTES THAT ROCK
SET THE STAGE

The process of note taking begins well before you enter a classroom or crack open a book. You can promote your success at the task by "psyching up"—setting the physical and mental stage to receive what your teachers have to offer. The following suggestions can help.

COMPLETE REQUIRED READING

Instructors usually assume that students complete reading assignments, and they construct their lectures accordingly. The more familiar you are with a subject, the easier it will be to understand in class. Nothing is more discouraging (or boring) than sitting through a lecture about the relationship of the Le Chatelier principle of kinetics if you have never heard of Le Chatelier or kinetics.

BRING THE RIGHT MATERIALS

A good pen does not make you a good observer, but the lack of a pen or a notebook can be distracting enough to take the fine edge off your concentration. Make sure you have a pen, pencil, notebook, and any other materials you will need. Bring your textbook to class, especially if the lectures relate closely to the text.

If you are consistently unprepared for a class, that might be a message about your intentions concerning the course. Find out if it is. The next time you're in a frantic scramble to borrow pen and paper 37 seconds before the class begins, notice the cost. Use the borrowed pen and paper to write a Discovery Statement about your lack of preparation. Consider whether you intend to be successful in the course.

ARRIVE EARLY TO PUT YOUR BRAIN IN GEAR

When students arrive at class late or with only seconds to spare, they create a level of stress that interferes with listening. You can avoid that interference by arriving at least five minutes before class begins. Use the spare time to warm up your brain by reviewing notes from the previous class.

SIT IN THE FRONT OF THE CLASSROOM

This signals your willingness to participate fully in class. The closer you sit to the front, the fewer the distractions. Also, material on the board is easier to read from up front, and the instructor can see you more easily when you have a question.

Instructors are usually not trained to perform. While some can project their energy to a large audience, some cannot. A professor who sounds boring from the back of the room might sound more interesting up close.

Sitting up front enables you to become a constructive force in the classroom. By returning the positive energy that

an engaged teacher gives out, you can reinforce the teacher's enthusiasm and enhance your experience of the class.

In addition, sound waves from the human voice begin to degrade at a distance of eight to 12 feet. If you sit more than 15 feet from the speaker, your ability to hear and take effective notes might be compromised. Get close to the source of the sound. Get close to the energy.

Sitting close to the front is a way to commit yourself to getting what you want out of school. One reason students gravitate to the back of the classroom is that they think the instructor is less likely to call on them. Sitting in back can signal a lack of commitment. When you sit up front, you are declaring your willingness to take a risk and participate.

TAKE CARE OF HOUSEKEEPING DETAILS

Write your name and phone number in each notebook in case you lose it. Class notes become more and more valuable as a term proceeds.

Develop the habit of labeling and dating your notes at the beginning of each class. Number the page, too. Sometimes the sequence of material in a lecture is important.

Devote a specific section of your notebook to listing assignments for each course. Keep all details about test dates here also, along with a course syllabus. You're less likely to forget assignments if you compile them in one place where you can review them all at a glance.

If you store notes on a computer, create one file where you list assignments for all your courses.

LEAVE BLANK SPACE

Notes tightly crammed into every corner of the page are hard to read and difficult to use for review. Give your eyes a break by leaving plenty of space, no matter what technology or note-taking format you use. Later, when you review, you can use the blank space in your notes to clarify points, write questions, or add other material. Often, instructors return to material covered earlier in the lecture. If you leave adequate space, you can add information.

CONSIDER THE PROS AND CONS OF RECORDERS

Some students are fond of recording lectures. Before you record, consider the potential pitfalls. For one, recorders can malfunction. Watching or listening to recorded lectures can take a lot of time—in fact, more time than reviewing written notes. And when you record a lecture, you may be tempted to daydream ("I'll just listen to this later.").

With those warnings in mind, you might be able to use recordings effectively. Recordings can help you:

- Catch up after an absence. Recordings can help you stay on track if you have to miss a class. Ask a classmate to record the lecture for you. Some teachers may even be willing to do this.

- **Review your written notes.** To create a useful review tool, record yourself as you review the notes you took in class. Using your notes as a guide, see if you can re-create the essence of the lecture. Pretend you're teaching the class.

- **Create review materials.** Use recordings to create and burn CDs to listen to while you drive.

Make sure that your recording equipment works. During class, set the volume high enough to pick up the speaker. Sitting close and up front can help.

Also back up your recording with written notes. Turn the recorder on and then take notes as if it weren't there. If the recording fails, you'll still have a record of what happened in class.

Note: Before recording, check with your instructors. Some prefer not to be recorded.

Laptop computers offer more technology for note taking, along with several benefits. As with recorders, however, there are downsides. Laptops can freeze, crash, or run out of battery power. You can get around these disadvantages in several ways.

- **Protect your work.** Save your data often while taking notes. Regularly back up all your computer files.

- **Bring paper and pen—just in case.** If you have computer problems, you can keep taking notes without missing a beat. Also, you may find it easier to enter diagrams and formulas by hand rather than by keyboard.

- **Combine handwritten notes with computer-based notes.** This option gives you the best of both worlds. During class, take notes by hand. After class, enter your notes into a word processing or database file. Or use the computer simply to outline or summarize your notes. In either case, save your handwritten notes as a backup.

When taking notes, you can always turn to the original word processors—pen or pencil and paper. If you do, keep the following in mind.

Use a three-ring binder. Three-ring binders have several advantages over other kinds of notebooks. First, pages can be removed and spread out when you review. This way, you can get the whole picture of a lecture. Second, the three-ring-binder format will allow you to insert handouts right into your notes easily. Third, you can insert your own out-of-class notes in the correct order.

Use only one side of a piece of paper. When you use one side of a page, you can review and organize all your notes by spreading them out side by side. Most students find the benefit well worth the cost of the paper. If you're concerned about the environmental impact of consuming more paper, use the blank side of old notes or buy recycled paper.

 You're One Click Away . . .
from more ways to set the stage for note taking.

Take effective notes for online learning

You can print out anything that appears on a computer screen—online course materials, articles, books, manuscripts, e-mail messages, chat room sessions, and more.

One potential problem: You might skip taking notes on this material altogether (*I can just print out everything!*). You then miss the chance to internalize a new idea by restating it in your own words. Result: Material passes from computer to printer without ever intersecting your brain.

To prevent this problem, find ways to actively engage with online course material:

- Talk about what you're learning (and consider running a recorder at the same time).

- Organize a study group with other members of your online class.

- Write summaries of online articles and chat room sessions.

- Save online materials in a word processing file on your computer and add your own notes.

- Keep a personal journal to capture key insights from the course and ways you plan to apply them outside the class.

- Print out online materials and treat them like a textbook, applying the suggestions for reading explained in Chapter Three.

SNOTES THAT ROCK
SHOW UP FOR CLASS

Your ability to take notes in any course—from American history to zoology—can instantly improve when you truly show up for class. That means taking a seat in the room *and* focusing your attention while you're there. Use the following suggestions to meet both goals.

LIMIT DISTRACTIONS

Listening can be defined as the process of overcoming distraction. In the classroom, you may have to deal with external distractions—noises from the next room, students who have side conversations, a lecturer who speaks softly, or audiovisual equipment that malfunctions. Internal distractions can be even more potent—for example, memories about last Saturday night's party, daydreams about what you'll do after class, or feelings of stress.

When the problem is an external distraction, you'll often know what to do about it. You can move closer to the front of the room, ask the lecturer to speak up, or politely ask classmates to keep quiet.

Internal distractions can be trickier. Some solutions follow:

- Flood your mind with sensory data. Notice the shape and color of the pen in your hand. Run your hand along the surface of your desk. Bring yourself back to class by paying attention to the temperature in the room, the feel of your chair, or the quality of light in the room.

- Don't fight daydreaming. If you notice that your attention is wandering from thermodynamics to beach parties, let go of the beach. Don't grit your teeth and try to stay focused. Just notice when your attention has wandered and gently bring it back.

- Pause for a few seconds and write distracting thoughts down. If you're distracted by thoughts of errands you want to run after class, list them on an index card and stick it in your pocket. Once your distractions are out of your mind and safely stored on paper, you can gently return your attention to taking notes.

Let go of judgments about lecture styles. Human beings are judgment machines. We evaluate everything, especially other people. If another person's eyebrows are too close together (or too far apart), if she walks a certain way or speaks with an unusual accent, we instantly make up a story about her. We do this so quickly that the process is usually not a conscious one.

Don't let your attitude about an instructor's lecture style, habits, or appearance get in the way of your education. You can decrease the power of your judgments if you pay attention to them and let them go.

You can even let go of judgments about rambling, unorganized lectures. Turn them to your advantage. Take the initiative and organize the material yourself. While taking notes, separate the key points from the examples and supporting evidence. Note the places where you got confused and make a list of questions to ask.

Participate in class activities. Ask questions. Volunteer for demonstrations. Join in class discussions. Be willing to take a risk or look foolish, if that's what it takes for you to learn. Chances are, the question you think is "dumb" is also on the minds of several of your classmates.

Relate the class to your goals. If you have trouble staying awake in a particular class, write at the top of your notes how that class relates to a specific goal. Identify the reward or payoff for reaching that goal.

REMEMBER THAT YOU CAN LISTEN *AND* DISAGREE

When you hear something you disagree with, notice your disagreement and let it go. If your disagreement is persistent and strong, make note of this and then move on. Internal debate can prevent you from receiving new information. Just absorb it with a mental tag: "I don't agree with this and my instructor says . . . ."

Later, as you review and edit your notes after class, think critically about the instructor's ideas. Take this time to list questions or write about your disagreements.

A related guideline is to avoid "listening with your answer running." This refers to the habit of forming your response to people's ideas *before* they've finished speaking. Give people the courtesy of letting them have their say, even when you are sure you'll disagree.

GIVE THE SPEAKER FEEDBACK

Speakers are human beings. They thrive on attention. They want to know that their audiences have a pulse. Give lecturers verbal and nonverbal feedback—everything from simple eye

contact to insightful comments and questions. Such feedback can raise an instructor's energy level and improve the class.

BRACKET EXTRA MATERIAL

Bracketing refers to separating your own thoughts from the lecturer's as you take notes. This is useful in several circumstances:

- Bracket your own opinions. For the most part, avoid making editorial comments in your lecture notes. The danger is that when you return to your notes, you may mistake your own ideas for those of the instructor. If you want to make a comment—either a question to ask later or a strong disagreement—clearly label it as your own. Pick a symbol or code and use it in every class. Brackets can work well.

- Bracket material that confuses you. Invent your own signal for getting lost during a lecture. For example,

write a circled question mark in the margin of the paper. Or simply leave space for the explanation or clarification that you will get later. The space will also be a signal that you missed something. As long as you are honest with yourself when you don't understand, you can stay on top of the course.

- Let go of judgments about rambling, unorganized lectures. Take the initiative and organize the material yourself. While taking notes, separate the key points from the examples and supporting evidence. Note the places where you got confused and make a list of questions to ask.

 You're One Click Away . . .

from more strategies for "showing up" as you take notes.

Cope with fast-talking teachers

Ask the instructor to slow down. This obvious suggestion is easily forgotten. If asking him to slow down doesn't work, ask him to repeat what you missed. Also experiment with the following suggestions.

Take more time to prepare for class. Familiarity with a subject increases your ability to pick out key points. Before class, take detailed notes on your reading and leave plenty of blank space. Take these notes with you to class and simply add your lecture notes to them.

Be willing to make choices. Focus your attention on key points. Instead of trying to write everything

down, choose what you think is important. Occasionally you will make a wrong choice and neglect an important point. Worse things could happen.

Exchange photocopies of notes with classmates. Your fellow students might write down something you missed. At the same time, your notes might help them.

Leave empty spaces in your notes. Allow plenty of room for filling in information you missed. Use a symbol that signals you've missed something, so you can remember to come back to it.

See the instructor after class. Take your class notes with you and show the instructor what you missed.

Learn shorthand. Some note-taking systems, known as shorthand, are specifically designed for getting ideas down fast. Books and courses are available to help you learn these systems.

Ask questions even if you're totally lost. There may be times when you feel so lost that you can't even formulate a question. That's OK. Just report this fact to the instructor. Or just ask any question. Often this will lead you to the question you really want to ask.

Listen for key points

KEY POINTS ARE the major ideas in a lecture—the "bottom-line" or "takeaway" messages. Lecturers usually provide verbal clues that they're coming up to a key point. Listen for phrases such as:

The following three factors ...

The most important thing is ...

What I want you to remember is ...

In conclusion ...

To illustrate and support key points, speakers offer supporting material in the form of examples, facts, statistics, quotations, anecdotes, and other details.

In short, there are two levels of material in a lecture: (1) key points and (2) details that support the key points. Your ability to examine evidence depends on making this distinction.

You can make this distinction in your notes with simple visual cues. For example:

- **Highlight key points.** As you take notes, graphically emphasize the key points. Underline them, write them in uppercase letters, write them in a different color of ink, or go over them with a highlighter. In your notes, record only the most vivid or important details used to support each key point.
- **Use numbered lists to record a sequence of key points.** When you want to indicate a series of events or steps that take place in time, number each one in chronological order.
- **Format your notes in two columns.** In the left-hand column, list the key points. On the right, include the most important details that relate to each point.

To experiment with these suggestions right away, complete the following steps to evaluate your note taking:

1 Select a page or two of class notes that you've taken recently.

2 Circle, underline, or highlight the key points.

3 If you were not able to distinguish the key points from supporting material in your notes, then do some revision. Recopy your notes using the two-column format described above. Show your revised notes to a classmate or to your instructor and ask for feedback.

Finally, reflect on this exercise. Complete the following sentences.

In reviewing my notes, I discovered that . . .

To take more effective notes in the future, I intend to . . .

You're One Click Away . . .

from more ways to capture key points and supporting details.

NOTES THAT ROCK
CAPTURE KEY WORDS

When it comes to notes, more is not necessarily better. Your job is not to write down all of a lecturer's words or even most of them. Taking effective notes calls for split-second decisions about which words are essential to record and which are less important.

An easy way to sort the less important from the essential is to take notes using key words. Key words or phrases contain the essence of communication. They include technical terms, names, numbers, equations, and words of degree: *most, least, faster,* and the like.

Key words are laden with associations. They evoke images and associations with other words and ideas. One key word can initiate the recall of a whole cluster of ideas. A few key words can form a chain: From those words, you can reconstruct an entire lecture.

FOCUS ON NOUNS AND VERBS

In many languages, there are two types of words that carry the essential meaning of most sentences—nouns and verbs. For example, the previous sentence could be reduced to: *nouns + verbs carry meaning. Carry* is a verb; the remaining words are all nouns.

There are additional ways to subtract words from your notes and still retain the lecturer's meaning:

- **Eliminate adverbs and adjectives**. The words *extremely interesting* can become *interesting* in your notes—or simply an exclamation mark (!).

- **Note the topic followed by a colon and key point**. For instance, *There are seven key principles that can help you take effective notes* becomes *Effective notes: 7 principles.*

- **Use lists**. There are two basic types. A numbered list expresses steps that need to be completed in a certain order. A simple list includes ideas that are related but do not have to follow a sequential order.

To find more examples of key words, study newspaper headlines. Good headlines include a verb and only enough nouns to communicate the essence of an event.

EXAMPLE: REDUCING SPEECH TO KEY WORDS

To see how key words can be used in note taking, take yourself to an imaginary classroom. You are enrolled in a course on world religion, and today's lecture is an introduction to Buddhism. The instructor begins with these words:

Okay, today we're going to talk about three core precepts of Buddhism. I know that this is a religion that may not be familiar to many of you, and I ask that you keep an open mind as I proceed. Now, with that caveat out of the way, let's move ahead.

First, let's look at the term anicca. By the way, this word is spelled a-n-i-c-c-a. Everybody got that? Great. All right, well, this is a word in an ancient language called Pali, which was widely spoken in India during the Buddha's time—about 600 years before the birth of Jesus. Anicca is a word layered with many meanings and is almost impossible to translate into English. If you read books about Buddhism, you may see it rendered as impermanence, and this is a passable translation.

Impermanence is something that you can observe directly in your everyday experience. Look at any object in your external environment and you'll find that it's constantly changing. Even the most solid and stable things—like a mountain, for example—are dynamic. You could use time-lapse photography to record images of a mountain every day for ten years, and if you did, you'd see incredible change—rocks shifting, mudslides, new vegetation, and the like.

Following is one way to reduce this section of the lecture to key words:

Buddhism: 3 concepts
#1 = anicca = impermanence.
Anicca = Pali = ancient Indian language (600 yrs b4 Jesus).
Example of anicca: time-lapse photos → changes in mountain.

This example might be a little sparse for your tastes. Remember that it shows only one possible option for abbreviating your notes. Don't take it as a model to imitate strictly.

A CAVEAT: USE COMPLETE SENTENCES AT CRUCIAL POINTS

Sometimes key words aren't enough. When an instructor repeats a sentence slowly and emphasizes each word, he's sending you a signal. Also, technical definitions are often worded precisely because even a slightly different wording will render the definitions useless or incorrect. Write down key sentences word for word.

ADDITIONAL SUGGESTIONS FOR CAPTURING THE ESSENTIAL INFORMATION

- **Use standard abbreviations.** Be consistent with your abbreviations. If you make up your own abbreviations or symbols, write a key explaining them in your notes. Avoid vague abbreviations. When you use an abbreviation such as *comm.* for *committee*, you run the risk of not being able to remember whether you meant *committee, commission, common, commit, community, communicate,* or *communist.*

- **Write notes in paragraphs.** When it is difficult to follow the organization of a lecture or to put information into outline form, create a series of informal paragraphs. These paragraphs will contain few complete sentences. Reserve complete sentences for precise definitions, direct quotations, and important points that the instructor

4

Discover Your Notes

emphasizes by repetition or other signals—such as the phrase "This is an important point." For other material, apply the suggestions in this article for using key words.

- **Listen for introductory, concluding, and transition words and phrases.** These include phrases such as "the following three factors," "in conclusion," "the most important consideration," "in addition to," and "on the other hand." These phrases and others signal relationships, definitions, new subjects, conclusions, cause and effect, and examples. They reveal the structure of the lecture. You can use these phrases to organize your notes.

- **Take notes in different colors.** You can use colors as highly visible organizers. For example, you can signal important points with red. Or use one color of ink for notes about the text and another color for lecture notes. Notes that are visually pleasing can be easier to review.

 You're One Click Away . . .

from more strategies for reducing ideas to their essence.

Short and sweet—the art of abbreviation

Abbreviations can greatly speed up your note taking—if you use them consistently. Some abbreviations are standard. If you make up your own abbreviations, write a key explaining them in your notes.

Avoid vague abbreviations. When you use an abbreviation like *comm.* for committee, you run the risk of not being able to remember whether you meant *committee, commission, common, commit, community, communicate, or communist.*

If you key your notes into word processing files, you can use the Find feature to replace abbreviations with full words. The following seven principles explain how to use abbreviation in your notes:

Principle: Leave out articles.
Examples: Omit *a, an, the.*

Principle: Leave out vowels.
Examples: Talk becomes *tlk, said* becomes *sd, American* becomes *Amrcn.*

Principle: Use mathematical symbols.
Examples: Plus becomes +, *minus* becomes -, *is more than* becomes >, *is less than* becomes <, *equals* or *is* becomes =.

Principle: Use arrows to indicate causation and changes in quantity.
Examples: Increase becomes ↑; *decrease* becomes ↓; *causes, leads to,* or *shows that* becomes →.

Principle: Use standard abbreviations and omit the periods.
Examples: Pound becomes *lb, Avenue* becomes *av.*

Principle: Create words from numbers and letters that you can sound out and combine.
Examples: Before becomes *b4, too* becomes *2.*

Principle: Use a comma in place of *and.*
Examples: Freud and Jung were major figures in twentieth-century psychology becomes *20th century psych: Freud, Jung = major figures.*

NOTES THAT ROCK
PREDICT TEST QUESTIONS

Predicting test questions can do more than help you get better grades. It can also keep you focused on the purpose of the course and help you design your learning strategies. Following are legal and constructive ways to outsmart your teacher and reduce surprises at test time.

CREATE A SIGNAL TO FLAG POSSIBLE TEST ITEMS IN YOUR NOTES

Use asterisks (**), exclamation points (!!), or a *T!* in a circle. Place these signals in the margin next to ideas that seem like possible test items.

LOOK FOR VERBAL CUES FROM YOUR TEACHER

Few teachers will try to disguise the main content of their courses. In fact, most offer repeated clues about what they want you to remember. Many of those clues are verbal. In addition to focusing on *what* lecturers say, pay attention to how they say it.

Repetition. Your teachers may state important points several times or return to those points in subsequent classes. They may also read certain passages word for word from their notes or from a book. Be sure to record all these points fully in your notes.

Common terms. Also note your teachers' "pet phrases"—repeated terms that relate directly to course content. You could benefit from using these terms in essay exams—along with explanations in your own words to show that you truly understand the concepts.

Questions. Pay attention to questions that the instructor poses to the class. These are potential test questions. Write them down, along with some answers.

Emphasis on certain types of content. Some teachers emphasize details—facts, names, dates, technical terms, and the like. Other teachers focus on broad themes and major events. Be alert to such differences. They are clues to the kind of tests you'll have.

Placement of content. Listen closely to material presented at the beginning and end of a lecture. Skilled speakers will often preview or review their key content at these points.

Comments on assigned readings. When material from reading assignments is also covered extensively in class, it is likely to be on the test. The opposite can also be true: When your teacher emphasizes material that does *not* appear in any assigned reading, that material is likely to be important.

LOOK FOR NONVERBAL CUES FROM YOUR TEACHER

Sometimes a lecturer's body language will give potent clues to key content. He might use certain gestures when making critical points—pausing, looking down at notes, staring at the ceiling, or searching for words. If the lecturer has to think hard about how to make a point, that's probably an important point. Also note the following.

Watch the board or overhead projector. If an instructor takes time to write something down, consider this to be another signal that the material is important. In short: If it's on the board, on a projector, or in a handout, put it in your notes. Use your own signal or code to flag this material.

Watch the instructor's eyes. If an instructor glances at his notes and then makes a point, it is probably a signal that the information is especially important. Anything he reads from his notes is a potential test question.

WRITE PRACTICE TEST QUESTIONS

Save all quizzes, papers, lab sheets, and graded material of any kind. Quiz questions have a way of appearing, in slightly altered form, on final exams. If copies of previous exams are available from your instructor, use them to predict test questions. For science courses and other courses involving problem solving, practice working problems using different variables.

Also brainstorm test questions with other students. This is a great activity for study groups.

REMEMBER THE OBVIOUS

Listen for these words: "This material will be on the test."

 You're One Click Away . . .

from more ways to predict test questions.

NOTES THAT ROCK
PLAY WITH FORMATS

USING THE CORNELL FORMAT

One option for note taking that has worked for students around the world is the Cornell format. Originally described by Walter Pauk, this approach is now taught across the United States and in other countries as well.[1]

The cornerstone of this system is simple: a wide margin on the left-hand side of the page. Pauk calls this the cue column, and using it is the key to the Cornell format's many benefits. To get started with this approach to note taking, take the following steps.

Format your paper. On each page of your notes, draw a vertical line, top to bottom, about two inches from the left edge of the paper. This line creates the cue column—the space to the left of the line. You will use this space later to condense and review your notes.

Pauk also suggests that you leave a two-inch space at the bottom of the page. He calls this the summary area. This space is also designed to be used at a later stage, as you review your notes.

Take notes, leaving the cue column and summary area blank. As you read or listen to a lecture, take notes on the right-hand side of the page. *Do not write in the cue column or summary area.* You'll use these spaces later.

Fill in the cue column. You can make several kinds of entries in the cue column:

- Reduce notes to key questions. Think of the notes you took on the right-hand side of the page as a set of answers. In the cue column, write the corresponding questions. Write one question for each major term or point in your notes.
- Reduce notes to key words. Writing key words will speed the review process later. Also, reading your notes and focusing on extracting key words will further reinforce your understanding of the lecture or reading assignment.
- Reduce notes to headings. Pretend that you are a copy editor at a newspaper, and that the notes you took are a series of articles about different topics. In the cue column, write a headline for each "article." Use actual newspaper headlines—and headings in your textbooks—as models.

Fill in the summary area. See if you can reduce all the notes on the page to a sentence or two. Add cross-references to topics elsewhere in your notes that are closely related. Explain briefly why the notes on this page matter; if you think the material is likely to appear on a test, note that fact here. Also use the summary area to list any questions that you want to ask in class.

USING OUTLINES

In addition to the Cornell format, another option for note taking is outlining. The Roman-numeral style represents just one option for outlining. By playing with other options, you can discover the power of outlining to reveal relationships between ideas and to categorize large bodies of information.

Outlines consist of *headings*—words, phrases, or sentences arranged in a hierarchy from general to specific:

- In the first or top level of an outline, record the major topics or points that are presented in a lecture or reading assignment.
- In the second level, record the key topics or points that are used to support and explain the first-level headings.
- In the third level, record facts, examples, and other details that relate to each of your second-level headings.

Following is an outline of this article, based on the above suggestions:

USING THE CORNELL FORMAT

Format paper in two vertical columns and summary
    area at bottom

Take notes; leave cue column and summary area blank

Fill in cue column with key questions, key words, or
    headings

Fill in summary area

USING OUTLINES

In the top level, record major topics or points

In the second level, record key supporting topics or points

In the third level, record other topics or points

USING CONCEPT MAPS

Choose one concept as a focus

List related concepts

Arrange concepts in a hierarchy

Add links

EXAMPLE: NOTES IN CORNELL FORMAT

CUE COLUMN	NOTES
	INTRO TO PHILOSOPHY 1/10/09
What is the origin of the word Philosophy?	Philosophy—from the Greek philosophia—"lover of wisdom"
What do philosophers do?	Philosophers have different views of their main task: --reflect on the nature of ultimate reality --create a framework to unite all fields of knowledge --critically evaluate all claims to knowledge
What are 5 traditional topics in philosophy?	Traditional topics in philisophy = 5 areas: 1. Determine when a series of assertions is coherent and consistent (logic) 2. Determine what is ultimately real (ontology) 3. Determine what constitutes real knowledge (epistemology) 4. Determine is what is truly valuable (axiology and aesthetics) 5. Determine what forms of behavior best sustain human society (ethics and politics)

SUMMARY

Even though philosophers have differing views of their task, there are 5 traditional topics in philosophy.

Notice that first-level headings in this outline are printed in all uppercase (capital) letters. Second-level headings appear in both uppercase and lowercase letters.

You could add a third level of headings to this outline by listing the topic sentences for each paragraph in the chapter. These third-level headings could be indented and listed underneath the second-level headings.

USING CONCEPT MAPS

Concept mapping—explained by Joseph Novak and D. Bob Gowin in their book *Learning How to Learn*—is a way to express ideas in a visual form.[2] The key elements are:

- A main concept written at the top of a page.
- Related concepts arranged in a hierarchy, with more general concepts toward the top of a page and more specific concepts toward the bottom.
- Links—lines with words that briefly explain the relationship between concepts.

When you combine concepts with their linking words, you'll often get complete sentences (or sets of coherent phrases). One benefit of concept maps is that they quickly, vividly, and accurately show the relationships between ideas. Also,

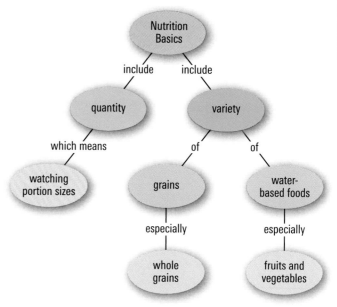

EXAMPLE: NOTES IN CONCEPT MAP FORMAT

The concept map shown above is an excerpt from notes on a reading assignment about nutrition.

concept mapping helps you think from general to specific. By choosing a main topic, you focus on the big picture, then zero in on subordinate details. And by using only key words, you can condense a large subject into a small area on a concept map. You can review more quickly by looking at the key words on a concept map than by reading notes word for word.

Use the following steps to create concept maps.

Choose one concept as a focus. To begin, limit the scope of your concept map. Choose one general concept as a focus—the main topic of a chapter, article, or lecture. Express this concept in one to three words. Concept words are usually nouns and adjectives, including key terms and proper names. Circle your main concept.

List related concepts. Next, brainstorm a list of concepts that are related to the main concept. Don't worry about putting these concepts in any order yet. Just list them—again, expressing each concept in a single word or short phrase. For ease in rearranging and ranking the concepts later, you might wish to write each one on a single index card—or on a single line in a word processing file.

Arrange concepts in a hierarchy. Rank concepts on a continuum from general to specific. Then create the body of your concept map by placing the main concept at the top and the most specific concepts at the bottom. Arrange the rest of the concepts in appropriate places throughout the middle. Again, circle each concept.

Add links. Draw lines that connect the concepts along with words that describe their relationships. Limit yourself to the fewest words needed to make accurate links. Linking words are often verbs, verb phrases, or prepositions.

COMBINING FORMATS

Feel free to use different note-taking systems for different subjects and to combine formats. Do what works for you.

For example, combine concept maps along with the Cornell format. You can modify the Cornell format by dividing your note paper in half, reserving one half for mind maps and the other for linear information, such as lists, graphs, and outlines, as well as equations, long explanations, and word-for-word definitions. You can incorporate a mind map into your paragraph-style notes whenever you feel one is appropriate. Minds maps are also useful for summarizing notes taken in the Cornell format.

John Sperry, a teacher at Utah Valley State College, developed a note-taking system that can include all of the formats discussed in this article:

- Fill up a three-ring binder with fresh paper. Open your notebook so that you see two blank pages—one on the left and one on the right. Plan to take notes across this entire two-page spread.

- During class or while reading, write your notes only on the left-hand page. Place a large dash next to each main topic or point. If your instructor skips a step or switches topics unexpectedly, just keep writing.

- Later, use the right-hand page to review and elaborate on the notes that you took earlier. This page is for anything you want. For example, add visuals such as mind maps. Write review questions, headlines, possible test questions, summaries, outlines, mnemonics, or analogies that link new concepts to your current knowledge.

- To keep ideas in sequence, place appropriate numbers on top of the dashes in your notes on the left-hand page. Even if concepts are presented out of order during class, they'll still be numbered correctly in your notes.

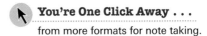 **You're One Click Away . . .**
from more formats for note taking.

TAKING NOTES WHILE READING

Taking notes while reading requires the same skills that apply to class notes: observing, recording, and reviewing. Use these skills to take notes for review and for research.

REVIEW NOTES

These will look like the notes you take in class. Take review notes when you want more detailed notes than writing in the margin of your text allows. You might want to single out a particularly difficult section of a text and make separate notes. You can't underline or make notes in library books, so these sources will require separate notes, too.

Use a variety of formats. Mind maps and concept maps are useful for review, especially for summaries of overlapping lecture and textbook materials. You can also outline or take notes in paragraph form. Another option is the Cornell method. Use the left-hand column for key words and questions, just as you do in your class notes.

When you read mathematic, scientific, or other technical materials, copy important formulas or equations. Recreate important diagrams and draw your own visual representations of concepts. Also write down data that might appear on an exam.

RESEARCH NOTES

Take research notes when preparing to write a paper or deliver a speech.

One traditional tool for research notes is the mighty index card. Create two kinds of cards: source cards and information cards.

Source cards. These cards identify where you found the information contained in your paper or speech. For example, a source card for a book will show the author, title, date and place of publication, and publisher. Ask your instructor what information to include for each type of source.

When you write source cards, give each source a code—the initials of the author, a number, or a combination of numbers and letters.

A key advantage of using source cards is that you create your bibliography as you do the research. When you are done, simply alphabetize the cards by author and—voilà!—instant bibliography.

Information cards. Write the actual research notes on information cards. At the top of each information card, write the code for the source of the information. For printed sources, also include the page numbers your notes are based on. When recording your own ideas, simply note the source as "me."

Write only one piece of information on each information card—a single quotation, fact, or concept. You can then sort the cards in various ways to construct an outline of your paper or speech.

Avoid plagiarism. When people take words or images from a source and present them as their own, they are committing plagiarism. Even when plagiarism is accidental, the consequences can be harsh.

Consider a computer. Another option is to take research notes using a computer. This offers the same flexibility as index cards when it comes to sorting and organizing ideas. However, be especially careful to prevent plagiarism. If you copy text or images from a Web site, separate these notes from your own ideas. Use a different font for copied material or enclose it in quotation marks.

THINK ABOUT NOTES

Whenever you take notes, use your own words as much as possible. When you do so, you are thinking about what you are reading. If you do quote your source word for word, put that material within quotation marks.

Close the book after reading an assignment and quickly jot down a summary of the material. This writing can be loose, without any structure or format. The important thing is to do it right away, while the material is still fresh in your mind. Restating concepts in this way helps you remember them.

SPECIAL CASES

The style of your notes can vary according to the nature of the material. If you are assigned a short story or poem, read the entire work once without taking any notes. On your first reading, simply enjoy the piece. When you finish, write down your immediate impressions. Then go over the piece and make brief notes on characters, images, symbols, settings, plot, point of view, or other aspects of the work.

NOTES THAT ROCK
Mine your notes for more value

The purpose of taking notes is to consult them later. To some students, that means scanning them once or twice before a test. By that time, however, the notes may raise more questions than they answer.

As an alternative, add value to your notes by updating, condensing, reorganizing, reviewing, and refining them.

The key is to see your notes as living documents—words and images that gain clarity as your understanding of a subject deepens. Create notes that you will understand for weeks, months, or years to come.

REVISE YOUR NOTES

Take your first pass through your notes as soon after each class as possible. Use this time to:

- Fix passages that are illegible.
- Check to see that your notes are labeled with the date and the name of the class.
- Make sure that the pages are numbered.
- Expand on passages that are hard to understand.
- Write out abbreviated words or phrases that might be unclear to you later.
- List questions that you need answered in order to make sense of your notes.

You might find it useful to distinguish between what you wrote in class and what you filled in later. With handwritten notes, edit using a different colored pen or pencil. If you key your notes into a computer, you can use different colored fonts for your edits.

Sometimes it helps to get a different perspective on the material. You can do that by re-creating your notes in a new format. If you took notes in Cornell format, for example, convert sections to outline format. Use all these formats at different points in your notes for a course, or invent new formats of your own.

The benefit of playing with all these formats is that they engage your mind in different ways. Taking notes in Cornell format can help you get a handle on details—key terms and facts. Outlines force you to pay attention to the way that material is structured. And maps are visual devices that help you see connections between many topics at once. Each format yields a different cross-section of the subject matter. And each format deepens your understanding.

REVIEW YOUR NOTES

In terms of reinforcing long-term memory, the process you use to review your notes can be just as crucial as the content or format of those notes. Think of notes that have not been reviewed as leaky faucets, constantly dripping, losing precious information until you shut them off with a quick review.

The sooner you review your notes, the better, especially if the class was difficult. In fact, you can start reviewing during class. When your instructor pauses to set up the overhead projector or erase the board, scan your notes. Dot the i's, cross the t's, and write out unclear abbreviations.

Another way to use this technique is to get to your next class as quickly as you can. Then use the four or five minutes before the lecture to review the notes you just took in the previous class.

If you do not get to your notes immediately after class, you can still benefit by reviewing later in the day. A review right before you go to sleep can also be valuable. And you can do it in just a few minutes—often 10 minutes or less.

Once a week, review all your notes again. The review sessions don't need to take a lot of time. Even a 20-minute weekly review period is valuable. Some students find that a weekend review, say, on Sunday afternoon, helps them stay in continuous touch with the material. Scheduling regular review sessions on your calendar helps develop the habit.

As you review, step back for the larger picture. In addition to reciting or repeating the material to yourself, ask questions about it:

- How does this relate to information I already know, in this field or another?
- Will I be tested on this material?
- What will I do with this material?
- How can I relate it to something that deeply interests me?
- Am I unclear on any points? If so, what exactly is the question I want to ask?

A third and equally important level of review is the kind of studying you do during the week before a major test. This is an intensive phase of learning that can involve many types of activity: creating course summaries, writing mock tests, and taking part in study groups.

REHEARSE YOUR NOTES

When you want to remember a fact or idea, you instinctively rehearse it. Rehearsal can be as simple as repeating the seven digits of a phone number a few times before you dial it—or as complex as an actor who practices lines to learn a one-hour monologue.

The point is this: Information that you rehearse moves into your long-term memory. And information that you do not rehearse can fade completely from your memory in anywhere from a few seconds to a few hours. In more common parlance: If you don't use it, you lose it.

For more effective rehearsal, try the following.

Use a variety of strategies. Recite the points in your notes that you want to remember. Explain these points to someone else. Lead a study group about the topic. Also look for ways to summarize and condense the material. See if you can take the language from your notes and make it more precise. If you succeed, edit your notes accordingly.

Involve your senses. Make rehearsal a rich, enjoyable experience. Read your notes out loud and use a variety of voices. Sing your notes, making up your own rhymes or songs. Record yourself as you recite your notes, and play music you like in the background.

Use elaborative rehearsal instead of rote memory. Rehearsal is a sophisticated learning strategy that goes well beyond rote repetition. As you review your notes, use rehearsal to move facts and ideas off the page and into your mind. See if you can elaborate on your notes by using more of your own words and by supplying your own examples.

Build a feedback cycle into your rehearsal. Create a list of key questions that cover the important sections of your notes. Then quiz yourself, or ask a friend to quiz you. To get maximum value from this exercise, evaluate the accuracy of your answers. If you're consistently missing key questions, then consider using a new strategy for reading or note taking.

Allow adequate time. Following the above suggestions means that rehearsal will take more time than mindlessly scanning your notes. It's worth it. Also remember that you can be selective. You don't have to rehearse everything in your notes. Save your most elaborate rehearsal for the most important material.

 You're One Click Away . . .

from more ways to revise, review, and rehearse your notes.

5 ways to improve your handwriting

Many people are resigned to writing illegibly for the rest of their lives. They feel that they have no control over their handwriting. Yet everyone's handwriting does change. Since handwriting undergoes change unconsciously, you can make a conscious effort to change it. The prerequisite for improving your handwriting is simply the desire to do so. Then you can explore the following possibilities.

1. Use creative visualizations. Find a quiet spot to sit, then relax your whole body, close your eyes, and see yourself writing clearly. Feel the pen as it moves over the page and visualize neat, legible letters as you write them.

2. Revise sloppy writing immediately. Use an erasable pen or pencil. When you write something sloppily, fix it immediately. At first, you might find yourself rewriting almost everything. This technique can help you learn to write legibly.

3. Dot all *i*'s and cross all *t*'s. The time you spend dotting and crossing will eliminate time spent scratching your head.

4. Notice problem letters. Go through your notes and circle letters that you have difficulty deciphering. Practice writing these letters.

5. Be willing to slow down. Weigh the costs and benefits of writing more slowly as a way to improve your handwriting. If you cannot read what you write, speed is of little use. Also, take fewer notes; write down only what's essential. Learning to take notes efficiently could allow you to improve your handwriting and spend less time writing and more time learning.

Commit to Action
Transform your note taking

THINK BACK ON the last few lectures you have attended. How would you rate your note taking skills? As you complete this exercise think of areas that need improvement.

First, recall a recent incident in which you had difficulty taking notes. Perhaps you were listening to an instructor who talked fast. Maybe you got confused and stopped taking notes altogether. Or perhaps you went to review your notes after class, only to find that they made no sense at all.

Discovery Statement

Describe an incident where note taking was challenging for you.

Intention Statement

Now review this chapter to find at least ten strategies that you can use right away to help you take better notes. Sum up each of those strategies in a few words and note page numbers where these strategies are explained.

Strategy   **Page number**

Action Statement

Now gear up for action. Describe a specific situation in which you will apply at least three of the strategies you listed above. If possible, choose a situation that will occur within the next 24 hours.

After experimenting with these strategies, evaluate how well they worked for you. If you thought of a way to modify any of the strategies so that they can work more effectively, describe those modifications here:

> **You're One Click Away . . .**
> from more ways to apply the cycle of discovery, intention, and action to note taking.

Discover Your Notes

4

Love your problems

4

Discover Your Notes

PROBLEMS OFTEN WORK LIKE BARRIERS. When we bump up against one of our problems, we usually turn away and start walking along a different path. And all of a sudden—bump!—we've struck another barrier. As we continue to bump into problems and turn away from them, our lives stay inside the same old boundaries. We stop learning.

One way of dealing with a barrier is to pretend it doesn't exist. A second approach is to fight the barrier, which usually makes it grow.

The third option is to love the barrier. Accept it. Totally experience it. Tell the truth about it. Describe it in detail. When you do this, the barrier loses its power. You can literally love it to death.

You might not actually eliminate the fear; however, your barrier *about* the fear might disappear. And you might discover that if you examine the fear, love it, accept it, and totally experience it, the fear itself also disappears.

Loving a problem does not stop us from solving it. In fact, fully accepting and admitting the problem usually helps us take effective action—which can free us of the problem once and for all.

 You're One Click Away . . .
from more ways to love your problems.

5 Discover...
Your Grades

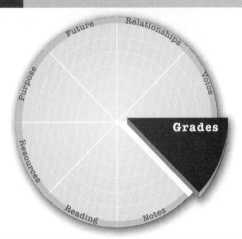

The Discovery Wheel on page 1 includes a section titled Grades. Before you read the rest of this chapter, take a few minutes to go beyond your initial responses to the Discovery Wheel. Reflect on the Skills Snapshot below to take a closer look at your skills. Complete these statements honestly, then flip to the articles or exercises highlighted for strategies that will promote your success.

Skills SNAPSHOT

If I get a high grade, it tells me that . . .
If I get a low grade, it tells me that . . . *

check out:
"Grades: The truth,"
page 79

If asked to rate, on a scale of 1 to 10, how well I'm usually prepared for tests, I'd choose a rating of _____ because . . . *

check out:
"Six R's for remembering," page 82

check out:
"Be ready for your next test," page 80

* I'd describe my skill at recalling information during tests as . . .

* To prevent making careless errors on tests, I . . .

check out:
"Test-taking errors and ways to avoid them,"
page 85

If I get a low grade on a test, my first response is to . . . *

check out:
Critical Thinking Experiment #6: "Turn 'F' into feedback," page 86

* If I feel worried or anxious about a test, I usually respond by . . .

check out:
"Relax—it's just a test,"
page 87

My overall strategy for succeeding in math courses is to . . . *

check out:
"Math essentials,"
page 90

* If I could change anything about the way that I experience tests, it would be . . .

check out:
Commit to Action:
"Transform your experience of tests,"
page 92

I can separate my grades from my overall opinion of myself: *
❏ Most of the time
❏ Some of the time
❏ Almost never

check out:
Power Process:
"Detach," page 93

GRADES: THE TRUTH

On the surface, tests don't look dangerous. Yet sometimes we treat them as if they are land mines.

Suppose a stranger walks up to you on the street and says, "Amiri Baraka first published under another name. What was it?"*

Would you break out in a cold sweat?

Would your muscles tense up?

Probably not—even if you've never heard of Amiri Baraka. However, if you find the same question on a test and you don't know the answer, your hands might get clammy.

That's because there are lots of misconceptions about grades. Here are some truths about grades that textbooks usually don't tell you:

Grades are not a measure of your intelligence or creativity.

Grades are not an indication of your ability to contribute to society.

Grades are not a measure of your skills or your worth as a human being.

The truth is, grades often result from test scores. And a test score is only a measure of how a student responded to items on a test.

Some people think that a test score measures what you accomplished in a course. This is false. If you are anxious about a test and blank out, the grade cannot measure what you've learned. The reverse is also true: If you are good at taking tests and you are a lucky guesser, the grade won't be an accurate reflection of what you know.

If you get a low grade on a test, you are simply a person who got a low grade on a test—nothing more.

Don't give the test some magical power over your worth as a human being. Academic tests are not a matter of life or death. Scoring low on important tests—entrance tests for college or medical school, bar exams, CPA exams—usually means only a delay.

There's another common confusion about grades—that the way to get good grades is to study for tests. That sounds logical, but what does that word *study* really mean? Skimming your textbooks? Skimming your notes?

One way to prevent hours of wasted time is to see each test as a performance. From this point of view, preparing for a test means *rehearsing*. Study in the way that a musician rehearses for a concert or an actor prepares for opening night—by simulating the physical and psychological conditions you'll encounter when you actually enter the exam room.

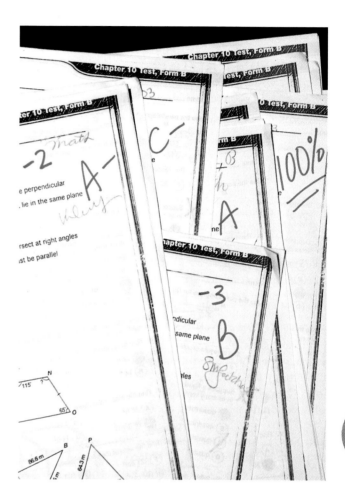

 Discover Your Grades

5

Rehearsing for a test means doing the kinds of tasks that you'll actually perform during a test: answering questions, solving problems, composing essays, and the like.

Start your rehearsal with regular reviews of course content. Also create special review materials, explore the power of study groups, and discover ways to reduce fears of tests. In this chapter, you'll find dozens of suggestions on these topics. Use them to transform your experience of tests—and discover for yourself the truth about grades.

> **You're One Click Away . . .**
> from information about integrity in test taking.

---

*Amiri Baraka has written more that 40 books, including essays, poems, and plays. He first published under the name LeRoi Jones.

BE READY
FOR YOUR NEXT TEST

When getting ready for tests, remember the key word—*review*. First create effective materials for review. Then use them often.

WRITE REVIEW CHECKLISTS
To begin your test preparation, make a list of what to review in each subject. Include items such as:

- Reading assignments by chapters or page numbers.
- Dates of lectures and major topics covered in each lecture.
- Skills you must master.
- Key course content—definitions, theories, formulas, sample problems, and laboratory findings.

A review checklist is not a review sheet; it is a to-do list. These checklists contain the briefest possible description of each type of material that you intend to review.

When you conduct your final review sessions, cross items off each checklist as you study them.

CREATE SUMMARY NOTES
Summary notes are materials that you create specifically to review for tests. They are separate from notes that you take throughout the term on lectures and readings. Summary notes tie together content from all sources—readings, lectures, handouts, lab sessions, and any other course elements.

You can create summary notes with a computer. Key in all your handwritten notes and edit them into outline form. Or simply create an annotated table of contents for your handwritten notes. Note the date of each lecture, the major topics covered in the lecture, and the main points about each topic.

Even if you study largely from summary notes, keep the rest of your notes on file. They'll come in handy as backup sources of information.

CREATE FLASH CARDS
Flash cards are like portable test questions. Write them on index cards. On one side of the cards, write key terms or questions. On the other side, write definitions or answers. It's that simple.

Buy an inexpensive card file to keep your flash cards arranged by subject. Then carry a pack of flash cards with you whenever you think you might have a spare minute to review them. Also keep a few blank cards with you. That way, you can make new flash cards whenever you recall new information to study.

CREATE A MOCK TEST
Write your own exam questions and take this "test" several times before the actual test. Before writing questions, make some predictions about the exam. Review your notes and find material that seems important, and recall the lecture for topics that your professor covered in detail.

Design your mock test so that it looks like the real thing. And if possible, write out your answers in the room where the test will actually take place. When you walk in for the real test, you'll be in familiar territory.

GET COPIES OF PREVIOUS TESTS
Copies of previous exams for a class may be available from the instructor, other students, the instructor's department, the library, or the counseling office. Old tests can help you plan a review strategy. In addition, keep a file of tests that have been returned to you.

Caution: If you rely on old tests exclusively, you may gloss over material the instructor has added since the last test. Also check your school's policy about making past tests available to students.

DO DAILY REVIEWS
Daily reviews include the short pre- and post-class reviews of reading and lecture notes. This is a powerful tool for moving ideas from short-term to long-term memory.

Short daily reviews are ideal tasks for small pockets of time, such as waiting for a bus or doing laundry. To make sure you complete these reviews, include them on your daily to-do list. Write down *5 min. review of biology* or *10 min. review of economics*. When you're done, give yourself the satisfaction of crossing each item off your list.

AMERICAN HISTORY TEST

Date: 11/1

Materials:

☐ Lecture notes: 9/14 – 10/29

☐ Textbook, pages 190–323

☐ *The Federalist*, chapters 1, 2, 4, 6

Topics:

☐ Hamilton and bank policies

☐ Frontier crisis

☐ Jay's treaty and foreign policy

☐ Election of 1796

☐ Alien and Sedition Acts

DO WEEKLY REVIEWS

Review each subject at least once a week. Revisit assigned readings and lecture notes and do something that forces you to rehearse the material. For example:

- Look over any course summaries you've created and see if you can re-create them from memory.
- Answer study questions and sample problems from your textbooks.
- Recite the points in your notes that you want to remember.
- Rewrite your notes for greater precision and clarity.

DO MAJOR REVIEWS

Major reviews are usually conducted during the week before finals or other major exams. They integrate concepts and deepen your understanding of material presented throughout the term. *To uncover gaps in knowledge, start major reviews at least three days before the test.*

Major reviews are longer review periods—several hours at a stretch, punctuated by breaks. During long sessions, study the most difficult subjects at the beginning, when you are most alert.

Remember that the effectiveness of your review begins to drop after an hour or so unless you give yourself a short rest. And after a certain point, short breaks every hour might not be enough to refresh you. That's when it's time to quit.

Learn your limits by being conscious of the quality of your concentration. When you find it difficult to focus your attention, quit for the day and come back to it tomorrow. Allowing yourself this leeway is a powerful reason for conducting major reviews over several days.

KNOW THE LIMITATIONS OF CRAMMING

Cramming won't work if you've neglected all of the reading assignments, or if you've skipped most of the lectures and daydreamed through the rest. The more courses you have to cram for, the less effective cramming will be. Also cramming is not the same as learning: you won't remember what you cram. The purpose of cramming is only to make the best of the situation. The key to cramming is repetition. Go over your material again and again.

 **You're One Click Away . . .**
from more strategies for test preparation.

Seven things to do with your study group

1. Compare notes. Make sure you all heard the same thing in class and that you all recorded the important information.

2. Work in groups of three at a computer to review a course. Choose one person to operate the keyboard. Others can dictate summaries of lectures and assigned readings.

3. Brainstorm test questions. You can add these to the "Test Questions" section of your notebook.

4. Take a mock test and share results. Ask each group member to bring four or five sample test questions to a meeting. Create a mock test from these questions, take the test under timed conditions, and share answers.

5. Practice teaching each other. Teaching is a great way to learn something. Turn the material you're studying into a list of topics. Then assign specific topics for each person to teach the group.

6. Create wall-size concept maps to summarize a textbook or series of lectures. Work on large sheets of butcher paper, or tape together pieces of construction paper.

7. Pair off to do "book reports." One person can summarize an assigned reading. The other person can act like an interviewer on a talk show, posing questions and asking for further clarification.

SIX R'S FOR REMEMBERING

Discover Your Grades

5

On a conscious level, a memory appears as a discrete mental event—an image, a series of words, the record of a sensation. On a biological level, each of those events involves millions of nerve cells firing chemical messages to each other. Memory is the *probability* that those nerve cells will fire together again in the future. The whole art of improving memory is increasing that probability.

Following are six strategies you can use for this purpose. They all begin with the letter *R*—a convenient hook for your memory.

RELAX

Stress in all its forms—including fear and anxiety—interferes with memory. You can learn about relaxation techniques from books, Websites, audio and video recordings, and workshops. Some of these techniques are sophisticated and take time.

However, you can reduce tension at any time simply by noticing your breathing. This will make it deeper and more regular. For a deeper relaxation, deliberately slow down your breathing. Take in more air with each inhalation and release more air with each exhalation.

When you're relaxed, you absorb new information quickly and recall it with greater ease and accuracy. Students who can't recall information under the stress of a final exam can often recite the same facts later when they are relaxed. Also remember that being relaxed is not the same as being drowsy, zoned out, or asleep. Relaxion is a state of alertness, free of tension, during which your mind can play with new information, roll it around, create associations with it, and apply many of the other memory techniques.

REDUCE

Start by reducing distraction. The simple act of focusing your attention at key moments can do wonders for your memory. Test this idea for yourself: The next time you're introduced to someone, direct 100 percent of your attention to hearing that person's name. Do this consistently and see what happens to your ability to remember names.

Study in a quiet place that is free from distraction. If there's a party at your house, go to the library. If you have a strong attraction to food, don't torture yourself by studying next to your refrigerator. Two hours of studying in front of the television might equal only 10 minutes of studying where it is quiet.

As an aid to focused attention, avoid marathon study sessions. Plan for shorter, spaced-out sessions. You may find that you can recall more from three two-hour sessions than one six-hour session.

Next, reduce the amount of material to master. Decide what's essential to remember from reading assignments and lectures. Extract core concepts and key examples. Ask what you'll be tested on, as well as what you want to remember.

When you've chosen what you want to remember, then divide the content into manageable chunks. Efficient rehearsal calls for limiting the number of items in your short-term memory at one time. As a rough guide, remember the number seven. When reading a long list of terms, for instance, stop after the first seven or so and see if you can write definitions for them.

Also study your most difficult subjects duing times when your energy peaks. Many people can concentrate more effectively during daylight hours. The early morning hours can be especially productive, even for those who hate to get up with the sun. Observe the peaks and valleys in your energy flow during the day and adjust times accordingly.

Perhaps you will experience surges in memory power during the late afternoon or evening.

RESTRUCTURE

Structure refers to the way that things are organized. When you're faced with a long list of items to remember, look for ways to organize them. Group them into larger categories or arrange them in chronological order.

You can apply this suggestion to long to-do lists. Write each item on a separate index card. Then create a pile of cards for calls to make, for errands to run, and for household chores. Within each of these categories, you can also arrange the cards in the order you intend to do them.

The same concept applies to the content of your courses. When reading a novel, for example, organize ideas and facts in categories such as plot, characters, and setting:

- To remember the plot, create a timeline. List key events on index cards and arrange the cards to parallel the order of events in the book.

- Group the people in the story into major and minor characters. Again, use index cards to list each character's name along with an identifying feature.

- If geographical setting is important, create a map of the major locations described in the story.

RELATE

The data already in your memory is arranged according to a scheme that makes sense to you. When you introduce new data, relate it to similar data:

- *Create visual associations.* Invent a mental picture of the information you want to remember. You can remember how a personal computer stores files by visualizing the hard disk as a huge filing cabinet. This cabinet is divided into folders that contain documents.

- *Associate course material with something you want.* If you're bogged down in quadratic equations, stand back for a minute. Think about how that math course relates to your goal of becoming an electrical engineer, or to gaining skills that open up new career options for you.

Mnemonics are verbal associations that can increase your ability to recall everything from grocery lists to speeches. There are several varieties, such as:

- *Acrostics:* For instance, the first letters of the words in the sentence *Every good boy does fine* (E, G, B, D, and F) are the music notes of the lines of the treble clef staff.

- *Acronyms:* You can make up your own acronyms to recall a series of facts. A common mnemonic acronym is Roy G. Biv, which has helped thousands of students remember the colors of the visible spectrum (**r**ed, **o**range, **y**ellow, **g**reen, **b**lue, **i**ndigo, and **v**iolet). IPMAT helps biology students remember the stages of cell division (**i**nterphase, **p**rophase, **m**etaphase, **a**naphase, and **t**elophase).

- *"Catchy" lists:* Theodore Cheney, author of *Getting the Words Right*, suggests that you remember the "three R's"

when editing a paper: *reduce* the paper to eliminate extraneous paragraphs, *rearrange* the paragraphs that remain into a logical order, and *reword* individual sentences so that they include specific nouns and active verbs.

- *Rhymes:* This simple technique is widely applied. Advertisers often use jingles—songs with rhyming lyrics—to promote products. You can invent original rhymes to burn course material into your long-term memory. Rhymes have been used for centuries to teach basic facts. "I before e, except after c" has helped many a student on spelling tests.

Mnemonics can be useful—but they have two potential drawbacks. First, they rely on rote memorization rather than understanding the material at a deeper level or thinking critically about it. Second, the mnemonic device itself is sometimes complicated to learn and time-consuming to develop. To get the most from mnemonic devices, keep them simple.

RECITE

Recitation is simply speaking about ideas and facts that you want to remember. An informal version of this technique is to inject summaries of your course work into ordinary conversation. When relatives or friends ask what you're studying, seize the moment as an opportunity to recite. Explain what a course is about and mention some of the key topics covered. Describe the three most important ideas or startling facts that you've learned so far.

Informal recitation gains its power from the fact that you need to be brief, distinguishing between major concepts and supporting details. Another option is formal recitation, where you can take more time and go into more depth. Pretend that you've been asked to speak about the topic you're studying. Prepare a brief presentation and deliver it, even if you're the only member of the audience.

Or agree to lead a study group on the topic. One of the best ways to learn something is to teach it.

Some points to remember about recitation include the following.

The "out loud" part is important. Reciting silently, in your head, may be useful—in the library, for example—but it can be less effective than making noise. Your mind can trick itself into thinking it knows something when it doesn't. Your ears are harder to fool.

When you repeat something out loud, you also anchor the concept in two different senses. First, you get the physical sensation in your throat, tongue, and lips when voicing the concept. Second, you hear it. In terms of memory, the combined result is synergistic.

Recitation works best when you use your own words. Say that you want to remember that the "acceleration of a falling body due to gravity at sea level equals 32 feet per second per second." You might say, "Gravity makes an object accelerate 32 feet per second faster for each second that it's in the air at sea level." Putting an idea in your own words forces you to think about it.

Recite in writing. Like speaking, the act of writing is multisensory, combining sight and touch. The mere act of writing down a series of terms and their definitions can help you remember the terms—even if you lose the written list. In addition, writing down what you know quickly reveals gaps in your learning, which you can then go back and fill in. When you're done writing summaries of books or lectures, read what you've written out loud—two forms of recitation.

Recite with visuals. Create diagrams, charts, maps, timelines, bulleted lists, numbered lists, and other visuals. Even the traditional outline is a visual device that separates major and minor points.

REPEAT

Students often stop studying when they think they know material just well enough to pass a test. Another option is to pick a subject apart, examine it, add to it, and go over it until it becomes second nature. Learn the material so well that you could talk about it in your sleep.

You're One Click Away . . .
from more memory strategies.

Keep your brain fit for life

Memories are encoded as physical changes in the brain. And your brain is an organ that needs regular care. Starting now, adopt habits to keep your brain lean and fit for life. Consider these research-based suggestions from the Alzheimer's Association.[1]

1. Challenge your brain with new experiences. Seek out museums, theaters, concerts, and other cultural events. Even after you graduate, consider learning another language or taking up a musical instrument. New experiences give your brain a workout, much like sit-ups condition your abs.

2. Exercise. Physical activity promotes blood flow to the brain. It also reduces the risk of diabetes and other diseases that can impair brain function.

3. Eat well. A diet rich in dark-skinned fruits and vegetables boosts your supply of antioxidants—natural chemicals that nourish your brain. Examples of these foods are raisins, blueberries, blackberries, strawberries, raspberries, kale, spinach, Brussels sprouts, alfalfa sprouts, and broccoli. Avoid foods that are high in saturated fat and cholesterol, which increase the risk of Alzheimer's disease. Drink alcohol moderately, if at all.

4. Nourish your social life. Having a network of supportive friends can reduce stress levels. In turn, stress management helps to maintain connections between brain cells. Stay socially active by working, volunteering, and joining clubs.

5. Protect your heart. In general, what's good for your heart is good for your brain. Protect both organs by eating well, exercising regularly, managing your weight, staying tobacco-free, and getting plenty of sleep. These habits reduce your risk of heart attack, stroke, and other cardiovascular conditions that interfere with blood flow to the brain.

5

TEST-TAKING ERRORS
AND WAYS TO AVOID THEM

If you think of a test as a sprint, remember that there are at least two ways that you can trip. Watch for errors due to carelessness and errors that result from getting stuck on a question.

ERRORS DUE TO CARELESSNESS

These kinds of errors are easy to spot. Usually you'll catch them immediately after your test has been returned to you—even before you see your score or read any comments from your teacher.

You can avoid many common test-taking errors simply with the power of awareness. Learn about them up-front and then look out for them. Examples are:

- Mistakes due to skipping or misreading test directions.
- Missing several questions in a certain section of the test—a sign that you misunderstood the directions for that section or neglected certain topics while studying for the test.
- Failing to finish problems that you knew how to answer—such as skipping the second part of a two-part question or the final step of a problem.
- Consistently changing answers that were correct to answers that were incorrect.
- Spending so much time on certain questions that you failed to answer others.
- Making mistakes when you copy an answer from scratch paper to your answer sheet.
- Turning in your test and leaving early—rather than taking the extra time to proofread your answers.

To avoid the above types of errors, read and follow directions more carefully—especially when tests are divided into several sections with different directions. Also, set aside time during the next test to proofread your answers.

ERRORS DUE TO GETTING STUCK

You might encounter a test question and discover that you have no idea how to answer it. If this occurs, accept your feelings of discomfort. Take a few deep breaths, and then use any of the following suggestions.

Read it again, Sam. Eliminate the simplest sources of confusion, such as misreading the question.

Skip the question for now. Simple, but it works. Let your subconscious mind work on the answer while you respond to other questions.

Look for answers in other test questions. A term, name, date, or other fact that escapes you might appear in another question on the test itself. Use other questions to stimulate your memory.

Treat intuitions with care. In quick-answer questions (multiple choice, true/false), go with your first instinct on which answer is correct. If you think your first answer is wrong because you misread the question, do change your answer.

Visualize the answer's "location." Think of the answer to any test question as being recorded someplace in your notes or assigned reading. Close your eyes, take a deep breath, and see if you can visualize that place—its location on a page in the materials you studied for the test.

Rewrite the question. See if you can put the question that confuses you into your own words. This might release the answer.

Just start writing anything at all. On scratch paper, record any response to the question, noting whatever pops into your head. Instead of just sitting there, stumped, you're doing something—a fact that can reduce anxiety. You may also trigger a mental association that answers the test question.

Write a close answer. If you simply cannot think of a direct, accurate answer to the question, then give it a shot anyway. Answer the question as best as you can, even if you don't think your answer is fully correct. This technique may help you get partial credit on some tests.

Eliminate incorrect answers. Cross off the answers that are clearly not correct. The answer you cannot eliminate is probably the best choice.

Before you write, make a quick outline. An outline can help speed up the writing of your detailed essay answer, you're less likely to leave out important facts, and if you don't have time to finish your answer, your outline could win you some points. To use test time efficiently, keep your outline brief. Focus on key words to use in your answer.

 You're One Click Away . . .
from more ways to avoid test-taking errors.

Discover Your Grades

5

6 Critical Thinking Experiment

Turn "F" into feedback

When some students get an F as a grade, they interpret that letter as a message: "You are a failure." That interpretation is not accurate.

Getting an F means only that you failed a test or an assignment—not that you failed your life.

From now on, experiment with a new way of thinking. Imagine that the letter *F* when used as a grade represents the word *feedback*. An F is an indication that you didn't understand the material well enough. It's an invitation to do something differently before you get your next grade.

The next time that a graded test is returned to you (no matter what the grade), spend at least five minutes reviewing it. Then write your answers to the following questions in the space provided. Use separate paper as needed.

On what material did the teacher base test questions—readings, lectures, discussions, or other class activities?

What types of questions appeared in the test—objective (such as matching items, true/false questions, or multiple choice), short-answer, or essay?

What types of questions did you miss?

Can you learn anything from the instructor's comments that will help you prepare for the next test?

Can you now correctly answer the questions that you missed?

Did you make any of the mistakes mentioned in "Test-taking errors and ways to avoid them" on page 85?

After answering the above questions, describe the major sources of lost points on the test.

▶ **You're One Click Away . . .**

from more strategies for turning tests into feedback.

RELAX—IT'S JUST A TEST

If you freeze during tests and flub questions when you know the answers, you might be suffering from test anxiety. A little tension before a test is good. That tingly, butterflies-in-the-stomach feeling you get from extra adrenaline can sharpen your awareness and keep you alert. You can enjoy the benefits of a little tension while you stay confident and relaxed. Sometimes, however, tension is persistent and extreme. It causes loss of sleep, appetite, and sometimes even hair. That kind of tension is damaging. It is a symptom of test anxiety, and it can prevent you from doing your best on exams.

Other symptoms include nervousness, fear, dread, irritability, and a sense of hopelessness. Boredom also can be a symptom of test anxiety. Frequent yawning immediately before a test is a common reaction. Though it suggests boredom, yawning is often a sign of tension. It means that oxygen is not getting to the brain because the body is tense. A yawn is one way the body increase its supply of oxygen.

You might experience headaches, an inability to concentrate, or a craving for food. For some people, test anxiety makes asthma or high blood pressure worse. During an exam, symptoms can include confusion, panic, mental blocks, fainting, sweaty palms, and nausea.

To perform gracefully under the pressure of exams, put as much effort into mastering fear as you do into mastering the content of your courses. Think of test taking as the "silent subject" on your schedule, equal in importance to the rest of your courses. If nervousness about tests is a consistent problem for you, that is an ideal point to begin "test taking 101."

OVERPREPARE FOR TESTS

Performing artists know that stage fright can temporarily reduce their level of skill. That's why they often overprepare for a performance. Musicians will rehearse a piece so many times that they can play it without thinking. Actors will go over their parts until they can recite lines in their sleep.

As you prepare for tests, you can apply the same principle. Read, recite, and review the content of each course until you know it cold. Then review again. The idea is to create a margin of mastery that can survive even the most extreme feelings of anxiety.

This technique—overlearning the material—is especially effective for problem solving in math and science courses. Do the assigned problems, then do more problems. Find another text and work similar problems. Make up your own problems and work those. When you pretest yourself in this way, the potential rewards are speed, accuracy, and greater confidence at exam time.

ACCEPT YOUR FEELINGS

Telling someone who's anxious about a test to "just calm down" is like turning up the heat on a pan that's already boiling over: The "solution" simply worsens the problem. Fear and anxiety tend to increase with resistance. The more you try to suppress them, the more intensity the feelings gain.

Roughly speaking, the problem has two levels. First, there's your worry about the test. Second, there's your worry about the fact that you're worried.

As an alternative, stop resisting your fear of tests. Simply accept your feelings, whatever they are. See fear as a cluster of thoughts and body sensations. Watch the thoughts as they pass through your mind. Observe the sensations as they wash over you. Let them arise, peak, and pass away. No feeling lasts forever. The moment you accept fear, you take the edge off the feeling and pave the way for its release.

EXAGGERATE YOUR FEAR UNTIL IT DISAPPEARS

Imagine the catastrophic problems that might occur if you fail the test. You might say to yourself, "Well, if I fail this test, I might fail the course, lose my financial aid, and get kicked out of school. Then I won't be able to get a job, so the bank would repossess my car, and I'd start drinking. Pretty soon I'd be a bum on Skid Row, and then . . . ."

Keep going until you see the absurdity of your predictions. Then you can backtrack to discover a reasonable level of concern.

Your worry about failing the entire course if you fail the test might be justified. At that point ask yourself, "Can I live with that?" Unless you are taking a skills test in parachute packing and the final question involves jumping out of a plane, the answer will almost always be yes.

ZOOM OUT

When you're in the middle of a test, zoom out. Think the way film directors do when they dolly a camera out and away from an action scene. In your mind, imagine that you're floating away and viewing the situation as a detached outside observer.

From this larger viewpoint, ask yourself whether this situation is worth worrying about. This is not a license to belittle or avoid problems; it is permission to gain some perspective.

Another option is to zoom out in time. Imagine yourself one week, one month, one year, one decade, or one century from today. Assess how much the current situation will matter when that time comes. Then come back to the test with a more detached perspective.

RESIGN YOURSELF TO FAILURE—AND CONTINUE

During a test, you may feel a panic so intense that you see no way out. You might apply all the suggestions listed above and find that none of them work for you in the moment.

If this happens, one option is to simply resign yourself to a low grade on this particular test. Most of the time, you'll be able to live with the consequences. They may not be ideal, but they won't be catastrophic either.

Once you've taken the pressure off yourself, find just one question you think you can answer, anywhere on the test. When you finish that one question, find another. Place 100 percent of your attention on answering the easier questions, one by one. This might be enough to gradually rebuild your confidence and help you complete the test.

TAKE SPECIAL CARE OF YOURSELF RIGHT BEFORE THE TEST

The actions you take in the 24 hours before a test can increase your worries—or reduce them. Ease the pressures with the following suggestions:

- During the day before a test, review only the content that you already know. Avoid learning facts and ideas that are entirely unfamiliar.
- On the night before a test, do a late review and then go directly to bed.
- Set up conditions to sleep well during the night before a test.
- On the morning of the test, wake up at your usual time and immediately do a quick review.

- Before a test, eat a nutritious breakfast. Go easy on caffeine, which can increase nervousness—and send you to the bathroom during the exam.

Show up just a few minutes before the test starts. Avoid talking to other students about how worried you are—which may only fan the fire of fear. If other people are complaining or cramming at the last minute, tune them out. Look out a window and focus on neutral sights and sounds. You don't have to take on other people's nervous energy.

USE STRESS-MANAGEMENT TECHNIQUES

While the following techniques were not specifically designed for test taking, they can help you achieve a baseline of relaxation in all of your activities. During the week before your next test, set aside a few minutes each day to practice one of the following suggestions.

Breathe. If you notice that you are taking short, shallow breaths, then begin to take longer and deeper breaths. Fill your lungs so that your abdomen rises, then release all the air. Imagine yourself standing on the tip of your nose. Watch the breath pass in and out as if your nose were a huge ventilation shaft for an underground mine.

Describe it. Focus your attention on your anxiety. Tell yourself how large it is, where it is located in your body, what color it is, what shape it is, what texture it is, how much water it might hold if it had volume, and how heavy it is. As you describe anxiety in detail, don't resist it. If you can completely experience a physical sensation, it will often disappear.

Tense and relax. Find a muscle that is tense and make it even more tense. If your shoulders are tense, pull them back, arch your back, and tense your shoulder muscles even more tightly; then relax. The net result is that you can be aware of the relaxation and allow yourself to relax more. You can use the same process with your legs, arms, abdomen, chest, face, and neck.

Use guided imagery. Relax completely and take a quick fantasy trip. Close your eyes, relax your body, and imagine yourself in a beautiful, peaceful, natural setting. Create as much of the scene as you can. Be specific. Use all your senses.

For example, you might imagine yourself at a beach. Hear the surf rolling in and the seagulls calling to each other. Feel the sun on your face and the hot sand between your toes. Smell the sea breeze. Taste the salty mist from the surf. Notice the ships on the horizon and the rolling sand dunes. Use all of your senses to create a vivid imaginary trip.

Some people find that a mountain scene or a lush meadow scene works well. You can take yourself to a place you've never been or re-create an experience out of your past. Find a place that works for you and practice getting there. When you become proficient, you can return to it quickly for trips that might last only a few seconds.

With practice, you can use this technique even while you are taking a test.

Focus. Focus your attention on a specific object. Examine the details of a painting, study the branches on a tree, or observe the face of your watch (right down to the tiny scratches in the glass). During an exam, take a few seconds to listen to the hum of the lights in the room. Touch the surface of your desk and notice the texture. Concentrate all your attention on one point. Don't leave room in your mind for fear-related thoughts.

Yell "Stop!" When you notice that your thoughts are racing, that your mind is cluttered with worries and fears, that your thoughts are spinning out of control ... mentally yell "Stop!" If you're in a situation that allows it, yell it out loud. Stay in the present moment. Release all thoughts beyond the test.

Exercise aerobically. This is one technique that won't work in the classroom or while you're taking a test. Yet it is an excellent way to reduce body tension. Do some kind of exercise that will get your heart beating at a higher rate and keep it beating at that rate for 15 or 20 minutes. Aerobic exercises include rapid walking, jogging, swimming, bicycling, playing basketball. Do these or another safe activity with the same effects.

Adopt a posture of confidence. Even if you can't control your feelings, you can control your posture. Avoid slouching. Sit straight, as if you're ready to sprint out of your seat. Look like someone who knows the answers. Notice any changes in your physical and mental alertness.

GET HELP FOR PROLONGED ANXIETY

When stress-management techniques don't work—and when anxiety persists well beyond test times—get help. If you become withdrawn, have frequent thoughts about death or suicide, or feel hopeless or sad for more than a few days, then talk to someone immediately. Seek out a trusted friend. Also see your academic advisor or a counselor at your student health center.

 You're One Click Away . . .
from more stress-management strategies.

Five myths about test anxiety

Myth	Reality
1. All nervousness relating to testing is undesirable.	Up to a certain point, nervousness can promote alertness and help you prevent careless errors.
2. Test anxiety is inevitable.	Test anxiety is a learned response—one that you can also learn to replace.
3. Only students who are underprepared feel test anxiety.	Anxiety and preparation are not always directly related. Students who are well-prepared may experience test anxiety. And students who underprepare for tests can be free of anxiety.
4. Successful students never feel nervous about tests.	Anxiety, intelligence, and skill are not always directly related. Gifted students may consistently feel stressed by tests.
5. Resisting feelings of test anxiety is the best way to deal with them.	Freedom from test anxiety begins with accepting your feelings as they exist in the present moment—whatever those feelings are.

Discover Your Grades

5

MATH ESSENTIALS

Consider a three-part program for math success. Begin with strategies for overcoming math anxiety. Next, boost your study skills. Finally, let your knowledge shine during tests.

OVERCOME MATH ANXIETY

Many schools offer courses in overcoming math anxiety. Ask your advisor about resources on your campus. Also experiment with the following suggestions.

Connect math to life. Think of the benefits of mastering math courses. You'll have more options for choosing a major and career—which can increase your earning power. Math skills can also put you at ease in everyday situations—calculating the tip for a waiter, balancing your checkbook, working with a spreadsheet on a computer. If you follow baseball statistics, cook, do construction work, or snap pictures with a digital camera, you'll use math. And speaking the language of math can help you feel at home in a world driven by technology.

Tell the truth. Math is cumulative. Concepts build upon each other in a certain order. If you struggled with algebra, you may have trouble with trigonometry or calculus.

To ensure that you have an adequate base of knowledge, tell the truth about your current level of knowledge and skill. Before you register for a math course, locate assigned texts for the prerequisite courses. If that material seems new or difficult for you, see the instructor. Ask for suggestions on ways to prepare for the course.

Remember that it's OK to continue your study of math from your current level of ability, whatever that level might be.

Change your conversation about math. When students fear math, they often say negative things to themselves about their abilities in these subjects. Many times this self-talk includes statements such as *I'll never be fast enough at solving math problems.* Or *I'm good with words, so I can't be good with numbers.*

Get such statements out in the open and apply some emergency critical thinking. You'll find two self-defeating assumptions lurking there: *Everybody else is better at math and science than I am.* And *Since I don't understand a math concept right now, I'll never understand it.* Both of these are illogical.

Replace negative beliefs with logical, realistic statements that affirm your ability to succeed in math: *Any confusion I feel now will be resolved. I learn math without comparing myself to others.* And *I ask whatever questions are needed to aid my understanding.*

Notice your pictures about math. Sometimes what keeps people from succeeding at math is their mental picture of mathematicians. They see a man dressed in a baggy plaid shirt and brown wingtip shoes. He's got a calcultor on his belt and six pencils jammed in his shirt pocket.

These pictures are far from the truth. Succeeding in math won't turn you into a nerd. Actually, you'll be able to enjoy school more, and your friends will still like you.

Mental pictures about math can be funny, and they can have serious effects. If math is seen as a field for white males, then women and people of color get excluded. Promoting math success for all students helps to overcome racism and sexism.

Choose your response to stress. Math anxiety is seldom just "in your head." It can also register as sweaty palms, shallow breathing, tighness in the chest, or a mild headache. Instead of trying to ignore these sensations, just notice them without judgment. Over time, simple awareness decreases their power.

In addition, use stress management techniques. "Relax—It's just a test" on page 87 offers a bundle of them.

No matter what you do, remember to breathe. You can relax in any moment just by making your breath slower and deeper. Practice doing this while you study math. It will come in handy at test time.

BOOST STUDY SKILLS FOR MATH

Choose teachers with care. Whenever possible, find a math teacher whose approach to math matches your learning style. Try several teachers until you find one whom you enjoy.

Another option is to ask around. Maybe your academic advisor can recommend math teachers. Also ask classmates to name their favorite math teachers—and to explain the reasons for their choices. Perhaps only one teacher is offering the math course you'll need.

Take math courses back to back. Approach math in the same way that you learn a foreign language. If you take a year off between Spanish I and Spanish II, you won't gain much fluency. To master a language, you follow each course with a related one. It works the same way with math, which is a language in itself.

Form a study group. During the first week of each math course, organize a study group. Ask each member to bring five problems to group meetings, along with solutions. Also exchange contact information so that you can stay in touch via e-mail, phone, and instant messaging.

Avoid short courses. Courses that you take during summer school or another shortened term are condensed. You might find yourself doing far more reading and homework each week than you do in longer courses. If you enjoy math, the extra intensity can provide a stimulus to learn. But if math is not your favorite subject, then give yourself extra time. Enroll in courses with more calendar days.

Participate in class. Success in math depends on your active involvement. Attend class regularly. Complete homework assignments *when they're due*—not just before the test. If you're confused, get help right away from an instructor, tutor, or study group. Instructor's office hours, free on-campus tutoring, and classmates are just a few of the resources available to you.

Also support class participation with time for homework. Make daily contact with math.

Ask questions fearlessly. It's a cliché, and it's true: In math, there are no dumb questions. Ask whatever questions will aid your understanding. Keep a running list of them and bring the list to class.

Make your text top priority. Math courses are often text-driven. Class activities closely follow the book. This makes it important to complete your reading assignments. Master one concept before going on to the next, and stay current with your reading. Be willing to read slowly and reread sections as needed.

Read actively. To get the most out of your math texts, read with paper and pencil in hand. Work out examples. Copy diagrams, formulas, and equations. Use chapter summaries and introductory outlines to organize your learning.

From time to time, stop, close your book, and mentally reconstruct the steps in solving a problem. Before you memorize a formula, understand the basic concepts behind it.

Practice solving problems. To get ready for math tests, work *lots* of problems. Find out if practice problems or previous tests are on file in the library, in the math department, or with your math teacher.

Isolate the types of problems that you find the most difficult. Practice them more often. Be sure to get help with these *before* exhaustion or frustration sets in.

To prepare for tests, practice working problems fast. Time yourself. This is a great activity for math study groups.

USE TESTS TO SHOW WHAT YOU KNOW

Practice test taking. Part of preparing for any math test is rehearsal. Instead of passively reading through your text or scanning class notes, do a practice test:

- Print out a set of practice problems and set a timer for the same length of time as your testing period.
- Whenever possible, work these problems in the same room where you will take the actual test.
- Use only the kinds of supporting materials—such as scratch paper or lists of formulas—that will be allowed during the test.
- As you work problems, use deep breathing or another technique to enter a more relaxed state.

Ask appropriate questions. If you don't understand a test item, ask for clarification. The worst that can happen is that an instructor or proctor will politely decline to answer your question.

Write legibly. Put yourself in the instructor's place and imagine the prospect of grading stacks of illegible answer sheets. Make your answers easy to read. If you show your work, underline key sections and circle your answer.

Do your best. There are no secrets involved in getting ready for math tests. Use some stress-management techniques, do your homework, get answers to your questions, and work sample problems. If you've done those things, you're ready for the test and deserve to do well. If you haven't done all those things, then just do the best you can.

Remember that your personal best can vary from test to test, and even day to day. Even if you don't answer all test questions correctly, you can demonstrate what you do know right now.[2]

 You're One Click Away . . .
from strategies for succeeding in math courses.

Discover Your Grades

5

Transform your experience of tests

NO MATTER HOW YOU'VE felt about tests in the past, you can wipe your mental slate clean. Use the following suggestions to transform the ways that you experience tests of all types, from the shortest pop quiz to the longest exam.

Discovery Statement

Mentally re-create a time when you had difficulty taking a test. Do anything that helps you re-experience this event. You could draw a picture of yourself in this situation, list some of the questions you had difficulty answering, or tell how you felt after finding out your score on the test.

Briefly describe that experience in the space below.

I discovered that I . . .

Intention Statement

Next, describe how you want your experience of test taking to change. For example, you might write: "I intend to walk into every test I take feeling well rested and thoroughly prepared."

I intend to . . .

Review this chapter, looking for five strategies that can help you turn your intention into reality. List those strategies below and note the page numbers where you read about them.

Strategy   Page number

Action Statement

Finally, prepare for a smooth transition from intention to action. Choose *one* strategy from the above list and describe exactly when and where you will use it.

I will . . .

 You're One Click Away . . .

from an exercise that relates learning styles to mastering tests.

Discover Your Grades

5

Detach

5

SUPPOSE YOU ARE ATTACHED to getting an A on your physics test. You feel as though your success in life depends on getting an A. It's not just that you want an A. You *need* an A. You MUST get an A.

This is a time to detach.

First, take a moment to consider the worst that could happen if you get a B, a C, or a lower grade. Even flunking the test will not ruin your life. An F is an inconvenience, not a tragedy. Put this circumstance into a broader perspective. Imagine the impact that this test will have on your life in five, 10, or 20 years.

Now take this strategy a little farther. See if you can practice mindful awareness. This is a place where you can simply watch an event unfold as if it is happening to someone else. When a thought about grades arises, just notice it. When a feeling about grades arises, just notice that as well. When you're simply present as an observer, you can release judgments about yourself. You can remember that you are much more than your grades.

Giving up an attachment to being an A student does not mean giving up being an A student. It simply means that you don't base your *entire* well-being

on your grades (or your job, or your car, or anything else you do or have).

When we are detached, we often perform better. When we think everything is at stake, the results might suffer. When we're free of the need to get an A on the physics test, we're more likely to remember formulas and solve problems.

Behind your attachments is a master student. By detaching, you release that quality in yourself.

Detach.

 You're One Click Away . . .
from more ways to detach.

6 Discover...
Your Voice

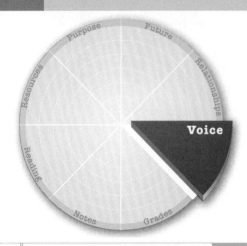

The Discovery Wheel on page 1 includes a section titled Voice. Before you read the rest of this chapter, take a few minutes to go beyond your initial responses to the Discovery Wheel. Reflect on the Skills Snapshot below to take a closer look at your skills. Complete these statements honestly, then flip to the articles or exercises highlighted for strategies that will promote your success.

Skills SNAPSHOT

✱ I define the word communication as . . .

check out:
"Your word creates your world," page 95

If someone asked me to explain what a thesis statement is, I'd say . . . ✱

check out:
"Take the mystery out of thesis statements," page 96

When researching a paper or presentation, I usually begin by . . . ✱

check out:
"Research: Digging for gold," page 98

I completed my last writing assignment with:
- ❏ Minutes to spare ✱
- ❏ Hours to spare
- ❏ Days to spare

check out:
Commit to Action: "Avoid last-minute writing projects," page 101

✱ In completing a writing assignment, I usually leave enough time to:
- ❏ Write a second draft
- ❏ Write a third draft
- ❏ Ask a friend to read my paper and give feedback
- ❏ Do careful proofreading

check out:
"Editing without fear: Revise for scope, structure, and style," page 102

check out:
"Take the panic out of public speaking," page 105

When asked to give a speech or presentation in class, I feel . . . ✱

In general, I view problems as: ✱
- ❏ Negative events to be avoided
- ❏ Neutral events that are simply part of life
- ❏ Potentially positive events

check out:
Power Process: "Find a bigger problem," page 109

YOUR WORD CREATES YOUR WORLD

Certain things are real for us because we can see them, touch them, hear them, smell them, or taste them. Books, pencils, tables, chairs, and food all are real in this sense. They enter our world in a straightforward, uncomplicated way.

Many other aspects of our lives, however, do not have this kind of reality. None of us can point to a *purpose*, for example. Nor would a purpose step up and introduce itself or buy us lunch.

The same is true about other abstract concepts, such as *quality, intelligence, trust, human rights,* or *master student.*

Concepts such as these shape our experience of life. Yet they exist for us only to the degree that we talk about them. Communication creates our experience of the world.

Communication can be defined as the process of creating meaning. This is a constant challenge. Each of us creates meaning in a highly personal way. Your past experiences, thoughts, feelings, drives, and desires are different than those of anyone else. This means that you attach a different meaning to events than anyone else. Even people who witness the same crime can give different accounts of the incident.

With our senses, we perceive sights, sounds, and other sensations. However, none of our sense organs is capable of perceiving *meaning*. We create meaning by finding patterns in our sensations and sharing them through reading and writing, speaking and listening. And the patterns you find will be unique to you.

Due to the unique ways that we create meaning, even the simplest message can get muddled. For some people, the word *chair* conjures up the image of an overstuffed rocking recliner. Others visualize a metal folding chair. If things like this can be misunderstood, it's easy to see how abstract ideas such as *love* and *peace* can wreak havoc.

When we speak or listen, read or write, we can only exchange *symbols*—words, images, gestures. And symbols are open to interpretation. This means that communication is always flawed to some extent. We can never be sure that the message we send is the message that others receive. Yet with practice we can overcome many of the difficulties inherent in human communication.

Modern technology only makes this practice more important. Society depends on creating shared meaning. Advertisers want us to spend money on their products. Political candidates want us to "buy" their stands on the issues. Teachers want us to agree that their classes are worthwhile. All of these people and organizations have meanings to share. The way that we respond will determine how we spend our money, our time, and our political power.

You can thrive in this environment by taking your communication skills to the next level. Text messaging is fun. E-mail is efficient. At the same time, you'll need deeper writing and speaking skills to persuade someone to fund your project, hire you, promote you, agree with you, or marry you.

In our daily contact with other people and the mass media, we are exposed to hundreds of messages. Yet the obstacles to receiving those messages accurately are numerous.

For one thing, only a small percentage of communication is verbal. We also send messages with our bodies and with the tone of our voices. Throw in a few other factors, such as a hot room or background noise, and it's a wonder we communicate at all.

Written communication adds a whole other set of variables. When you speak, you supplement the meaning of your words with the power of body language and voice inflection. When you write, those nonverbal elements are absent. Instead, you depend on your skills at word choice, sentence construction, and punctuation to get your message across. The choices that you make in these areas can aid—or hinder—communication.

In communication theory, the term *noise* refers to any factor that distorts meaning. When noise is present, the channels of communication start to close. Noise can be external (a lawn mower outside a classroom) or internal (the emotions of the sender or receiver, such as speech anxiety). To a large extent skillful communication means reducing noise and keeping channels open.

One powerful technique for doing this is to separate the roles of sending and receiving. Communication channels get blocked when we try to send and receive messages at the same time. Instead, be aware of when you are the receiver and when you are the sender. If you are receiving (listening or reading), just receive; avoid switching into the sending (speaking or writing) mode. When you are sending, stick with it until you are finished.

Communication works best when each of us has plenty of time to receive what others send *and* the opportunity to send a complete message when it's our turn. This is a two-way street. When someone else talks, just listen. Then switch roles so that you can be the sender for a while. Keep doing this until you do a reasonably complete job of creating shared meaning.

This is more challenging than it sounds. When emotions run high, people can totally forget when it's their job to receive and when it's their turn to send. Everyone talks and nobody listens. The results can range from a simple misunderstanding to a declaration of war.

As you develop your communication skills, you add your voice to the human community. You can create a new experience of the world. You can make ideas come alive and persuade people to take positive action. That's what this chapter is about.

 You're One Click Away . . .

from more strategies for reducing confusion when you communicate.

Discover Your Voice

6

TAKE THE MYSTERY OUT OF THESIS STATEMENTS

One purpose of communication is to reduce confusion. And it's hard to make an idea clear to others when it's unclear to *you*. Start down the path to clarity by writing a thesis statement for any paper you write or presentation you give.

A thesis statement is a one-sentence summary of a longer piece of communication, such as a speech or paper. You can boil even the longest and most complex article, chapter, or book down to a single statement that will fit on one side of an index card. When you can do that, you know that you truly understand the message. Writing thesis statements helps to develop critical thinking skills—and increases the persuasive power of your ideas.

DEFINE YOUR TOPIC FIRST

Sometimes your instructors will assign the topic for a paper or speech. At other times, however, you'll get to choose the topic. Take time for this step. Doing it effectively can save hours of research and writing time up front.

A common pitfall is selecting a topic that's too broad. As a topic for a paper in an American history course, for instance, *Harriet Tubman* offers little to guide your research. Instead, consider *Harriet Tubman's activities as a Union spy during the Civil War.*

Topics that are too broad create practical problems. You might start your research and say to yourself, "There's so much to say about this that I could write 100 pages." That's a clear message to narrow down your topic.

WRITE A COMPLETE SENTENCE ABOUT YOUR TOPIC

A thesis statement is different than a topic statement. Like newspaper headlines, a thesis statement makes an assertion or describes an action. It is expressed in a complete sentence, including a verb.

For example, *diversity* is a topic. *Cultural diversity is valuable* is a thesis statement.

Another topic is *new drugs for breast cancer chemotherapy*. A sample thesis statement about this topic is: *New drugs for breast cancer chemotherapy may prevent as well as treat this common disease.*

When writing a thesis statement, you might find that it helps to do some initial research about your topic. At this stage, research is not about mining for facts or conducting extensive interviews. That comes later. For now, just get an overview. Discover the overall structure of your topic—its major divisions or subtopics. It's fine to consult sources such as encyclopedias and almanacs for this purpose.

USE YOUR THESIS TO CLARIFY YOUR PURPOSE

When you've got a working thesis statement, take a few minutes to reflect on it. Consider the purpose behind your thesis—how you want your readers or listeners to be changed by what you write or say.

Psychologists often speak about three dimensions of personal change:

- *Cognitive* change means gaining knowledge or changing an opinion.

- *Affective* change refers to feeling differently about something or altering a deeply held attitude.

- *Behavioral* change refers to modifying the way you act.

These terms also point to three different purposes for speaking or writing: Do you want your audience to *think* differently (cognitive change), to *feel* differently (affective change), or *act* differently (behavioral change)?

Of course, you may initially have more than one purpose in mind. To focus your thinking and make a stronger impression on your audience, choose one of these as your primary purpose.

Narrowing your topic

Topics that are too broad	Topics with more focus
War	The concept of the "just war"
Feminism	The social impact of Betty Friedan's writing about feminism
Agriculture in developing countries	Coffee growers in Latin America

Most of the writing and speaking that you'll be assigned to do in higher education will have a cognitive purpose. The aim is to inform your readers or listeners.

Another common purpose is persuasion—to change opinion. Persuasion is the purpose behind a thesis statement such as: *Stricter gun control will reduce violent crime.*

One way to state your purpose is to begin your thesis statement with the words *I intend to.* Follow this with a key word such as *explain, persuade,* or *convince* that clarifies your purpose. For example, *I intend to convince my audience that stricter gun control will reduce violent crime.* Some other ways to begin your purpose statement include:

I intend to *analyze* . . . .

I intend to *compare* . . . .

I intend to *contrast* . . . .

I intend to *defend* . . . .

I intend to *define* . . . .

I intend to *describe* . . . .

I intend to *explain* . . . .

I intend to *prove* . . . .

If you want your audience to take a specific action, then consider opening words such as:

I want my audience to *buy* . . . .

I want my audience to *call* . . . .

I want my audience to *go to* . . . .

I want my audience to *send* . . . .

I want my audience to *write an e-mail in support of* . . . .

BE WILLING TO REVISE YOUR THESIS

Getting to the stage where you've refined your topic, completed some research, and crafted a thesis takes real intellectual effort. Given that investment of time and energy, you might be tempted to see your thesis as etched in stone. However, your thesis can still change. In fact, it's a good idea to do this as you do more research and gain more understanding of your topic.

Keep in mind that being *flexible* about your thesis is not the same as being *indefinite.* At any point in your research or writing, make sure that your thesis reflects a clear and definite stand on your topic.

KEEP YOUR THESIS IN FRONT OF YOU

As a way to stay focused and save research time, keep your thesis in front of you—literally—as you work. Write your thesis on an index card and tape it to your computer. Or open a file on your computer that includes only your thesis statement; keep that window open.

If you're ever in doubt about whether to pursue a certain line of research or include a particular fact in your final paper, ask yourself: "Does this relate directly to my thesis?"

If not, let it go.

You're One Click Away . . .

from more strategies for preparing to write.

Sample topics and thesis statements

Topics	Possible thesis statements
The concept of the "just war"	Definitions of the "just war" shifted with each generation of new weapons.
The social impact of Betty Friedan's writing	Betty Friedan's book *The Feminist Mystique* convinced more women to enter the work force.
Coffee growers in Latin America	Fair-trade policies for coffee growers in Latin America will benefit consumers as well as farmers.

Discover Your Voice

6

RESEARCH
DIGGING FOR GOLD

To many students, the word *research* conjures up images of a lonely scholar trapped among stacks of decaying, dusty manuscripts—a hermit who's taking notes on subjects that nobody cares about.

If that's your image, think again. The process of research is more like climbing Mount Everest. You'll make observations, gather facts, trek into unfamiliar intellectual terrain, and ascend from one plateau of insight to another.

Ideas come alive through details. This is especially important when your purpose is persuasion. If you want people to support your favorite candidate, then provide the details about that person's experience and stands on key issues. If you want people to stop eating beef, then present facts about the health and environmental costs of the meat industry. Research will help you make a case that begs for agreement.

Before digging in the stacks at the library or mining the Internet for information, know what questions you want to answer. Also find published sources of ideas and information. And don't forget about people—living, breathing beings who can answer your questions with ease and expertise.

DISCOVER YOUR MAIN QUESTION

Every paper or presentation calls on you to answer one question above all others. This is your main question—one that gets to the heart of your topic and your purpose. This is the question that will guide and direct your research at each stage.

To discover your main question, simply take your thesis statement and turn it into a question. For example, *Fair-trade policies for coffee growers in Latin America will benefit consumers as well as farmers* is a thesis statement. Stated as a main question, it becomes: *Will fair-trade policies for coffee growers in Latin America benefit consumers as well as farmers?*

LIST SUPPORTING QUESTIONS

Chances are that you can think of some questions that you'll need to answer *before* you can fully answer your main question. You may also be able to predict the questions that your audience will ask after reading or hearing your thesis statement. These are your *supporting questions*. The next step in your research is to consult sources of information that answer these questions.

Following is an example of the thinking that leads from a choice of topic all the way to supporting questions:

Topic:

Dot-com companies during the 1990s

Thesis:

Investors in dot-com companies during the 1990s failed to predict certain problems with online retailing.

Purpose:

I intend to explain how investors in dot-com companies during the 1990s failed to predict certain problems with online retailing.

Main question:

Did investors in dot-com companies during the 1990s fail to predict certain problems with online retailing?

Supporting questions:

Who were some of the major online retailers and what did they sell?

How does online retailing differ from other forms of retailing?

What gaps existed in the marketing plans for online retailers?

Could anyone have predicted these gaps?

Did some online retailers succeed? If so, how did they differ from their competitors?

The cool thing about main and supporting questions is that you can turn them into an outline of your paper or speech. Start your outline with a statement of your topic and thesis. Then use answers to your questions as headings in your outline. Continuing the above example, those headings might include: *Major online retailers sold a variety of products.* And *Online retailing differs from other kinds of retailing.*

FIND PUBLISHED SOURCES

When researching, remember that much published material is available only in print. The book—a form of information technology that's been with us for hundreds of years—still has something to offer the twenty-first-century researcher.

This fact means that you can often benefit from a trip to your campus or community library. To discover the joy of research, pick one library as your first stop for information. Get to know it well.

Next, keep in mind that any library—from the smallest one in your hometown to the massive Smithsonian in Washington, D.C.—consists of just three basic elements:

- *Catalogs*—online databases that list all of the library's accessible sources.

- *Collections*—materials, such as periodicals (magazines and newspapers), books, pamphlets, audiovisual materials, and materials available from other collections via interlibrary loans.

- *Computer resources*—Internet access; connections to campuswide computer networks; and databases stored on CD-ROMs, CDs, DVDs, or online.

Before you start your next research project, take some time to investigate all three elements of your library. Start with a library orientation session or tour.

ASK A LIBRARIAN

Libraries give you access to a resource that goes beyond the pages of a book or a Website—a librarian. Librarians are trained explorers who can guide your expedition into the information jungle. Asking a librarian for help can save you hours.

FIND EXPERTS

Making direct contact with people as you complete your research can offer a welcome relief from hours of solitary time. Here's your chance to conduct interviews—to pose real questions to a real human being rather than a lifeless search engine.

Your research will uncover the names of experts on your chosen topic. Consider doing an interview with one of these people—in person, over the phone, or via e-mail.

Respect the expert's time by posing a few precise questions. Then follow up with a thank-you note.

CAPTURE YOUR OWN IDEAS

Don't forget one of the most important people to consult—yourself. As you gather and digest the ideas of others, you'll come to conclusions of your own. This is the ultimate goal of the research process. Capture your insights in writing, treating them as notes and citing yourself as the source.

Instead of using a direct quote, you might choose to paraphrase an author's words. Paraphrasing means restating the original passage in different words, usually making it shorter and simpler. Students who copy a passage word for word and then just rearrange or delete a few phrases are running a serious risk of plagiarism. Consider this paragraph:

Higher education also offers you the chance to learn how to learn. In fact, that's the subject of this book. Employers value the person who is a "quick study" when it comes to learning a new job. That makes your ability to learn a marketable skill.

Following is an improper paraphrase of that passage:

With higher education comes the chance to learn how to learn. Employers value the person who is a "quick study" when it comes to learning a new job. Your ability to learn is a marketable skill.

A better paraphrase of the same passage would be:

The author notes that when we learn how to learn, we gain a skill that is valued by employers.

Cite a source for paraphrases, just as you do for direct quotes.

When you use the same sequence of ideas as one of your sources—even if you have not paraphrased or directly quoted—cite that source.

 You're One Click Away . . .
from more strategies that save research time.

Discover Your Voice

6

Take notes that won't get you into trouble

Using another person's words or images without giving proper credit is called *plagiarism*. Plagiarism can have big-time consequences, ranging from a failing grade to expulsion from school.

If your paper includes a passage, identifiable phrase, or visual image created by another person, then acknowledge this fact:

- Put any passage or phrase that you take word for word within quotation marks.

- Note the source of the quotation.

- When you summarize or paraphrase ideas from a source, also note the source.

- When you use the same sequence of ideas as one of your sources—even if you haven't summarized, paraphrased, or quoted—note that source.

Keep a list of your sources with details about each one. For books, these details include the author, title, publisher, publication date, and page number.

For articles from print sources, record the title and the name of the magazine as well.

If you found the article in an academic or technical journal, also record the volume and number of the publication. A librarian can help identify these details.

If your source is a Web page, record as many identifying details as you can find—author, title, sponsoring organization, URL, publication date, and revision date. In addition, list the date that you accessed the page.

WRITING WITHOUT TEARS
REDUCE RESISTANCE

Adding your voice to the human community boils down to the humble task of putting one word after another. Many students find that the hardest part of writing is not writing a thesis or researching a topic—it's getting a first draft done. Any of the following techniques can help you get the words flowing with ease.

Freewrite. According to Natalie Goldberg, teacher and author of *Writing Down the Bones*, there are only two rules in freewriting: Keep your hands moving, and don't think. In other words, write without stopping.[1]

For optimum results, begin your freewriting session by picking any topic that interests you and setting a timer—say, for 10 minutes. Then keep your pencil in motion across paper (or your fingers in motion over a keyboard) until the timer goes off. Write anything that pops into your head. Put yourself on automatic pilot until the words start happening on their own.

The trick is to give yourself permission to keep writing—even if you don't think your work is very good, even if you want to stop and rewrite. It's OK if you stray from your initial topic. Just keep writing and let the ideas flow.

Freewriting can help you draft a lot of material in a relatively short time. That material will be rough. You might end up using none of it, or only a small part of it. Even so, this technique can solve a common problem with writing—getting started.

Write an e-mail. Instead of writing an "official" draft, write an e-mail message about your draft. Describe what your writing project is about and, in general, what you want to say. You can send this message to someone, keep it to yourself, or even trash it—whatever seems most appropriate. The only purpose of the message is to get unblocked and unleash ideas for your draft.

Speak, then write. Talk to a friend or family member about what you intend to write. Encoding your message in speech instead of text activates a different part of your brain. This is a way to stimulate creativity. Consider asking a friend to take notes as you speak. Or run a recorder and then go back to it later to transcribe what you said.

Go back to prewriting. Sometimes a problem is diagnosed as writer's block when it's actually lack of preparation. If you sit

down to create a first draft and repeatedly draw a blank, go back to a prewriting task, such as toying with your outline or doing some more research. This can get your creative juices flowing.

 You're One Click Away . . .

from more ways to get started on your next writing assignment.

Write e-mails that people actually read

Target content to readers. Send e-mail messages only to the people who need them, and only when necessary.

Write an informative subject line. Rather than writing a generic description, include a capsule summary of your message. "Biology 101 report due next Tuesday" packs more information than "Report."

Think short. Keep your subject line short, your paragraphs short, and your message as a whole short.

Put the point first. To make sure your main idea or request gets across, put it in the first sentence after the greeting in your message.

Avoid last-minute writing projects

YOU CAN BREAK A LARGE GOAL—a finished paper—into a series of smaller steps that you can start right away. The purpose of this exercise is to get started on one of your current writing assignments, and to finish it with time to spare.

Start by reviewing the following list of common steps in the writing process:

Prewriting
Define your topic.
Consider your purpose.
Do initial research.
Create a thesis and purpose statement.
List questions to answer.

Do in-depth research.
Outline your paper.

Writing
Complete the first draft.

Revising
Complete the second draft.
Complete the third draft.
Prepare the final manuscript (including title page, bibliography, and footnotes or endnotes) as directed by your instructor.
Proofread.

Discovery Statement

Think about the way that you typically approach writing assignments. Do you include all of the above steps? Are there any steps not listed above that you do include? Summarize your answers by completing the following sentence.

I discovered that I . . .

Intention Statement

Next, write the date that your next paper is due:

Due date: _____

Plan to finish your assigned paper with at least one day to spare. State your intention in the space below, including a specific date.

I intend to . . .

Now, prepare to make this miracle happen. Schedule dates to complete major steps in the writing process. Choose your steps from the list above, along with any others that occur to you.

For example: Say that you intend to finish your paper one month from today. You could write notes on your calendar to:

- Finish your research one week from today.
- Finish your first draft two weeks from today.
- Finish your second draft three weeks from today.

Pull out your calendar and start scheduling dates now.

Action Statement

Finally, choose one task related to your paper that you will complete *within the next 24 hours*. This can be a small step—such as checking just one Website that's related to your topic—or a slightly more complex task, such as writing a thesis statement. Describe your task in the space below.

I will . . .

If it's appropriate for you to do so, close this book and start the above task immediately.

 You're One Click Away . . .
from more strategies for planning a writing project.

Discover Your Voice

6

EDITING WITHOUT FEAR
REVISE FOR SCOPE, STRUCTURE, AND STYLE

One definition of a writer is simply anyone who rewrites. People who write for a living might rewrite a piece seven, eight, or even more times. Ernest Hemingway rewrote the last page of *A Farewell to Arms* 39 times before he was satisfied with it. When asked what the most difficult part of this process was, he said, "Getting the words right."[2]

There's a difference in pace between writing a first draft and revising it. Keep in mind the saying: "Write in haste, revise at leisure." When you revise, slow down and take a microscope to your work.

Before you start revising, consider sharing your writing with a few people and asking them for feedback. Ask teachers, classmates, or members of your target audience to review your draft. This takes courage, but the resulting suggestions are often worth it.

Next, revise your writing in three broad stages.

EDIT FOR SCOPE

At the level of scope, the most common type of revision is to reduce the number of words in your paper. Cut passages that don't contribute to your purpose or support your thesis.

At this point, don't worry about polishing individual words, phrases, and sentences. That time will only be wasted if you choose to delete them later on. Rather, decide now which passages you want to let go. Then come back to what remains and revise it.

Approach your rough draft as if it is a chunk of granite from which you will chisel the final product. In the end, much of your first draft will be lying on the floor. What is left will become the clean, clear, polished product.

Note: For maximum efficiency, make the larger cuts first—sections, chapters, pages. Then go for the smaller cuts—paragraphs, sentences, phrases, words.

EDIT FOR STRUCTURE

Structure is all about flow—putting the sections of your paper in a logical order and crafting smooth transitions between them. If your draft doesn't hang together, then you may need to reorder your ideas.

For the structural draft, imagine yourself with a pair of scissors and glue. You're going to cut the paper into scraps—one scrap for each point and its supporting material. Then you're going to paste these points down in a new, more logical order. That's the essential process, even if you do the cutting and pasting with a computer rather than paper, scissors, and glue.

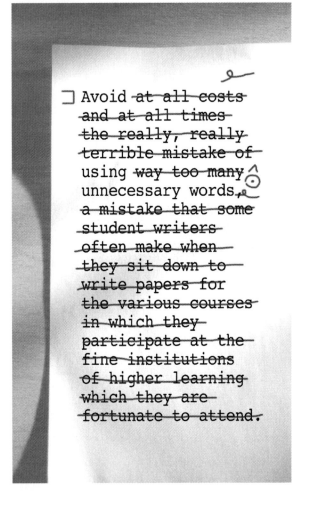

Avoid ~~at all costs and at all times the really, really terrible mistake of~~ using ~~way too many~~ unnecessary words. ~~a mistake that some student writers often make when they sit down to write papers for the various courses in which they participate at the fine institutions of higher learning which they are fortunate to attend.~~

EDIT FOR STYLE

After you've revised your draft for scope and structure, focus on style. The main concerns here are effective word choice, variety in sentence structure, and fixing errors.

In general, write with nouns and verbs. Using too many adjectives and adverbs weakens your message and adds unnecessary bulk to your writing. Use nouns to point out specific details. And put verbs in the active rather than the passive voice. Simply by doing these two things, you'll find that your writing becomes more lean and forceful. For example:

Instead of writing with vague nouns:

The speaker made effective use of the television medium, asking in no uncertain terms that we change our belief systems.

Discover Your Voice

6

You can include specifics:

The reformed criminal stared straight into the television camera and shouted, "Take a good look at what you're doing! Will it get you what you really want?"

Instead of writing in the passive voice:

A project was begun.

You can switch to the active voice:

She began the project.

Instead of piling on adverbs and adjectives:

The diminutive woman had enough strength to quickly propel objects over vast distances.

Cut words and create an image in the reader's mind:

She stood only five feet tall, but she could throw a baseball from home plate into the stands over right field.

Next, pay attention to *mechanics*—the details of grammar, punctuation, and spelling. To catch errors in your drafts, proofread on paper. Print out your manuscript in double-spaced format, grab a pencil, and mark up your draft at a location away from your computer. As you do, watch carefully for six common errors:

Run-on sentence

Original: Cassandra Wilson's vocal range is stunning, her only peer in the history of jazz singers is Ella Fitzgerald.

Revised: Cassandra Wilson's vocal range is stunning. Her only peer in the history of jazz singers is Ella Fitzgerald.

Sentence fragment

Original: Wilson's peer in jazz history: Ella Fitzgerald.

Revised: Wilson has a notable peer in jazz history: Ella Fitzgerald.

Comma missing after a long introductory phrase

Original: As a jazz musician who combines the talents of vocalist and pianist Diana Krall has few peers.

Revised: As a jazz musician who combines the talents of vocalist and pianist, Diana Krall has few peers.

Dangling modifier

Original: Ambling down the city street, the parking ramps seemed so dingy.

Revised: Ambling down the city street, I noticed that the parking ramps seemed so dingy.

Disagreement between pronoun and antecedent

Original: Each citizen should pay the full amount of income tax that they owe.

Revised: Each citizen should pay the full amount of income tax that he or she owes.

Revised again: Citizens should pay the full amount of income tax that they owe.

Disagreement between subject and verb

Original: The problem with her drafts are structure.

Revised: The problem with her drafts is structure.

Finally, prepare your work for submission. In a sense, any paper is a sales effort. If you hand in a paper with wrinkled jeans, its hair tangled and unwashed, and its shoes untied, your instructor is less likely to buy it. To avoid this situation, present your paper following an acceptable format for title pages, margin widths, fonts, footnotes or endnotes, and bibliographies.

 You're One Click Away . . .

from more ways to make your writing sparkle.

Checklist for effective revision

Scope

☐ Your introduction captures the audience's attention, states your topic, and previews the body of your paper or presentation.

☐ Your writing presents a clear thesis statement—or narrates a series of events unified by a consistent point of view.

☐ Your writing answers the main questions implied by your title and thesis statement.

☐ You support each of your main points with adequate details—quotations; examples; statistics; and vivid descriptions of people, places, or things.

☐ Your conclusion leaves the reader or listener with a sense of resolution—and it isn't mechanical or forced.

Structure

☐ The major sections of your paper or presentation flow in a logical sequence.

☐ The paragraphs within each section of your paper or presentation flow in a logical sequence.

☐ Your paragraphs include topic sentences that are developed in a clear and logical way.

Style

☐ Your writing is concise—purged of needless words.

☐ Your sentences are filled with action verbs and concrete, specific nouns.

☐ You use variety in sentence structure.

☐ Your sentences are free of mechanical errors.

Focus on solutions

MANY STUDENTS FIND it easy to dwell on complaints about roommates, instructors, classes, homework loads, or some other aspect of school. Yet they seldom, if ever, talk about ways to resolve those complaints. This exercise is about changing that habit.

The key is to focus on solutions rather than problems. Moving your conversation in this direction can raise your sense of possibility. It is one way to unleash the master student within you.

In the space below, describe a problem that could interfere with your success as a student. The problem can be related to courses, teachers, personal relationships, finances, or anything else that might get in the way of your success.

The problem is that . . .

Now do some creative thinking (which you will soon put to practical use). In the space below, brainstorm *at least* 10 possible solutions to the problem that you just described.

Don't stop there. See if you can come up with 10 or 20 *additional* solutions. If you get stuck, share your problem with friends or family members and ask them to contribute their ideas.

When you're done brainstorming, take a five-minute break. Then come back to your list and do some critical thinking:

• Circle three solutions that particularly appeal to you.

• From these three, choose one that you could implement within the next week.

• Write an Intention Statement that describes exactly what you intend to do.

Keep your brainstormed list of solutions on hand. It could prove handy if you choose to implement more than one solution, or if you face a similar problem in the future.

 You're One Click Away . . .
from more problem-solving strategies.

TAKE THE PANIC OUT OF
PUBLIC SPEAKING

Some people tune out during a speech. Just think of all the times you've listened to instructors, lecturers, and politicians. Remember all the wonderful daydreams you had during their speeches.

Your audiences are like you. The way you plan and present your speech can determine the number of audience members who will stay with you until the end. Polishing your speaking and presentation skills can also help you think on your feet and communicate clearly. These are skills that you can use in almost any course—and in any career you choose.

PLAN YOUR PRESENTATION

Consider the length of your presentation. Plan on delivering about 100 words per minute. This is only a general guideline, however, so time yourself as you practice your presentation.

Aim for a lean presentation—enough words to make your point but not so many that your audience becomes restless. Leave your listeners wanting more. Be brief and then be seated.

Speeches are usually organized in three main parts: the introduction, the main body, and the conclusion. The introduction is especially important.

Rambling speeches with no clear point or organization put audiences to sleep. Solve this problem with your introduction. The following introduction, for example, reveals the thesis and exactly what's coming. The speech will have three distinct parts, each in logical order:

Dog fighting is a cruel sport. I intend to describe exactly what happens to the animals, tell you who is doing this, and show you how you can stop this inhumane practice.

Whenever possible, talk about things that hold your interest. Include your personal experiences and start with a bang! Consider this introduction to a speech on the subject of world hunger:

I'm honored to be here with you today. I intend to talk about malnutrition and starvation. First, I want to outline the extent of these problems, then I will discuss some basic assumptions concerning world hunger, and finally I will propose some solutions.

You can almost hear the snores from the audience. Following is a rewrite:

More people have died from hunger in the past five years than have been killed in all of the wars, revolutions, and murders in the past 150 years. Yet there is enough food to go around. I'm honored to be here with you today to discuss solutions to this problem.

Though some members of an audience begin to drift during any speech, most people pay attention for at least the first few seconds. Highlight the main points in your beginning sentences.

Some professional speakers recommend writing out your speech in full, then putting key words or main points on a few index cards. Number the cards so that if you drop them, you can quickly put them in order again. As you finish the information on each card, move it to the back of the pile. Write information clearly and in letters large enough to be seen from a distance.

A disadvantage of the index card system is that it involves card shuffling. Some speakers prefer to use standard outlined notes. Another option is concept mapping as explained in Chapter Four. Even an hour-long speech can be mapped on one sheet of paper.

PRACTICE YOUR PRESENTATION

Use your "speaker's voice." When you practice, do so in a loud voice. Your voice sounds different when you talk loudly, and this can be unnerving. Get used to it early on.

Practice in the room in which you will deliver your speech. Hear what your voice sounds like over a sound system. If you can't practice your speech in the actual room, at least visit the site ahead of time. Also make sure that the materials you will need for your speech, such as an overhead projector and screen, will be available when you want them.

Discover Your Voice

6

Avoid power-pointlessness

Use slides generated with presentation software such as PowerPoint to *complement* rather than *replace* your speaking. If you use too many slides—or slides that are too complex—your audience may focus on them and forget about you. To avoid this fate, do the following.

Keep text simple. Limit the amount of text on each slide. Stick to key words presented in short sentences and bulleted or numbered lists. Use a consistent set of plain fonts that are large enough for all audience members to see.

Keep colors simple. PowerPoint offers a wide spectrum of colors that you can combine in countless patterns. Don't feel obligated to use all that computing power. To create clear and memorable slides, stick with a simple, coherent color scheme. Use light-colored text on dark background, or dark text on a light background.

Maintain consistency. Make sure that the terminology you use in your speaking, in your handouts, and in your slides is consistent. Inconsistency can lead people to feel lost—or question your credibility.

Proofread. Check for spelling errors yourself. Then ask someone else to proofread your slides as well.

Watch your timing. Show each slide at an appropriate point in your presentation. If you're showing a chart or graph and want the audience to notice a particular piece of information, then point to it. When slides are no longer relevant, change them or fade the screen to black.

Stay out of the way. As you start feeling comfortable on stage, you might get enthusiastic, gesture freely, and start moving around. That's fine, but don't stand in front of your slides. Keep to the side of the screen while maintaining eye contact with your audience.

Make a recording. Many schools have recording equipment available for student use. Use it while you practice, then view the finished recording to evaluate your presentation.

Listen for repeated phrases. Examples include *you know, kind of,* and *really,* plus any little *uh's, umm's,* and *ah's.* To get rid of these, tell yourself that you intend to notice every time they pop up in your daily speech. When you hear them, remind yourself that you don't use those words anymore.

Keep practicing. Avoid speaking word for word, as if you were reading a script. When you know your material well, you can deliver it in a natural way. Practice your presentation until you could deliver it in your sleep. Then run through it a few more times.

PRESENT WITH CONFIDENCE

Research your topic thoroughly. Knowing your topic inside and out can help you step up to the front of the room with a baseline of confidence. Then use the following suggestions to reduce nervousness at any point during your presentation.

Accept your physical sensations. You've probably experienced physical sensations that are commonly associated with stage fright: dry mouth, a pounding heart, sweaty hands, muscle jitters, shortness of breath, and a shaky voice. One immediate way to deal with such sensations is to simply notice them. Tell yourself, "Yes, my hands are clammy. Yes, my stomach is upset. Also, my face feels numb." Trying to deny or ignore such facts can increase your fear. When you fully accept sensations, however, they start to lose power.

Focus on content, not delivery. Michael Motley, a professor at the University of California at Davis, distinguishes between two orientations to speaking.[3] People with a *performance orientation* believe that the speaker must captivate their audiences with flashy techniques not used in normal conversation.

In contrast, speakers with a *communication orientation* see public speaking simply as an extension of one-to-one conversation. The goal is not to perform but to communicate your ideas in the same way that you would explain them to a friend.

Adopting a communication orientation can reduce your fear of public speaking. Instead of thinking about yourself, focus on your message. Your audiences are more interested in *what* you have to say than *how* you say it. Give them valuable ideas and information that they can use.

DELIVER YOUR PRESENTATION

Before you begin, get the audience's attention. If people are still filing into the room or adjusting their seats, they're not ready to listen. When all eyes are on you, then begin.

Project your voice. When you speak, talk loudly enough to be heard. Avoid leaning over your notes or the podium.

Maintain eye contact. When you look at people, they become less frightening. Remember, too, that it is easier for the audience to listen to someone when that person is looking at them. Find a few friendly faces around the room and imagine that you are talking to each person individually.

6

Notice your nonverbal communication. Be aware of what your body is telling your audience. Contrived or staged gestures will look dishonest. Be natural. If you don't know what to do with your hands, notice that. Then don't do anything with them.

Notice the time. You can increase the impact of your words by keeping track of the time during your speech. Better to end early than run late.

Pause when appropriate. Beginners sometimes feel that they have to fill every moment with the sound of their voice.

Release that expectation. Give your listeners a chance to make notes and absorb what you say.

Have fun. Chances are that if you lighten up and enjoy your presentation, so will your listeners.

 You're One Click Away . . .
from more ways to master public speaking.

Three ways to win over your audience

Aristotle, the ancient Greek philosopher, wrote a text on rhetoric (the art of persuasion) that is still widely quoted.[4] He recommends that any persuasive speech include three main elements, presented in the following order.

First, establish credibility. *Ethos* is a Greek word for character. Aristotle believed that audiences want to know whether a speaker is credible and honest. So your first goal is to establish that you know what you're talking about—and that you can be trusted. Do this by talking briefly about your qualifications. Mention any association with people whom your audience already trusts.

Ironically, you can sometimes gain credibility by being modest or even cracking a joke about your qualifications. Audiences may perceive this as honesty.

Next, engage emotions. Aristotle also spoke about *pathos*, the Greek word for passion or emotion. He emphasized that human beings have instinctive desires for security, appreciation, recognition, pleasure, and love.

Whenever possible, tie your presentation to one of these basic drives. Show that adopting your ideas or acting on your recommendation will help audience members get something that they want. Deliver a benefit that people feel strongly about.

Finally, provide reasons. *Logos*, the Greek word for logic, comes last in Aristotle's system. Aristotle believed that rational arguments in favor of your point of view have little force unless your audience first trusts you and feels emotionally engaged.

Logic and evidence are important. For maximum impact, present them after you've established *ethos* and *pathos*.

Discover Your Voice

6

Take the next step in finding your speaking voice

WHAT DO YOU WANT to improve about your presentation skills? Thinking about past speeches you have made can help you with future speeches you may need to make in the classroom or in the workplace.

Being honest about your current skills will open you up to new strategies that will help you succeed. Think beyond this textbook, as well. Look to successful speakers in your community or in the public eye. What traits do they have as speakers that you'd like to adapt?

Discovery Statement

Think back to the last time you were called upon to speak before a group. In the space below, write down what you remember about that situation.

For example, describe the physical sensations you experienced before and during your presentation, the overall effectiveness of your presentation, and any feedback you received from the audience.

I discovered that . . .

Intention Statement

Based on what you wrote above, what would you like to do differently the next time you speak? Describe the most important thing that you could do to become a more effective speaker.

I intend to . . .

Action Statement

Now, review this chapter for five suggestions that could help you make your intention a reality. Summarize each suggestion here along with the related page number.

Strategy   Page number

Finally, choose *one* strategy from the list above that you will definitely use for your next presentation.

I will . . .

 You're One Click Away . . .

from ways to apply learning styles to the challenge of finding your voice.

Find a bigger problem

Discover Your Voice

PROBLEMS SEEM TO follow the same law of physics that gases do: They expand to fill whatever space is available. Say that your only problem today is to write a thank-you note after a job interview. You could spend the entire day thinking about what you're going to say, writing the note, finding a stamp, going to the post office—and then thinking about all of the things you forgot to say.

But if, on that same day, you also need to go food shopping, the problem of the letter shrinks to make room for a trip to the grocery store. If you want to buy a car, too, it's amazing how quickly and easily the letter and the shopping tasks are finished.

One way to handle little problems is to find bigger ones. This helps us solve smaller problems in less time and with less energy.

Bigger problems are not in short supply. In fact, there are plenty of *big* ones: world hunger, child abuse, environmental pollution, terrorism, human rights violations, drug abuse, street crime, energy shortages, poverty, and wars throughout the world. These problems await your attention and involvement. Use your voice to offer a solution in any arena and make it happen.

From this perspective, the goal becomes not to eliminate problems, but to find problems that are worthy of us.

Worthy problems are those that draw on our talents and increase our skills. Instead of viewing problems as barriers to eliminate, we see them as opportunities to participate in life.

Take responsibility for problems that are bigger than you are sure you can handle. Then notice how your other problems dwindle in importance—or even vanish.

 You're One Click Away . . .
from more ways to find a bigger problem.

7 Discover ...
Your Relationships

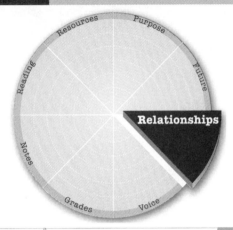

The Discovery Wheel on page 1 includes a section titled Relationships. Before you read the rest of this chapter, take a few minutes to go beyond your initial responses to the Discovery Wheel. Reflect on the Skills Snapshot below to take a closer look at your skills. Complete these statements honestly, then flip to the articles or exercises highlighted for strategies that will promote your success.

Skills SNAPSHOT

check out:
"Thriving in a diverse world," page 111

My friends include people from races and cultures such as . . .

If asked to describe how well I listen, my family and friends would say . . .

check out:
"Twelve tools for deep listening," page 113

check out:
"Create relationships with integrity," page 115

I am aware of how often I say the words:
- ❏ Can't
- ❏ Have to
- ❏ Must
- ❏ Ought to
- ❏ Should

check out:
Commit to Action: "Practice the art of saying *no*," page 116

check out:
"Five ways to resolve conflict," page 117

When someone asks me to do something that I truly have no intention of doing, my usual response is . . .

When I'm in conflict with someone, my usual response is to . . .

check out:
Commit to Action: "Write an 'I' message," page 118

check out:
"Notice your 'people pictures'—and let them go," page 119

If I could speak freely to someone I'm in conflict with right now, the first thing I would say is . . .

Before describing someone as rude, I would look for behaviors such as . . .

check out:
Critical Thinking Experiment #8: "Try on a new interpretation," page 120

When I feel angry or otherwise upset with someone, my first response is usually to . . .

check out:
"Victory through surrender—asking for help," page 121

When faced with a problem that persists despite all my attempts to solve it, my response is to . . .

check out:
Commit to Action: "Renew a relationship through gratitude," page 122

During the past year, I have expressed gratitude for my relationship with . . .

check out:
"You are already a leader," page 123

check out:
Power Process: "Choose your conversations," page 125

The leadership skills I demonstrate include . . .

When I'm in a conversation that seems to be going nowhere, I usually . . .

THRIVING IN A DIVERSE WORLD

Higher education could bring you into the most diverse environment of your life. Your fellow students could come from many different ethnic groups, cultures, and countries. Consider the larger community involved with your school—faculty members, staff members, alumni, donors, and their families. This community can include anyone from an instructor's newborn infant (age 0) to a retired instructor (age 80). Think of all the possible differences in their family backgrounds, education, job experience, religion, marital status, sexual orientation, and political viewpoints. Few institutions in our society can match the level of diversity found on some campuses.

To get the most from your education, use this environment to your advantage. Through your encounters with many types of people, gain new perspectives and new friends. Acquire skills for living in multicultural neighborhoods and working in a global economy.

You can cultivate friends from other cultures. Do this through volunteering, serving on committees, or any other activity in which people from other cultures are also involved. Then your understanding of other people unfolds in a natural, spontaneous way. Also experiment with the following strategies.

Switch cultural lenses. Diversity skills begin with learning about yourself and understanding the lenses through which you see the world. One way to do this is to intentionally switch lenses—that is, to consciously perceive familiar events in a new way.

For example, think of a situation in your life that involved an emotionally charged conflict among several people. Now mentally put yourself inside the skin of another person in that conflict. Ask yourself: "How would I view this situation if I were that person? Or if I were a person of

the opposite gender? Or if I were a member of a different racial or ethnic group? Or if I were older or younger?"

Do this consistently and you'll discover that we live in a world of multiple realities. There are many different ways to interpret any event—and just as many ways to respond, given our individual differences.

Reflect on experiences of privilege and prejudice. Someone might tell you that he's more likely to be promoted at work because he's white and male—and that he's been called "white trash" because he lives in a trailer park.

See if you can recall incidents such as these from your own life. Think of times when you were favored due to your gender, race, or age. Also think of times when you were excluded or ridiculed based on one of those same characteristics. In doing this, you'll discover ways to identify with a wider range of people.

To complete this process, turn your self-discoveries into possibilities for new behaviors. For example, if you're a younger student, you might usually join study groups with people who are about the same age as you. Make it your intention to invite an older learner to your group's next meeting. When choosing whether to join a campus organization, take into account the diversity of its membership. And before you make a statement about anyone who differs significantly from you, ask yourself: "Is what I'm about to say accurate, or is it based on a belief that I've held for years but never examined?"

Look for common ground. Students in higher education often find that they worry about many of the same things—including tuition bills, the quality of dormitory food, and the shortage of on-campus parking spaces. More important, our fundamental goals as human beings—such as health, physical safety, and economic security—are desires that cross culture lines.

The key is to honor the differences among people while remembering what we have in common. Diversity is not just about our differences—it's about our similarities. On a biological level, less than 1 percent of the human genome accounts for visible characteristics such as skin color. In terms of our genetic blueprint, we are more than 99 percent the same.[1]

Look for individuals, not group representatives. Sometimes the way we speak glosses over differences among individuals and reinforces stereotypes. For example, a student worried about her grade in math expresses concern over "all those Asian students who are skewing the class curve." Or a white music major assumes that her African American classmate knows a lot about jazz or hip hop music. We can avoid such errors by seeing people as individuals—not spokespersons for an entire group.

Discover Your Relationships

7

Be willing to accept feedback. Members of another culture might let you know that some of your words or actions had a meaning other than what you intended. Perhaps a comment that seems harmless to you is offensive to them. And they may tell you directly about it.

Avoid responding to such feedback with comments such as "Don't get me wrong," "You're taking this way too seriously," or "You're too sensitive."

Instead, listen without resistance. Open yourself to what others have to say. Remember to distinguish between the *intention* of your behavior from its actual *impact* on other people. Then take the feedback you receive and ask how you can use it to communicate more effectively in the future.

If you are new at responding to diversity, then expect to make some mistakes along the way. As long as you approach people in a spirit of tolerance, your words and actions can always be changed.

Speak up against discrimination. You might find yourself in the presence of someone who tells a racist joke, makes a homophobic comment, or utters an ethnic slur. When this happens, you have a right to state what you observe, share what you think, and communicate how you feel.

Depending on the circumstance, you might say:

- "That's a stereotype and we don't have to fall for it."
- "Other people are going to take offense at that. Let's tell jokes that don't put people down."
- "I realize that you don't mean to offend anybody, but I feel hurt and angry by what you just said."
- "As members of the majority culture around here, we can easily forget how comments like that affect other people."
- "I know that an African American person told you that story, but I still think it's racist and creates an atmosphere that I don't want to be in."

This kind of speaking may be the most difficult communicating you ever do. And if you *don't* do it, you give the impression that you agree with biased speech.

In response to your candid comments, many people will apologize and express their willingness to change. Even if they don't, you can still know that you practiced integrity by aligning your words with your values.

Speak and listen with cultural sensitivity. After first speaking to someone from another culture, don't assume that you've been understood or that you fully understand the other person. The same action can have different meanings at different times, even for members of the same culture. Check it out. Verify what you think you have heard. Listen to see if what you spoke is what the other person received.

If you're speaking to someone who doesn't understand English well, keep the following ideas in mind:

- Speak slowly and distinctly.
- To clarify your statement, don't repeat individual words over and over again. Restate your entire message in simple, direct language. Avoid slang.

- Use gestures to accompany your words.
- Since English courses for non-native speakers often emphasize written English, write down what you're saying. Print your message in capitalized block letters.
- Stay calm and avoid sending nonverbal messages that you're frustrated.

If you're unsure about how well you're communicating, ask questions: "I don't know how to make this idea clear for you. How might I communicate better?" "When you look away from me during our conversation, I feel uneasy. Is there something else we need to talk about?" "When you don't ask questions, I wonder if I am being clear. Do you want any more explanation?" Questions such as these can get culture differences out in the open in a constructive way.

Remember diversity when managing conflict. While in school or on the job, you might come into conflict with a person from another culture. Conflict is challenging enough to manage when it occurs between members of the same culture. When conflict gets enmeshed with cultural differences, the situation can become even more difficult.

Keep the following suggestions in mind when managing conflict:

- *Keep your temper in check.* People from other cultures might shrink from displays of sudden, negative emotion—for example, shouting or pointing.
- *Deliver your criticisms in private.* People in many Asian and Middle Eastern cultures place value on "saving face" in public.
- *Give the other person space.* Here the word *space* has two definitions. The first is physical space, meaning that standing close to people can be seen as a gesture of intimidation. The second is conversation space. Give people time to express their point of view. Allowing periods of silence might help.
- *Address people as equals.* For example, don't offer the other person a chair so that she can sit while you stand and talk. Conduct your conversation at eye level rather than from a position of superiority. Also refer to people by their first names only if they use *your* first name.
- *Stick to the point.* When feeling angry or afraid, you might talk more than usual. A peron from another culture—especially one who's learning your language—might find it hard to take in everything you're saying. Pause from time to time so that others can ask clarifying questions.
- *Focus on actions, not personalities.* People are less likely to feel personally attacked when you request specific changes in behavior. "Please show up for work right at 9 a.m." is often more effective than "You're irresponsible."

 You're One Click Away . . .
from more strategies for succeeding in a diverse world.

12 TOOLS FOR DEEP LISTENING

People love a good listener. The most popular salespeople, managers, coworkers, teachers, parents, and friends are the best listeners.

To listen well, begin from a clear intention. *Choose* to listen well. Then you can use the following twelve techniques to take your listening to deeper levels.

1. BE QUIET

Silence is more than staying quiet while someone is speaking. Allowing several seconds to pass before you begin to talk gives the speaker time to catch her breath and gather her thoughts. If the message being sent is complete, this short break gives you time to form your response and helps you avoid the biggest barrier to listening—listening with your answer running. If you make up a response before the person is finished, you might miss the end of the message, which is often the main point.

2. DISPLAY OPENNESS

You can display openness through your facial expression and body position. Uncross your arms and legs. Sit up straight. Face the other person and remove any physical barriers between you, such as a pile of books.

3. SEND ACKNOWLEDGMENTS

Let the speaker know periodically that you are still there. Words and nonverbal gestures of acknowledgment convey to the speaker that you are interested and that you are receiving her message. Examples are "Uh hum," "OK," "Yes," and head nods. These acknowledgments do not imply your agreement. They just indicate that you are listening.

4. RELEASE DISTRACTIONS

Even when your intention is to listen, you might find your mind wandering. Thoughts about what *you* want to say or something you want to do later might claim your attention.

There's a simple solution: notice your wandering mind without judgment. Then bring your attention back to the act of listening.

There are times when you might not want to listen. You might be distracted with your own concerns. Be honest. Don't pretend to listen. You can say, "What you're telling me is important, but I'm pressed for time right now. Can we set aside another time to talk about this?" Sometimes it's OK not to listen.

5. SUSPEND JUDGMENTS

Listening and agreeing are two different activities. As listeners, our goal is to fully receive another person's message. This does not mean that we're obligated to agree with the message. Once you're confident that you accurately understand a speaker's point of view, you are free to agree or disagree with it. One key to effective listening is understanding *before* evaluating.

6. LISTEN FOR REQUESTS AND INTENTIONS

An effective way to listen to complaints is to look for the request hidden in them. "This class is a waste of my time" can be heard as "Please tell me what I'll gain if I participate actively in class." "The instructor talks too fast" might be asking "What strategies can I use to take notes when the instructor covers material rapidly?"

We can even transform complaints into intentions. Take this complaint: "The parking lot by the dorms is so dark at night that I'm afraid to go to my car." This complaint can lead to "I intend to talk to someone who can see that a light gets installed in the parking lot."

Viewing complaints as requests and intentions gives us more choices. We can stop responding with defensiveness ("What does he know anyway?"), resignation ("It's always been this way and always will be"), or indifference ("It's not my job"). We can choose whether to grant the request or help people translate their complaint into an action plan.

7. ALLOW EMOTION

In the presence of full listening, some people will share things that they feel deeply about. They might cry, shake, or sob. If you feel uncomfortable when this happens, see if you can accept the discomfort for a little while longer. Emotional release can bring relief and trigger unexpected insights.

8. NOTICE VERBAL AND NONVERBAL MESSAGES

You might point out that the speaker's body language seems to be the exact opposite of her words. For example: "I noticed you said you are excited, but to me you look bored."

Keep in mind that the same nonverbal behavior can have various meanings across cultures. Someone who looks bored might simply be listening in a different way.

Discover Your Relationships

7

9. FEED BACK MEANING

Summarize the essence of that person's message: "Let me see if I understood what you said ..." or "What I'm hearing you say is ... ." Often, the other person will say, "No, that's not what I meant. What I said was ... ."

There will be no doubt when you get it right. The sender will say, "Yeah, that's it," and either continue with another message or stop sending when she knows you understand.

When you feed back meaning, be concise. This is not a time to stop the other person by talking on and on about what you think you heard.

10. BE CAREFUL WITH QUESTIONS AND ADVICE

Questions are directive. They can take conversations in a new direction, which may not be where the speaker wants to go. Ask questions only to clarify the speaker's message. Later, when it's your turn to speak, you can introduce any topic that you want.

Also be cautious about advice. Unsolicited advice can be taken as condescending or even insulting. Skilled listeners recognize that people are different, and they do not assume that they know what's best for someone else.

11. ASK FOR MORE

Full listening with unconditional acceptance is a rare gift. Many people have never experienced it. They are used to being greeted with resistance, so they habitually stop short of saying what they truly think and feel. Help them shed this habit by routinely asking, "Is there anything more you want to say about that?" This sends the speaker a message that you truly value what she has to say.

12. STAY OPEN TO THE ADVENTURE OF LISTENING

Receiving what another person has to say is an act of courage. Listening fully—truly opening yourself to the way another person sees the world—means taking risks. Your opinions may be challenged. You may be less certain or less comfortable than you were before.

Along with the risks come rewards. Listening in an unguarded way can take your relationships to a new depth and level of honesty. This kind of listening can open up new possibilities for thinking, feeling, and behavior. And when you practice full listening, other people are more likely to listen when it's your turn to speak.

 You're One Click Away . . .
from more strategies for deep listening.

7 steps to effective complaints

Sometimes relationship building involves making a complaint. Whining, blaming, pouting, screaming, and yelling insults usually don't get results. Here are some guidelines for complaining effectively:

1. Go to the source. Start with the person who is most directly involved with the problem.

2. Present the facts without blaming anyone. Your complaint will carry more weight if you document the facts. Keep track of names and dates. Note which actions were promised and which results actually occurred.

3. Go up the ladder to people with more responsibility. If you don't get satisfaction at the first level, go to that person's direct supervisor. Requesting a supervisor's name will often get results. Write a letter to the company president.

4. Ask for commitments. When you find someone who is willing to solve your problem, get him to say exactly what he is going to do and when.

5. Use available support. There are dozens of groups, as well as government agencies, willing to get involved in resolving complaints. Contact consumer groups or the Better Business Bureau. Trade associations can sometimes help. Ask city council members, county commissioners, state legislators, and senators and representatives. All of them want your vote, so they are usually eager to help.

6. Take legal action, if necessary. Small-claims court is relatively inexpensive, and you don't have to hire a lawyer. These courts can handle cases involving small amounts of money (usually up to a few thousand dollars). Legal-aid offices can sometimes answer questions.

7. Don't give up. Assume that others are on your team. Many people are out there to help you. State what you intend to do and ask for their partnership.

7

CREATE RELATIONSHIPS WITH INTEGRITY

When you speak and give your word, you are creating—literally. Your speaking brings life to your values. In large part, others know who you are by the words you speak and the agreements you make. You can learn who you are by observing which commitments you choose to make and which ones you choose to avoid.

There are over 6 billion people on Earth. This complex planetary network is held together by people keeping their word. Based on agreements, projects are finished. Deals are signed. Goods are exchanged. Treaties are made. When people keep their word, the world works.

RELATIONSHIPS WORK BY AGREEMENT

The same is true on a personal level. Relationships are built on integrity. When we break a promise to be faithful to a spouse, to help a friend move to a new apartment, or to pay a bill on time, relationships are strained. When we keep our word, relationships work.

Perhaps our most important relationship is the one we have with ourselves. Trusting ourselves to keep our word is enlivening. As we experience success, our self-confidence increases.

When we commit to complete a class assignment and then keep our word, our understanding of the subject improves. So does our grade. We experience satisfaction and success. If we break our word, we create a gap in our learning, a lower grade, and possibly negative feelings.

WAYS TO MAKE AND KEEP AGREEMENTS

Integrity means making agreements that we fully intend to keep. However, the only way to ensure that we keep *all* of our agreements is either to make none—or to play it safe and only make agreements that pose no risk.

Examining our agreements can improve our effectiveness. Perhaps we took on too much—or too little. Perhaps we did not use all the resources that were available to us—or we used too many. Perhaps we did not fully understand what we were promising. When we learn from our mistakes and our successes, we can become more effective at employing our word.

By making ambitious agreements, we can stretch ourselves into trying out new possibilities. If we end up breaking an agreement, we can quickly admit our mistake, deal with the consequences, and negotiate a new agreement.

MOVE UP THE LADDER OF POWERFUL SPEAKING

The words used to talk about our agreements fall into several different levels. Think of each level as one rung on a ladder—the ladder of powerful speaking. As we move up this ladder, our speaking becomes a more effective link to action.

Obligation. The lowest rung on the ladder is *obligation*. Words used at this level include *I should, he ought to, someone better, they need to, I must*, and *I had to*. Speaking this way implies that people and circumstances other than ourselves are in control of our lives. When we live at the level of obligation, we often feel passive and helpless to change anything.

Note: When we move to the next rung, we leave behind obligation and advance to self-responsibility. All of the rungs work together to reinforce this characteristic.

Possibility. The next rung up is *possibility*. At this level, we examine new options. We play with new ideas, possible solutions, and alternative courses of action. As we do, we learn that we can make choices that dramatically affect the quality of our lives. We are not the victims of circumstance. Phrases that signal this level include *I might, I could, I'll consider, I hope to*, and *maybe*.

Preference. From possibility we can move up to *preference*. Here we begin the process of choice. The words *I prefer* signal that we're moving toward one set of possibilities over another, perhaps setting the stage for eventual action.

Passion. Above preference is a rung called *passion*. Again, certain words signal this level: *I want to, I'm really excited to do that, I can't wait*. Possibility and passion are both exciting places to be. Even at these levels, though, we're still far from action. Many of us want to achieve lots of things and have no specific plan for doing so.

Planning. Action comes with the next rung—*planning*. When people use phrases such as *I intend to, my goal is to, I plan to*, and *I'll try like mad to*, they're at the level of planning. The Intention Statements you write in this book are examples of planning.

Promising. The highest rung on the ladder is *promising*. This is where the power of your word really comes into play. At this level, it's common to use phrases such as these: *I will, I promise to, I am committed, you can count on it*. This is where we bridge from possibility and planning to action. Promising brings with it all of the rewards of integrity.

 You're One Click Away . . .
from more ways to speak toward success.

Discover Your Relationships

7

Commit to Action
Practice the art of saying *no*

ALL YOUR STUDY PLANS CAN go down the drain when a friend says, "Time to party." Sometimes, succeeding in school means replying with a graceful *no*. Saying no helps you to prevent an overloaded schedule that compromises your health, your relationships, and your grade point average.

Discovery Statement

We find it hard to say no when we make certain assumptions—when we assume that others will think we're rude, or that we'll lose friends if we turn down a request.

But think about it: If you cannot say *no,* then you are not in charge of your time. You've given that right to whoever wants to interrupt you. This is not a relationship based on equality. People who care about you will respect your wishes.

Recall a situation when you wanted to say *no* to someone but did not. Were you making assumptions about how the other person would react? If so, describe what you were thinking.

I discovered that I ...

Intention Statement

Next, consider some strategies for giving someone a *no* that's both polite and firm. For instance, you can wait for the request. People who worry about saying *no* often give in to a request before it's actually been made. Wait until you hear a question: "Would you go to a party with me?"

You can also remind yourself that one *no* leads to another *yes.* Saying *no* to a movie allows you to say *yes* to getting a paper outlined or a textbook chapter read.

Then you can give an unqualified *yes* to the next social activity.

Describe any strategies that you plan to use the next time you find it difficult to say *no*.

I intend to ...

Action Statement

You might find it easier to act on your intention when you don't have to grasp for words. Choose some key phrases in advance. For example: "That doesn't work for me today." "Thanks for asking; my schedule for today is full." Or "I'll go along next time when my day is clear."

To effectively deliver my next *no,* I will say ...

 You're One Click Away . . .
from more ways to say *no* gracefully.

Discover Your Relationships

7

FIVE WAYS TO RESOLVE CONFLICT

When conflict occurs, we often make statements about another person. We say such things as:

"You are rude."

"You make me mad."

"You must be crazy."

"You don't love me anymore."

These are "You" messages. Usually they result in defensiveness. The responses might be:

"I am not rude."

"I don't care."

"No, *you* are crazy."

"No, *you* don't love *me*!"

"You" messages are hard to listen to. They label, judge, blame, and assume things that might or might not be true. They demand rebuttal.

The next time you're in conflict with someone, consider replacing "You" messages with "I" messages:

"You are rude" might become "I feel upset."

"You make me mad" could be "I feel angry."

"You must be crazy" can be "I don't understand."

"You don't love me anymore" could become "I'm afraid we're drifting apart."

"I" messages don't judge, blame, criticize, or insult. They don't invite the other person to counterattack. "I" messages are also more accurate. They stick to the facts and report our own thoughts and feelings.

Suppose a friend asks you to pick her up at the airport. You drive 20 miles and wait for the plane. No friend. You decide your friend missed her plane, so you wait three hours for the next flight. No friend. Perplexed and worried, you drive home. The next day, you see your friend downtown.

"What happened?" you ask.

"Oh, I caught an earlier flight."

"You are a rude person," you reply.

When you saw your friend, you might have chosen an "I" message instead: "I waited and waited at the airport. I was worried about you. I didn't get a call. I feel angry and hurt. I don't want to waste my time. Next time, you can call me when your flight arrives, and I'll be happy to pick you up."

An "I" message can include any or all of the following five elements.

1. Observations. Describe the facts—the indisputable, observable realities. Talk about what you—or anyone else—can see, hear, smell, taste, or touch. Avoid judgments, interpretations, or opinions. Instead of saying, "You're a slob," say, "Last night's lasagna pan was still on the stove this morning."

2. Feelings. Describe your own feelings. It is easier to listen to "I feel frustrated" than to "You never help me." Stating how you feel about another's actions can be valuable feedback for that person.

3. Wants. You are far more likely to get what you want if you *say* what you want. If someone doesn't know what you want, she doesn't have a chance to help you get it. Ask clearly.

Avoid demanding or using the word *need*. Most people like to feel helpful, not obligated. Instead of saying, "Do the dishes when it's your turn, or else!" say, "I want to divide the housework fairly."

4. Thoughts. Communicate your thoughts, and use caution. Beginning your statement with the word "I" doesn't make it an "I" message. "I think you are a slob" is a "You" judgment in disguise. Instead, say, "I'd have more time to study if I didn't have to clean up so often."

5. Intentions. The last part of an "I" message is a statement about what you intend to do. Have a plan that doesn't depend on the other person. For example, instead of "From now on we're going to split the dishwashing evenly," you could say, "I intend to do my share of the housework and leave the rest."

 You're One Click Away . . .
from more ways to resolve conflict.

Discover Your Relationships

7

Commit to Action
Write an "I" message

THE PURPOSE OF THIS EXERCISE is to help you experiment with "I" messages. Practice in the space below but also start practicing this with the next person you communicate with, whether it's a professor, roommate, friend, a parent, or a child. Watch how making this relatively easy shift in language can improve your relationships in your life.

Discovery Statement

Pick something about school that irritates you. Then pretend that you are talking to the person who is associated with this irritation. In the space below, write down what you would say to this person as a "You" message.

I discovered that I would say ...

Action Statement

Give some thought to exactly what you'll say if you *do* use this technique. Take the "You" message above and rewrite it as an "I" message. Include at least the first three elements suggested in "Five ways to resolve conflict" on page 117.

I will say ...

Intention Statement

Now consider the possibility of sending a different message. How interested are you in actually using "I" messages with the person described above?

There are several possible levels of commitment. For example, you might choose to deliver a few "I" messages to this person and then see how well they work. Or you might commit to using "I" messages on a permanent basis with this person—and with other key people in your life.

Describe your current level of commitment to using "I" messages in the space below.

I intend to ...

▶ **You're One Click Away . . .**

from more ways to deliver an effective "I" message.

Discover Your Relationships

7

NOTICE YOUR "PEOPLE PICTURES" AND LET THEM GO

One of the brain's primary jobs is to manufacture images. We use mental pictures to make predictions about the world, and we base much of our behavior on those predictions.

When an artist is creating a painting or sculpture, he has a mental picture of the finished piece. Novelists often have mental images of the characters that they're about to bring to life. Many parents have a picture about what they want their children to become.

These kinds of pictures and many more have a profound influence on us. Our pictures direct our thinking, our conversations, and our actions—all of which help affect our relationships. That's amazing, considering that we often operate with little, if any, conscious knowledge of our pictures.

A PROBLEM WITH PICTURES

The pictures we make in our heads are survival mechanisms. Without them, we couldn't get from one end of the town to the other. We couldn't feed or clothe ourselves. Without a picture of a socket, we couldn't screw in a light bulb.

Pictures can get in our way. Take the case of a student who plans to attend a school she hasn't visited. She chose this school for its strong curriculum and good academic standing, but her brain didn't stop there. The professors, she imagines, will be as humorous as Jon Stewart and as entertaining as Oprah Winfrey. Her roommate will be her best friend. The cafeteria will be a cozy nook serving delicate quiche and fragrant teas. She will gather there with fellow students for hours of stimulating, intellectual conversation. The library will have every book, while the computer lab will boast the newest technology.

The school turns out to be four gray buildings downtown, next to the bus station. The first class she attends is taught by an overweight, balding professor who is wearing a purple-and-orange bird of paradise tie and has a bad case of the sniffles. And the student's roommate is a tuba player whose instrument takes up a sizable area of their apartment. The cafeteria is a nondescript hall with machine-dispensed food.

This hypothetical student gets depressed. She begins to think about dropping out of school.

The problem with pictures is that they can prevent us from seeing what is really there. That happened to the student in this story. Her pictures prevented her from noticing that the professor with the weird tie is not only an expert in his field but is also a superior teacher. The student's pictures also prevented her from seeing that her roommate is a considerate person who plays her tuba only in the band room at school—never at home.

Anger and disappointment with people are often the results of our pictures. We set up expectations for their appearance and their behavior, which can lead to disappointment. Sometimes we don't even realize that we have these expectations. The next time you discover you are angry, disappointed, or frustrated, look to see which of your pictures aren't being fulfilled.

TAKE CHARGE OF YOUR PICTURES

Having pictures is unavoidable. Letting these pictures control our lives *is* avoidable. Some techniques for dealing with pictures are so simple and effortless, they might seem silly.

One way to deal with pictures is to be aware of them. Open up your mental photo album and notice how the pictures there influence your thoughts, feelings, and actions. Just becoming aware of your pictures—and how they affect you—can help you take a huge step toward dealing with them effectively.

When you notice that pictures are getting in your way, then, in the most gentle manner possible, let your pictures go. Let them drift away like wisps of smoke picked up by a gentle wind.

Pictures are persistent. They come back over and over. Notice them again and let them go again. At first, a picture might return repeatedly and insistently. Pictures are like independent beings. They want to live. If you can see the pictures as a thought independent from you, you will likely find it easier to let it go.

You are more than your pictures. Many images and words will pop into your head in the course of a lifetime. You do not have to identify with these picture. You can let pictures go without giving up yourself.

Sometimes we can let go of old pictures and replace them with new ones. We stored all of those pictures in the first place. We can replace them. Our student's new picture of a great education can include the skimpy cafeteria, the professor with the weird tie, and the roommate with the tuba.

We can take charge of the images that float through our minds. We don't have to be ruled by an album of outdated pictures. We can stay aware of our pictures and keep looking for new ones. And when *those* new pictures no longer serve us, we can also let them go.

 You're One Click Away . . .
from more ways to benefit from releasing mental pictures.

Discover Your Relationships

7

Try on a new interpretation

THIS EXERCISE IS ABOUT the difference between behaviors and interpretations. Understanding this difference can help you think more accurately about what other people say and do. And in turn, this thinking skill can help you prevent and resolve conflict.

A *behavior* is a physical action that we can directly observe. For example, someone enters a classroom 10 minutes after a lecture starts. Or another person gets up during a conversation and runs out of the room. These are behaviors. When we describe them, we're making statements of fact.

In contrast, an *interpretation* is subjective. It is a statement of opinion about what a behavior means: "She's too irresponsible to get to a lecture on time." "He ran out of the room because he was so angry with me."

There are often several ways to interpret someone's behavior. Perhaps the person arrived late because her car broke down and she took a bus to campus. Or maybe that person left the room suddenly because he got a text message about an emergency.

With this distinction in mind, think of a recent situation when you were in conflict with someone. In the space below, brainstorm a list of the behaviors that you observed during this event.

Now, review what you just wrote. Circle any items on your list that are actually *interpretations* rather than behaviors. Choose one of those interpretations and see if you can list the actual behaviors involved.

Finally, see if you can list any other possible interpretations for the behaviors you just listed. Again, use the space below.

You're One Click Away . . .
from more examples of the differences between observations and interpretations.

Discover Your Relationships

7

VICTORY THROUGH SURRENDER
ASKING FOR HELP

Life can be magnificent and satisfying. It can also be devastating.

Sometimes there is too much pain or confusion. Problems can become too big and too numerous. A broken relationship with a loved one, a sudden diagnosis of cancer, or even the prospect of several long years of school are situations that can leave us feeling powerless.

In these troubling situations, the first thing we can do is to admit that we don't have the resources to handle the problem. No matter how hard we try and no matter what skills we bring to bear, some problems remain out of our control. When this is the case, we can tell the truth: "It's too big and too mean. I can't handle it."

RELEASING CONTROL, RECEIVING HELP

These are times when we can benefit most from admitting our limitations, connecting to the human community, and asking for help. This is the kind of surrender that leads to victory.

Once you acknowledge your lack of control, all that remains is to surrender. Many traditions make note of this. Western religions speak of surrendering to God. Hindus speak of surrender to the Self. Members of Alcoholics Anonymous talk about turning their lives over to a Higher Power. Atheists and agnostics might suggest surrendering to the facts, to reason, to their intuition, their inner guide, or their conscience.

In any case, surrender means opening up to a source of help that's larger than ourselves. Surrender works for many of life's barriers.

An alcoholic admits that he just can't control his drinking. He surrenders. This allows him to finally seek treatment.

A student with financial problems admits that her school loans and credit cards are spiraling out of control. She surrenders to this fact and talks to a financial advisor about it. Now she can get a plan for controlling her situation and stay in school.

A man is devastated when his girlfriend abandons him. He is a "basket case," unable to work for days. Instead of struggling against this fact, he simply admits the full extent of his pain. In that moment of surrender, he is able to trust. He knows that one day he will be OK again. He trusts that new opportunities for love will come his way.

After finding out she has terminal cancer, a woman shifts between panic and depression. Nothing seems to console her. Finally, she accepts the truth and stops fighting her tragedy. She surrenders. Now at peace, she invests her remaining years in meaningful moments with the people she loves.

In such cases, people learn the power of surrender.

Once we admit that we're at the end of our rope, we open ourselves up to receiving help. We learn that we don't have to go it alone. We find out that other people have faced similar problems and survived. We give up our old habits of thinking and behaving as if we have to be in control of everything. We stop acting as general manager of the universe. We surrender. And that creates a space for something new in our lives.

WHAT SURRENDER IS NOT

Surrender is not resignation. It is not a suggestion to quit and do nothing about your problems. You have many skills and resources. Use them. You can apply all of your energy to handling a situation and surrender at the same time. Surrender includes doing whatever you can in a positive, trusting spirit. Giving up is fatalistic and accomplishes nothing. So let go, keep going, and know that the true source of control lies beyond you.

This article says, in effect, don't fight the current. Imagine a person rafting down a flowing river with a rapid current. She's likely to do fine if she surrenders control and lets the raft flow with the current. After all, the current always goes around the rocks. If she tries to fight the current, she could end up in an argument with a rock about where the current is going—and lose.

 You're One Click Away . . .
from more strategies for getting help when you need it.

Discover Your Relationships

7

Renew a relationship through gratitude

ONE STRATEGY FOR renewing relationships is both simple and often forgotten. This strategy is expressing appreciation.

We often assume that people know how we feel about them. Often they don't. Telling them how we feel can add a new level of depth and joy to the relationship. You can test this idea for yourself.

Discovery Statement

Begin by filling out the chart below. Under the column titled *Name*, write the names of five people who have positively influenced your life. They might be relatives, friends, teachers, coworkers, fellow students, or anyone else you appreciate.

In the next column, rate your gratitude for this person's influence. Use a scale from 1 to 5, with 1 being a little grateful and 5 being extremely grateful.

In the third column, rate how fully you have communicated your gratitude to this person. Again, use a scale of 1 to 5, with 1 meaning "not communicated" and 5 meaning "fully communicated."

Name	Gratitude	Communicated

Intention Statement

Now select one person from the chart. Consider how you will express your gratitude to this person. Describe when you will do this and how you will do it—for example, through a personal visit, phone call, e-mail, letter, or thank-you note.

I intend to . . .

Action Statement

Finally, to ease your transition from intention to action, write out exactly what you plan to say to this person.

What I appreciate about you is . . .

You're One Click Away . . .
from more ways to cultivate an "attitude of gratitude."

YOU ARE ALREADY A LEADER

No matter our station in life, at some point most of us become leaders. In fact, it's impossible to escape leadership. Every time you speak, you lead others in some small or large way. Every time you take action, you lead others through your example. Every time you ask someone to do something, you are leading that person.

To take your leadership skills to an even higher level, experiment with the following suggestions.

EMBRACE CHANGE

Leaders change the status quo. They create new products, develop new services, start new businesses, found new organizations, and pass new legislation. They recognize good ideas early on and then tirelessly promote them.

This calls for the willingness to be uncomfortable. Leadership is a courageous act. Leaders often are not appreciated or even liked. They can feel isolated, cut off from their colleagues. This can sometimes lead to self-doubt and even fear. Before you take on a leadership role, be aware that you might experience such feelings. Also remember that none of them needs to stop you from leading.

KEEP THE END IN MIND

Long-term goals usually involve many intermediate steps. Unless we're reminded of the purpose for those day-to-day actions, our work can feel like a grind.

Keeping the vision alive helps spirits soar again. Leadership is the art of helping others lift their eyes to the horizon—keeping them in touch with the ultimate value and purpose of a project. When you lead a project, speak a lot about the end result and the potential value of what you're doing.

MOVE PEOPLE INTO ACTION

A leader's vision has little power until people get behind it. That vision cannot be forced on anyone. Instead, leaders enlist wide support for new projects through the sheer force of enthusiasm. Their passion for a new project spreads to people at all levels of an organization.

In addition to sharing your passion, you can move people into action with several strategies:

- Make requests—lots of them. An effective leader is a request machine. Making requests, both large and small, is an act of respect. When we ask a lot from others, we demonstrate our respect for them and our confidence in their abilities.

- Delegate. Ask a coworker or classmate to take on a job that you'd like to see done. Ask the same of your family or friends. Delegate tasks to the mayor of your town, the governor of your state, and the leaders of your country. Suggest projects that are important to you. Then find people who can lead the effort.

- Follow up. What we don't inspect, people don't respect. When other people agree to do a job for you, follow up to see how it is going. This can be done in a way that communicates your respect and interest—not your fear that the project might flounder.

Effective leaders also know that "we" goes beyond a small group of people at the top of an organization. Leaders involve everyone who will be affected by a change—managers, customers, clients, and citizens.

Today this calls on leaders to implement diversity policies—and to go beyond them by preventing *micro-inequities*. These are small, subtle behaviors that over time create an atmosphere of intolerance. They occur, for example, when a manager continually glances at her watch while talking to a person of color, when a team leader consistently mispronounces the name of an employee from another country, or when a supervisor habitually interrupts women who speak during a meeting.

SHARE CREDIT

As a leader, take the praise and acknowledgment that you receive and give it away. When you're congratulated for your performance, pass it on to others. Share the credit with the group.

As a leader, you can sustain enthusiasm for a project by constantly acknowledging others. Express genuine appreciation for the energy and creativity that others put into their work. Take the time to be interested in what they do and to care about the results they produce. Thank and acknowledge them with your eyes, your words, and the tone of your voice.

When you're a leader, the results you achieve depend on the efforts of many others. Acknowledging that fact often is more than telling the truth—it's essential if you want to continue to count on their support in the future.

ALLOW MISTAKES

The more you practice leadership, the more likely it is that you'll make mistakes. And the more influential you are, the more likely it is that your mistakes will have huge consequences. The chief financial officer for a large company can make a mistake that costs thousands or even millions of dollars. A physician's error could cost a life.

At the same time, these leaders are in a position to make huge changes for the better—to save thousands of dollars or many lives through their skill and influence.

MODEL THE WAY

"Be the change you want to see" is a useful motto for leaders. Perhaps you want to see integrity, focused attention, and productivity in the people around you. Begin by modeling these qualities yourself. It's easy to excite others about a goal when you are enthusiastic about it yourself. Having fun while being productive is contagious. If you bring these qualities to a project, others might follow suit.

START NOW

At times, leadership is a matter of trial and error and flying by the seat of your pants. As a leader, you might sometimes feel that you don't know what you're doing. That's OK. A powerful course of action can be discovered in midstream. You can *act* as a leader even when you don't *feel* like a leader. As a process of constant learning, leadership calls for all of the skills of master students.

Look for areas in which you can make a difference and experiment with these strategies. Begin now, while you are in higher education. Campuses offer many opportunities to gain leadership skills. Volunteer for clubs, organizations, and student government. Look for opportunities to tutor, or to become a peer advisor or mentor. No matter what you do, take on big projects—those that are worthy of your time and leadership talents.

 You're One Click Away . . .
from more leadership strategies.

7

Leading high-performance teams

In the workplace, teams abound. To research their book *When Teams Work Best*, Frank LaFasto and Carl Larson studied 600 teams. These ranged from the Mount Everest climbing team to the teams that produced the Boeing 747 airplane—the world's largest aircraft and a product of 75,000 blueprints.[2]

LaFasto and Larson found that empowered teams set their own goals, plan their own schedule, and make decisions democratically. They also design their workspace and choose their own members.

You might wonder how to make all this happen. To get down to specifics, take the four learning styles questions presented in Chapter One of this book and reword them slightly when joining a team:

- *Why* is this project being done?
- *What* would a successful outcome for this project look like?
- *How* are we going to create a bridge from our current reality to that successful outcome?

- *What if* we truly make this outcome a high priority? What is the very next action that each of us would take to make it happen?

You can start using these questions right away. Prepare for effective teamwork now. While you are in school, seize opportunities to work collaboratively. Form study groups. Enroll in classes that include group projects. Show up for your next job with teamwork skills already in place.

Choose your conversations

CONVERSATIONS HAVE POWER over what we think, feel, and do. They shape our attitudes, our decisions, our opinions, our emotions, and our actions. If you want clues about what a person will be like tomorrow, listen to what she's talking about today. We become our conversations.

Given that conversations are so powerful, it's amazing that few people act on this fact. Most of us swim in a constant sea of conversations, almost none of which we carefully and thoughtfully choose. Of course, there are the conversations we have with friends, relatives, and other people. And if we flip on the radio or television, or if we surf the Web, millions of other conversations await us. Thanks to modern digital technology, many of these conversations take place in high-quality sound, high-resolution images, and living color, 24 hours each day.

We always have the power to choose our conversations. Certain conversations create real value for us. They give us fuel for reaching our goals. Others distract us from what we want. We can choose more of the conversations that exhilarate and sustain us.

The conversations you have are dramatically influenced by the people you associate with. If you want to change your attitudes about almost anything—prejudice, politics, religion, humor—choose your conversations by choosing your community. Spend time with people who speak about and live consistently with the attitudes you value. Use conversations to change habits. Use conversations to create new options in your life. Choose your conversations.

 You're One Click Away . . .
from more ways to choose your conversations.

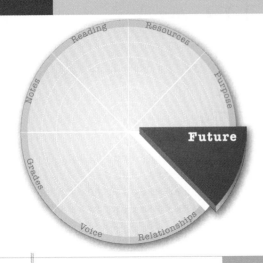

The Discovery Wheel on page 1 includes a section titled Future. Before you read the rest of this chapter, take a few minutes to go beyond your initial responses to the Discovery Wheel. Reflect on the Skills Snapshot below to take a closer look at your skills. Complete these statements honestly, then flip to the articles or exercises highlighted for strategies that will promote your success.

Skills SNAPSHOT

I know that I'm really living the meaning of my life when I . . . *

check out:
"Give up the myth of 'some day,'" page 127

If someone asked me to list the top skills that I already have, I would respond by . . . *

* The most important factors to consider when choosing a major are . . .

check out:
"Four ways to choose your major," page 131

check out:
"Discovering the skilled person you already are," page 128
Commit to Action: "Inventory your skills," page 130

check out:
"Create your career," page 134

If I had to declare a major today, I would choose . . . *

check out:
Commit to Action: "Declare your major today," page 133

* My career goals are to . . .

check out:
"Finding your place in the new world of work," page 137

If someone asked me to write a career plan, I would include . . . *

check out:
Commit to Action: "Plan your career now," page 136

* To increase my job security and long-term career prospects, I can . . .

check out:
Commit to Action: "Create your future," page 142

My usual strategies for finding a job include . . . *

check out:
Critical Thinking Experiment #9: "Examine beliefs about careers and jobs," page 138

Since starting this course, I've gained skills in . . . *

* My goals for next term include . . .

check out:
Power Process: "I create it all," page 143

I would define the term self-responsibility as . . . *

check out:
"The Discovery Wheel, reloaded," page 139

GIVE UP THE MYTH OF "SOME DAY"

It's tempting to postpone changes in our lives until we're really feeling "ready" for them—perhaps next week, next month, next year, or some other day that's more convenient.

Other people reinforce this notion by telling you that your life will *really* start on the day when you ... . (Fill in the blank with phrases such as *graduate from college, get married, have kids, get promoted,* or *retire.*)

Agreeing with these statements can condemn us to a life of perpetual waiting. Using this logic, we could wait our whole life to start living.

There's a mistaken idea about planning that adds to the problem. This is the assumption that life really works only when you complete your to-do list. Happiness, fulfillment, and satisfaction remain distant. They recede farther and farther into the future, to the time when you achieve your next goal, then the next one, and the one after that.

Giving up the myth of "some day" means taking a new attitude toward the future. In fact, one of the best ways to get what you want in the future is to realize that you do not have a future. The only time you have is right now.

Consider this: The only time to do anything is now. You can think about doing something next Wednesday. You can write about doing something next Wednesday. You can daydream, discuss, ruminate, speculate, and fantasize about what you will do next Wednesday. But you can't do anything on Wednesday until it *is* Wednesday.

The problem with this idea is that some students might think: "No future, huh? Terrific! Party time!"

Being in the here and now, however, is not the same as living for today and forgetting about tomorrow. Nor is "be here now" a call to abandon goals. Goals are useful tools when we use them to direct our actions right now. Goals allow us to live fully in the present.

The word *goal* comes from the Anglo-Saxon *gaelan*, which means "to hinder or impede," as in the case of a boundary. That's what a goal does. It restricts, in a positive way, our activity in the here and now. It channels our energy into present-moment actions that are more likely to get us what we really want.

Remembering this can help you avoid the fate of postponing happiness and living for that ethereal "some day." You can make commitments for the future that change your action in the present. You can live your life as if your life depended on it, starting right now. Use this chapter as a guide to choosing your major, planning your career, finding your place in the global economy, and otherwise creating the life of your dreams.

Just start doing it today.

 You're One Click Away . . .

from more suggestions about choosing what's next in your life.

Discover Your Future

8

DISCOVERING THE SKILLED PERSON YOU ALREADY ARE

When meeting with an academic advisor, some students say, "I've just been taking general education and liberal arts courses. I haven't got any marketable skills."

Think again.

TWO KINDS OF SKILLS

Few words are as widely misunderstood as *skill*. Defining it carefully can have an immediate and positive impact on your career planning.

One dictionary defines *skill* as "the ability to do something well, usually gained by training or experience." Some skills—such as the ability to speak a second language, repair fiber-optic cables, or do brain surgery—are acquired through formal schooling, on-the-job training, or both. These abilities are called *content skills*. People with such skills have mastered a specialized body of knowledge needed to do a specific kind of work.

However, there is another category of skills that we develop through experiences both inside and outside the classroom. We may never receive formal training to develop these abilities, yet they are key to success in the workplace. These are *transferable skills*. Transferable skills are the kinds of abilities that help people thrive in any job—no matter what work-content skills they have.

Perhaps you've heard someone described this way: "She's really smart and knows what she's doing, but she's got lousy people skills." People skills—such as *listening* and *negotiating*—are prime examples of transferable skills.

SUCCEEDING IN MANY SITUATIONS

Transferable skills are often invisible to us. The problem begins when we assume that a given skill can be used in only one context, such as being in school or working at a particular job. Thinking in this way places an artificial limit on our possibilities.

As an alternative, think about the things you routinely do to succeed in school. Analyze your activities to isolate specific skills and how they might apply in other situations.

Consider, for example, the task of writing a research paper. This calls for skills such as:

- *Planning*—setting goals for completing your outline, first draft, second draft, and final draft.

- *Managing time* to meet your writing goals.

- *Interviewing* people who know a lot about the topic of your paper.

- *Researching*—using the Internet and campus library to discover key facts and ideas to include in your paper.

- *Writing* to present those facts and ideas in an original way.

- *Editing* your drafts for clarity and correctness.

Now consider the kinds of jobs that draw on these skills.

For instance, you could transfer your skill at writing papers to a possible career in journalism, technical writing, or advertising copywriting. You could use your editing skills to work in the field of publishing as a magazine or book editor. Interviewing and research skills could help you enter the field of market research. And the abilities to plan, manage time, and meet deadlines will help you succeed in all the jobs mentioned so far.

Here's another example. Say that you work part-time as an administrative assistant at a computer dealer that sells a variety of hardware and software. You take phone calls from potential customers, help current customers solve problems using their computers, and attend meetings where your coworkers plan ways to market new products. You are developing skills at *selling, serving customers*, and *working on teams*.

The basic idea is to take a cue from the word *transferable*. Almost any skill you use to succeed in one situation can *transfer* to success in another situation.

The concept of transferable skills opens you up to discovering how skilled you already are. Almost everything you do in school can be applied to your career—if you consistently pursue this line of thought.

In addition to thinking about the skills you already have, consider the skills you'd like to acquire. Describe them in detail and list experiences that can help you develop them. Let your list of transferable skills grow and develop as you do.

 You're One Click Away . . .
from more information about the nature of skills.

Discover Your Future

8

T⁷⁵RANSFERABLE SKILLS

There are literally hundreds of transferable skills. Expand the list below based on your own experience.

Self-discovery skills

Assessing knowledge and skills

Selecting strategies to acquire new knowledge and skills

Showing flexibility by adopting new attitudes and behaviors

Career planning skills

Setting goals

Discovering career-related values

Discovering content and transferable skills

Updating career goals to reflect new insights and experience

Time-management skills

Scheduling due dates for projects

Choosing technology and applying it to goal-related tasks

Developing processes or procedures to meet goals

Working independently to meet goals

Planning projects for teams

Managing multiple projects at the same time

Persisting in order to meet goals

Delivering projects on schedule

Planning special events

Reading skills

Reading for major ideas and themes

Reading for detail

Reading to synthesize ideas and information from several sources

Reading to follow instructions

Note-taking skills

Taking notes on material presented verbally, in print, or online

Creating pictures, graphs, and visuals to summarize and clarify

Organizing information and ideas in digital and paper-based forms

Researching by finding information online or in the library

Test-taking and related skills

Assessing personal performance

Working cooperatively in study groups and project teams

Managing stress

Applying scientific findings and methods to solve problems

Using mathematics to do basic computations and solve problems

Thinking skills

Thinking to create new ideas, products, or services

Thinking to evaluate ideas, products, or services

Evaluating material presented verbally, in print, or online

Choosing appropriate strategies for making decisions

Choosing ethical behaviors

Stating problems accurately

Generating possible solutions to problems

Weighing the benefits and costs of potential solutions

Interpreting information for problem solving or decision making

Communication skills

Assigning and delegating tasks

Coaching

Consulting

Counseling

Demonstrating empathy

Editing publications

Entertaining people

Giving people feedback about the quality of their performance

Interpreting and responding to nonverbal messages

Interviewing people for assessment purposes

Leading meetings

Leading project teams

Listening fully

Managing relationships with vendors or suppliers

Preventing conflicts

Conducting focus groups

Conducting interviews

Resolving conflicts

Responding to complaints

Responding to requests

Selling products or services

Serving clients and customers

Speaking to diverse audiences

Speaking to explain ideas, information, or procedures clearly

Teaching

Working with difficult people

Writing instructional materials

Writing sales, marketing, or promotional materials

Money skills

Monitoring income and expenses

Raising funds

Estimating costs

Skills for adapting to work environments

Answering job interview questions

Finding and working with a mentor

Finding potential employers or clients

Networking with contacts

Understanding the culture of an organization

Using a computer for common tasks

Working well with people from a variety of backgrounds

👆 **You're One Click Away . . .**
from more information about identifying skills.

Discover Your Future

8

Commit to Action

Inventory your skills

THIS EXERCISE IS ABOUT discovering your skills. Before you begin, gather 100 blank index cards. Allow about one hour to complete the following three steps.

Note: This exercise is a detailed Discovery Statement. Commit to Action: "Plan your career now," on page 136, functions as a related Intention Statement. And Commit to Action: "Declare your major today," on page 133, guides you to taking a next step based on your discoveries and intentions.

① Step 1

Recall your activities during the past week or month. Write down as many activities as you can, listing each one on a separate index card. Include work-related activities, school activities, household activities, and hobbies. Some of your cards might read "washed dishes," "tuned up my car," or "tutored a French class."

In addition to daily activities, recall any rewards or recognition of your achievements that you've received within the last year. Examples include scholarships, athletic trophies, or letters of thanks for volunteer work. Again, list the activities that were involved.

Spend 20 minutes on this step, listing all of the activities you can recall.

② Step 2

Next, look over your activity cards. Then take another 20 minutes to list any specialized knowledge or procedures needed to complete those activities. These are your *content skills*. (See "Discovering the skilled person you already are" on page 128 for a definition of content skills.) You might be able to list several content skills for any one activity.

List your content skills below. Continue on additional paper as needed.

③ Step 3

Go over your activity cards one more time. Now look for examples of *transferable skills*. ("Discovering the skilled person you already are" defines these as well.) List your transferable skills below, continuing on additional paper if necessary.

Congratulations—you now have a detailed picture of your current skills. Keep your lists of content and transferable skills on hand when planning your career, choosing your major, writing your résumé, and preparing for job interviews. As you gain new skills, be sure to add them to your lists.

 You're One Click Away . . .

from more information about identifying skills.

Discover Your Future

8

FOUR WAYS TO CHOOSE YOUR MAJOR

One decision that concerns many students in higher education is the choice of an academic major. Here is an opportunity to apply your skills at critical thinking, decision making, and problem solving. Use the following four suggestions as a guide.

1. DISCOVER OPTIONS

Follow the fun. Perhaps you look forward to attending one of your classes and even like completing the assignments. This is a clue to your choice of major. See if you can find lasting patterns in the subjects and extracurricular activities that you've enjoyed over the years. Look for a major that allows you to continue and expand on these experiences.

Also, sit down with a stack of index cards and brainstorm answers to the following questions.

- What do you enjoy doing most with your unscheduled time?
- Imagine that you're at a party and having a fascinating conversation. What is this conversation about?
- What Websites do you frequently visit or have bookmarked in a Web browser?

- What kind of problems do you enjoy solving—those that involve people? Products? Ideas?
- What interests are revealed by your choices of reading material, television shows, and other entertainment?
- What would an ideal day look like for you? Describe where you'd live, who would be with you, and what you'd do throughout the day. Do any of these visions suggest a possible major?

Questions like these are not frivolous. They can uncover a "fun factor" that energizes you to finish the work of completing a major.

Consider ability. In choosing a major, ability counts as much as interest. Einstein enjoyed playing the violin, but his love of music didn't override his choice of a physics career. In addition to considering what you enjoy, think about times and places when you excelled. List the courses that you "aced," the work assignments that you mastered, and the hobbies that led to rewards or recognition. Let your choice of a major reflect a discovery of your passions *and* potentials.

Use formal techniques for self-discovery. Consider questionnaires that are designed to correlate your interests with specific majors. Examples include the Strong Interest Inventory and the Self-Directed Search. Your academic advisor or someone at your school's career-planning office can give you more details.

Remember that questionnaires can help you gain self-knowledge. However, what you *do* with that knowledge is entirely up to you. No one else can choose your major for you.

Link to long-term goals. Your choice of a major might fall into place once you determine what you want in life. Before you choose a major, back up to a bigger picture. List your core values, such as contributing to society, achieving financial security and professional recognition, enjoying good health, or making time for fun. Also write down specific goals that you want to accomplish in five years, 10 years, or even 50 years from today.

Many students find the prospect of getting what they want in life justifies all of the time, money, and day-to-day effort invested in going to school. Having a major gives you a powerful incentive for attending classes, taking part in discussions, reading textbooks, writing papers, and completing other assignments. When you see a clear connection between finishing school and creating the life of your dreams, the daily tasks of higher education become charged with meaning.

Ask other people. Key people in your life might have valuable suggestions about your choice of major. Ask for their ideas and listen with an open mind.

At the same time, distance yourself from any pressure to choose a major or career that fails to interest you. If you make a choice based solely on the expectations of other people, you could end up with a major or even a career you don't enjoy.

Gather information. Check your school's catalog or Website for a list of available majors. Here is a gold mine of information. Take a quick glance and highlight all the majors that interest you. Then talk to students who have declared them.

Also read descriptions of courses required for these majors. Chat with instructors who teach courses in these areas and ask for copies of their class syllabi. Go the bookstore and browse required texts.

Based on all this information, write a list of prospective majors. Discuss them with an academic advisor and someone at your school's career-planning center.

Invent a major. When choosing a major, you do not need to limit yourself to those listed in your school catalog. Many schools now have flexible programs that allow for independent study. Through such programs you might be able to combine two existing majors, or invent an entirely new one of your own.

Consider a complementary minor. You can add flexibility to your academic program by choosing a minor to complement or contrast with your major. The student who wants to be a politician could opt for a minor in English; all of those courses in composition can help in writing speeches. Or the student with a major in psychology might choose a minor in business administration, with the idea of managing a counseling service someday. An effective choice of a major can expand your skills and career options.

Think critically about the link between your major and your career. Your career goals might largely dictate your choice of a major. On the other hand, you might be able to pursue a rewarding career by choosing among *several* different majors. Remember that many people work happily in jobs with little relationship to their major.

2. MAKE A TRIAL CHOICE

At many schools, declaring a major offers some benefits. For example, you might get priority when registering for certain classes and qualify for special scholarships or grants.

Don't delay such benefits. Even if you feel undecided today, you probably have many ideas about what your major will be. Choose one soon.

Do a simple experiment. Pretend that you have to choose a major today. Based on the options that you've already discovered, write down the first three ideas that come to mind. Review the list for a few minutes and then just choose one.

Hold onto your list. It reflects your current intuition or "gut feelings," and it may come in handy during the next step. This step might confirm your trial choice of major—or return you to one of the majors that you had originally listed.

3. EVALUATE YOUR TRIAL CHOICE

When you've made a trial choice of major, take on the role of a scientist. Treat your choice as a hypothesis and then design a series of experiments to evaluate and test it. For example, you can try the following suggestions:

- Schedule office meetings with instructors who teach courses in the major. Ask about required course work and career options in the field.

- Discuss your trial choice with an academic advisor or career counselor.

- Enroll in a course related to your possible major. Remember that introductory courses might not give you a realistic picture of the workloads involved in advanced courses. Also, you might not be able to register for certain courses until you've actually declared a related major.

- Find a volunteer experience, internship, part-time job, or service-learning experience related to the major.

- Interview students who have declared the same major. Ask them in detail about their experiences and suggestions for success.

- Interview someone who works in a field related to the major.

- Think about whether you can complete your major given the amount of time and money that you plan to invest in higher education.

- Consider whether declaring this major would require a transfer to another program or even another school.

If these factors confirm your choice of major, celebrate that fact. If they result in choosing a new major, celebrate that outcome as well.

Also remember that higher education represents a safe place to test your choice of major. As you sort through your options, help is always available from administrators, instructors, advisors, and peers.

4. CHOOSE AGAIN

Keep your trial choice of a major in perspective. There is no single "correct" choice. Your unique collection of skills is likely to provide the basis for majoring in several fields.

Odds are that you'll change your major at least once—and that you'll change careers several times during your life.

One benefit of higher education is mobility. You can gain skills and knowledge that help you move into a new major or career field at any time.

Viewing a major as a one-time choice that determines your entire future can raise your stress levels. Instead, look at choosing a major as the start of a continuing path that involves discovery, intention, and passionate action, a decision that evolves during the rest of your life.

 You're One Click Away . . .
from more ways to choose your major.

Declare your major today

PRETEND THAT YOU ARE REQUIRED TO choose a major today. Of course, your choice is not permanent. You can change it in the future. The purpose of this exercise is simply to *begin* a process that will lead to declaring an official major.

1 To begin, review your responses to Commit to Action: "Inventory your skills" on page 131.

2 Next, look at your school's catalog (print or online) for a list of majors. Print out this list or make a copy of it.

3 Based on knowledge of your skills and your ideas about your future career, cross out all of the majors that do not interest you. You will probably eliminate well over half the list.

4 From the remaining majors on the list, circle those that you're willing to consider.

5 Now, scan the majors that you circled and look for those that interest you the most. See if you can narrow your choices down to three. List those majors here.

6 Write an asterisk next to the major that interests you most right now. *This is your trial choice of major.*

Don't stop there. Now, move into action. Review the article "Four ways to choose your major" on page 132. Then list the suggestions from this article that you will definitely use. List those suggestions below, including at least one action that you will take within the next 24 hours.

I will . . .

 You're One Click Away . . .
from more ways to choose your major.

Discover Your Future

8

CREATE YOUR CAREER

There's an old saying: "If you enjoy what you do, you'll never work another day in your life." A satisfying and lucrative career is often the goal of education. If you clearly define your career goals and your strategy for reaching them, then you can plan your education effectively.

Career planning involves continuous exploration. There are dozens of effective paths to take. Begin now with the following ideas.

YOU ALREADY KNOW A LOT ABOUT YOUR CAREER PLAN

When people go to school to gain skills, they often start discovering things that they don't know. Career planning is different. You can begin by realizing how much you know right now.

In fact, you've already made many decisions about your career. This is true for young people who say, "I don't have any idea what I want to be when I grow up." It's also true for midlife career changers.

Consider the student who can't decide if he wants to be a cost accountant or a tax accountant and then jumps to the conclusion that he is totally lost when it comes to career planning. Or take the student who doesn't know if he wants to be a veterinary assistant or a nurse.

These people forget that they already know a lot about their career choices.

The person who is debating tax accounting versus cost accounting already knows that he doesn't want to be a doctor, playwright, or taxicab driver. He also knows that he likes working with numbers and balancing books.

The person who is choosing between veterinary assistance and nursing has already ruled out becoming a lawyer, computer programmer, or teacher. He just doesn't know yet whether he has the right bedside manner for horses or for people.

Such people have already narrowed their list of career choices to a number of jobs in the same field—jobs that draw on the same core skills. In general, they already know what they want to be when they grow up.

Demonstrate this for yourself. Find a long list of occupations. (One source is *The Dictionary of Occupational Titles*, a government publication available at many libraries.) Using a stack of index cards, write down randomly selected job titles, one title per card. Then sort through the cards and divide them into two piles. Label one pile "Careers I've Definitely Ruled Out for Now." Label the other pile "Careers I'm Willing to Consider."

You might go through a stack of 100 such cards and end up with 95 in the "definitely ruled out" pile and five in the "willing to consider" pile. This demonstrates that you already have many ideas about the career you want.

YOUR CAREER IS A CHOICE, NOT A DISCOVERY

Many people approach career planning as if they were panning for gold. They keep sifting through dirt, clearing away dust, and throwing out rocks. They are hoping to strike it rich and discover the perfect career.

Other people believe that they'll wake up one morning, see the heavens part, and suddenly know what they're supposed to do. Many of them are still waiting for that magical day to dawn.

We can approach career planning in a different way. Instead of seeing a career as something we discover, we can see it as something we choose. We don't find the right career. We create it.

There's a big difference between these two approaches. Thinking that there's only one "correct" choice for your career can lead to a lot of anxiety: "Did I discover the right one?" "What if I made a mistake?"

Viewing your career as your creation helps you relax. Instead of anguishing over finding the right career, you can stay open to possibilities. You can choose one career today, knowing that you can choose again later.

Discover Your Future

8

Suppose that you've narrowed your list of possible careers to five, and you're still unsure. Then just choose one. Any one. Many people will have five careers in a lifetime anyway. You might be able to pursue all five of your careers, and you can do any one of them first. The important thing is to choose.

One caution is in order. Choosing your career is not something to do in an information vacuum. Rather, choose after you've done a lot of research. That includes research into yourself—your skills and interests—and a thorough knowledge of what careers are available.

YOU'VE GOT A WORLD OF CHOICES

Our society offers a limitless array of careers. You no longer have to confine yourself to a handful of traditional categories, such as business, education, government, or manufacturing. People are constantly creating new products and services to meet new demands. The number of job titles is expanding so rapidly that we can barely keep track of them.

For instance, there are people who work as *ritual consultants*, helping people to plan weddings, anniversaries, graduations, and other ceremonies. *Auto brokers* visit dealers, shop around, and buy a car for you. *Professional organizers* walk into your home or office and advise you on managing workflow and organizing your space. *Pet psychologists* help you raise a happy and healthy animal. *Life coaches* assist you in setting and achieving goals.

In addition to choosing the *content* of your career, you have many options for the *context* in which you work. You can work full-time. You can work part-time. You can commute to a cubicle in a major corporation. Or you can work at home and take the one-minute commute from your bedroom to your desk. You can join a thriving business—or create one of your own.

PLAN BY NAMING NAMES

One key to making your career plan real and to ensuring that you can act on it is naming. Go back over your plan to see if you can include specific names whenever they're called for.

Name your job. Take the skills you enjoy using and find out which jobs use them. What are those jobs called? List them. Note that one job might have different names.

Name your company—the agency or organization you want to work for. If you want to be self-employed or start your own business, then name the product or service you'd sell.

Name your contacts. Take the list of organizations you just compiled. Which people in these organizations are responsible for hiring? List those people and contact them directly. If you choose self-employment, list the names of possible customers or clients.

Name more contacts. Expand your list of contacts by brainstorming with your family and friends. Come up with a list of names—anyone who can help you with career planning and job hunting. Write each of these names on an index card or Rolodex card. Or use a contact manager on a computer.

Name your location. Ask if your career choices are consistent with your preferences about where to live and work. For example, someone who wants to make a living as a studio musician might consider living in a large city such as New York or Toronto. This contrasts with the freelance graphic artist who conducts his business mainly by phone and e-mail. He might be able to live anywhere and still pursue his career.

Name your career goal for others to hear. Develop a "pitch"—a short statement of your career goal that you can easily share with your contacts. For example: "After I graduate, I plan to work in the travel business. I'm looking for an internship in an international travel agency for next summer. Do you know of any agencies that take interns?" Consider everyone you meet a potential member of your job network, and be prepared to talk about what you do.

TEST YOUR CHOICE—AND BE WILLING TO CHANGE

Read books about careers and search for career-planning Websites. Ask career counselors about skills assessments that can help you discover your skills and identify jobs that call for those skills. Take career-planning courses and workshops sponsored by your school. Visit the career-planning and job placement offices on campus.

On the basis of all this information, you can make a trial career choice. Look for experiences that can help you evaluate the choice. For example, you can try the following:

- Contact people who are actually doing the job you're researching and ask them a lot of questions about what it's like (an *information interview*).
- Choose an internship or volunteer position in a field that interests you.
- Get a part-time or summer job in your career field.

If you enjoy such experiences, then you've probably made a wise career choice. The people you meet are possible sources of recommendations, referrals, and employment in the future.

If you did *not* enjoy your experiences, then celebrate what you learned about yourself. Now you're free to refine your initial career choice or go in a new direction.

Career planning is not a once-and-for-all proposition. Rather, career plans are made to be changed and refined as you gain new information about yourself and the world.

Career planning never ends. If your present career no longer feels right, you can choose again—no matter what stage of life you're in. The process is the same, whether you're choosing your first career or your fifth.

You're One Click Away . . .
from more career-planning strategies.

Commit to Action
Plan your career now

WRITE YOUR CAREER PLAN. Now.

That's right—*now*. Get started with the process of career planning, even if you're not sure where to begin.

Your response to this exercise can be just a rough draft of your plan, which you can revise and rewrite many times. The point is to start a conversation about taking charge of your career—and to get your ideas in writing.

The format of your plan is up to you. You could include many details, such as the next job title you'd like to have, the courses required for your major, and other training that you want to complete. You could list the names of companies to research and people that could hire you. You could also include target dates to complete each of these tasks.

Another option is to represent your plan visually. Consider using charts, timelines, maps, or drawings. You can generate these by hand or use computer software.

To prime your thinking, complete the following sentences. Use the space below and continue on additional paper as needed.

The skills I most enjoy using include . . .

Careers that require these skills include . . .

Of those careers, the one that interests me most right now is . . .

The educational and work experiences that would help me prepare for this career include . . .

The immediate steps I will take to pursue this career are . . .

You're One Click Away . . .

from more suggestions for writing a career plan.

FINDING YOUR PLACE IN THE NEW WORLD OF WORK

One generation ago, only factory workers worried about automation—being laid off and replaced by machines. Today, employees in a variety of fields might fear losing their jobs to computer-driven robots, or to workers across the globe who will do the same job for a fraction of the wages.

You are entering a global economy. Your toughest competitors for a new job might be people from India or China with technical skills and a blazing fast Internet connection.

Employers can now hire from a global work force. Project teams in the future will include people from several nations who connect via e-mail, cell phones, teleconferencing, and digital devices that have yet to be invented.

You can thrive in this global economy. It will take foresight and a willingness to learn, along with the following strategies.

Complete your education. According to *Tough Choices or Tough Times: The Report of the New Commission on the Skills of the American Workforce*, the United States will remain an economic powerhouse only if its citizens are educated to do creative work-research, development, design, marketing, sales, and management. Careers in these areas are the least likely to be outsourced.[1] The authors of *Tough Choices* also note that people with computer skills and strong backgrounds in mathematics and science will have key tools to succeed in the new global economy. They will also need to work with abstract ideas, think creatively, learn quickly, write well, develop new products, and work on culturally diverse project teams. These skills are all potential benefits of higher education.

Create a long-term career plan. When planning your career, look beyond your next job. Think in terms of a career *path*. Discover opportunities for advancement and innovation over the long term.

If you're a computer programmer, think about what you could do beyond writing code—perhaps by becoming a systems analyst or software engineer.

If you're a musician, find out how you could use the Internet to promote your band, book gigs, and distribute recordings.

And if you're a stockbroker, plan to offer more than advice about buying and selling. Help your clients plan their retirement and fund their children's college education as well.

No matter what your plan, consider gaining sales and marketing skills. Every organization depends on people who can bring in new customers and clients. If you can attract new sources of revenue, you'll be harder to replace.

Develop two key sets of skills. In *The New Division of Labor: How Computers Are Creating the Next Job Market*, Frank Levy and Richard J. Murnane describe two sets of skills that will not be taken over by robots or computers.[2]

First is *expert thinking*. This is the ability to work with problems that cannot be solved simply by applying rules. The doctor who successfully treats a person with a rare set of symptoms offers an example of expert thinking. So does the mechanic who repairs an engine defect that the computer diagnostics missed.

Second is *complex communication*—the ability to find information, explain it to other people, and persuade them how to use it. An example is the engineer who convinces his colleagues that his design for a DVD player will outstrip the competition and reduce production costs. Complex communication is essential to education, sales, marketing, and management.

Even in a high-tech world, there will always be a need for the human touch. Learn to lead meetings, guide project teams, mentor people, nurture new talent, and create long-term business relationships. Then you'll offer employers something that they cannot get from a software package or contract worker.

 You're One Click Away . . .
from more strategies for succeeding in a global economy.

Discover Your Future

8

9 Critical Thinking Experiment

Examine beliefs about careers and jobs

BELIEF #1: The best way to plan a career is to enter a field that's in demand.

This statement sounds reasonable. However, you might find it practical to choose a career that's not in demand right now. Even in careers that are highly competitive, job openings often exist for qualified people who are passionate about the field. Also, jobs that are "hot" right now might be "cool" by the time you complete your education. In a constantly changing job market, your own interests and values could guide you as reliably as current trends.

BELIEF #2: The best way to find a job is through "want ads" and online job listings.

There's a problem with these job-hunting strategies: *Many job openings are not advertised*. According to Richard Bolles, author of *What Color Is Your Parachute? A Practical Manual for Job-Hunters and Career-Changers,* employers turn to help wanted listings, résumés, and employment agencies only as a last resort. When jobs open up, they prefer instead to hire people they know—or people who walk through the door and prove that they're excellent candidates for available jobs.[3] Based on the above examples, do some critical thinking of your own. Evaluate each of the following beliefs, stating whether or not you agree with them.

Belief #3: Writing a career plan now is a waste of time. I'll just have to change it later.

Belief #4: I can't plan a career now. I can't afford to take time from my schoolwork.

Belief #5: Writing a résumé is a waste of time until you're actually ready to hunt for a job.

▶ **You're One Click Away . . .**
from strategies for successful job hunting, including résumé writing and job interviewing.

8

THE DISCOVERY WHEEL, RELOADED

The purpose of this book is to give you the opportunity to change your behavior. This exercise gives you a chance to see what behaviors you have changed on your journey toward becoming a master student. Answer each question quickly and honestly. Record your results on the Discovery Wheel that follows and then compare it with the one you completed in the Introduction.

As you complete this self-evaluation, keep in mind that *your scores might be lower here than on your earlier Discovery Wheel.* That's OK. Lower scores might result from increased self-awareness and honesty, and other valuable assets.

As you did with the earlier Discovery Wheel, read the following statements and give yourself points for each one. Use the point system described below. Then add up your point total for each category and shade the Discovery Wheel on page 141 to the appropriate level.

5 points
This statement is always or almost always true of me.

4 points
This statement is often true of me.

3 points
This statement is true of me about half the time.

2 points
This statement is seldom true of me.

1 points
This statement is never or almost never true of me.

1. _____ I can clearly state my overall purpose in life.

2. _____ I can explain how school relates to what I plan to do after I graduate.

3. _____ I can clearly describe what I want to experience in major areas of my life, including my career, relationships, financial well-being, and health.

4. _____ I consider different points of view and choose from alternative solutions.

5. _____ I use my knowledge of learning styles to support my success in school.

_____ Total score (1) *Purpose*

1. _____ I set goals and periodically review them.

2. _____ I plan each day and often accomplish what I plan.

3. _____ I have enough energy to study, attend classes, and enjoy other areas of my life.

4. _____ I have a plan for having enough money to complete my education.

5. _____ I make regular deposits to a savings account.

_____ Total score (2) *Resources*

1. _____ When reading, I ask myself questions about the material.

2. _____ When I read, I am alert and awake.

3. _____ I relate what I read to my life.

4. _____ I select reading strategies to fit the type of material I'm reading.

5. _____ When I don't understand what I'm reading, I note my questions and find answers.

_____ Total score (3) *Reading*

1. _____ When I am in class, I focus my attention.

2. _____ I take notes in class.

3. _____ I can explain various methods for taking notes, and I choose those that work best for me.

4. _____ I distinguish key points from supporting examples.

5. _____ I put important concepts into my own words.

_____ Total score (4) *Notes*

1. _____ The way that I talk about my value as a person is independent of my grades.

2. _____ I often succeed at predicting test questions.

3. _____ I review for tests throughout the term.

4. _____ I manage my time during tests.

5. _____ I use techniques to remember key facts and ideas.

_____ Total score (5) *Grades*

Discover Your Future

8

1. _____ I plan large writing assignments.
2. _____ When researching, I find relevant facts and properly credit their sources.
3. _____ I write brief, clear, and useful e-mail messages.
4. _____ I edit my writing for clarity, accuracy, and coherence.
5. _____ I prepare and deliver effective speeches.

_____ Total score (6) *Voice*

1. _____ Other people tell me that I am a good listener.
2. _____ I communicate my upsets without blaming others.
3. _____ I build rewarding relationships with people from other backgrounds.

4. _____ I effectively resolve conflict.
5. _____ I regularly take on a leadership role.

_____ Total score (7) *Relationships*

1. _____ I have a detailed list of my skills.
2. _____ I have a written career plan and update it regularly.
3. _____ I use the career-planning services offered by my school.
4. _____ I participate in internships, extracurricular activities, information interviews, and on-the-job experiences to test and refine my career plan.
5. _____ I have declared a major related to my interests, skills, and core values.

_____ Total score (8) *Future*

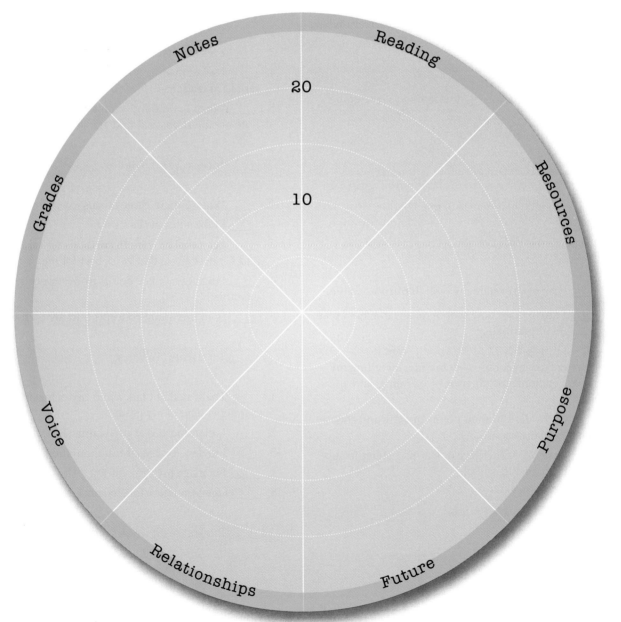

Discover Your Future

8

Using the total score from each category, shade in each section of the blank Discovery Wheel. If you want, use different colors. For example, you could use green for areas you want to work on.

REFLECT ON YOUR DISCOVERY WHEEL

Take this opportunity to review both of the Discovery Wheels you completed in this book. Write your scores from each section of the Discovery Wheel from the Introduction in the chart below. Then add your scores for each section of the Discovery Wheel that you just completed.

	Introduction	Chapter 8
Purpose		
Resources		
Reading		
Notes		
Grades		
Voice		
Relationships		
Future		

Finally, summarize your insights from doing the Discovery Wheels. Then declare how you will use these insights to promote your continued success.

Comparing the Discovery Wheel in this chapter with the Discovery Wheel in Chapter One, I discovered that I ...

_____

_____

_____

_____

In the next six months, I intend to review the following articles from this book for additional suggestions I could use:

_____

_____

_____

_____

You're One Click Away . . .
from an online version of this exercise.

Discover Your Future

8

Commit to Action

Create your future

THIS EXERCISE OFFERS a chance to celebrate your successes during the the past term—and to think in specific ways about what you want to create next term.

Part 1: Discover your successes

Looking back on this past term, you might be surprised at how quickly it went by. You might also be surprised at how much you learned, both inside and outside the classroom.

In the space below, list three things that you did well during the current term. Perhaps you took the initiative to meet a new person or created an effective way to take notes in class. Write down any success that you find personally significant, no matter how small you think it might seem to others. Use additional paper as needed.

❶

❷

❸

Part 2: Do some truth telling

Now take a moment to write about three things that did not go as well as you wanted during the past term. Explore whatever comes to mind—anything from a simple embarrassment to a major mistake. If you missed a class because you set your alarm for 7 P.M. instead of 7 A.M., you can write about that. If you failed a test, you might describe that experience as well.

As you practice truth telling, remember to keep it light. It's fine to acknowledge breakdowns and to laugh at yourself as you do.

❶

❷

❸

Part 3: Determine what you want next

Now, reflect on ways to maintain or expand on the successes you listed in Part 1. Also consider ways to change the outcomes listed in Part 2. For instance, you could set a goal to raise your grade point average to a specific number, or to declare your major by a certain date. Perhaps you want to resolve a conflict with an instructor or roommate. Or you might want to deepen a connection with someone you already know and make this person a friend for life. In any case, complete the following sentence, using additional paper as needed.

I intend to . . .

Part 4: Move into action

Finally, brainstorm a list of specific actions you can take to meet the goals you just wrote. Record these actions separately in your calendar or on a to-do list.[4]

 You're One Click Away . . .

from creating a master timeline for completing your education.

I create it all

THIS POWER PROCESS IS ABOUT the difference between two distinct positions in life: being a victim or being responsible.

Consider a student who flunks a test. "Another F!" the student says. "That teacher couldn't teach her way out of a wet paper bag. How could I read with a houseful of kids making noise all the time? And then friends came over ... ."

The problem with this viewpoint is that, in looking for excuses, the student is robbing himself of the power to get any grade other than an F. He's giving all of his power to a bad teacher, noisy children, and friends.

Instead, the student could react like this: "Another F! Well, hmmm... . How did I choose this F? What did I do to create it? I didn't review my notes after class. That might have done it." Or "I studied in the same room with my children while they watched TV. Then I went out with my friends the night before the test. Well, that probably helped me fulfill some of the requirements for getting an F."

You can apply this example to many circumstances in your life. Accidents happen. There are events that you cannot predict or control. And if you're willing to look, you'll find that other events followed from choices that you made.

Responsibility is "response-ability"—the ability to choose a response. When faced with any circumstance, you can choose what you say next, and what you do next. This does not mean that you have divine powers. It simply means that you always have a choice.

Whenever you feel like a victim, remember "I create it all." It's simply a tool for creative thinking. When you use it, you instantly open up a world of choices. You give yourself power.

You're One Click Away . . .

from more ways to master self-responsibility.

Discover Your Future

8

IMPORTANT NOTE

This book is continued on page i.

In other words, consider reading and doing any part of this book again. You can get even more value from it the second or third time around.

Discover Head Head

8

Photo and Illustration Credits

Introduction

p. 4, left to right: Pierre Desrosiers/Photographer's Choice/RF/Getty Images; Aaron Lindberg/Lifesize/RF/Getty Images; Hola Images/RF/Getty Images; Jamie Grill/Tetra Images/RF/Getty Images; Jose Luis Pelaez, Inc./Blend Images RF/Jupiter Images; p. 7: Steve Cole/RF/Getty Images; p. 10 (top left): Photo courtesy of Jennie Long.; p. 10 (top right): Photo courtesy of Jennifer Jarding.; p. 10 (bottom): Photo courtesy of Alex Denizard.; p. 11 (top): Photo Courtesy of the Washington Speaker's Bureau. Reprinted by permission of Liz Murray; p. 11 (center): © Bettmann/Corbis; p. 11 (bottom): Photo courtesy of the HistoryMakers; p. 13: Edmond Van Hoorick/Digital Vision/Getty Images.

Chapter 1

p. 15: (man) Tanya Constantine/Blend Images/RF/Getty Images, (fern) Tim Laman/National Geographic RF/Getty Images, (ballet shoes) Scott T. Baxter/Photodisc/RF/Getty Images, (protractor) Vladimir Godnick/fStop/RF/Getty Images, (meditating woman) Meg Takamura/RF/Getty Images, (holding hands) Doug Menuez/Photodisc/RF/Getty Images, (music) Gregor Schuster/PC/RF/Getty Images, (microphone) George Doyle/Stockbyte/RF/Getty Images; p. 23: © Masterfile Royalty Free; p. 25: Ted Humbie-Smith/RF/Getty Images.

Chapter 2

p. 28: © Deborah Jaffe/TSI/Getty Images; p. 33: © Jamie Grill/RF/Corbis; p. 35: Photodisc/RF/Getty Images; p. 39: © Michele Constantini/PhotoAlto/RF/Getty Images; p. 43: © Luca Tettoni/Corbis.

Chapter 3

p. 45: © Masterfile Royalty Free; p. 47: © Masterfile Royalty Free; p. 49: © Masterfile Royalty Free; p. 52: Moodboard/RF/Corbis; p. 59: DAJ/RF/Getty Images.

Chapter 4

p. 64: Greg Hinsdale/RF/Corbis; p. 69: Image Source/RF/Getty Images; p. 77: Angelo Cavalli/Digital Vision/RF/Getty Images.

Chapter 5

p. 79: Bill Aron/PhotoEdit, Inc.; p. 82: © Image Source/RF/Corbis; p. 87: © Masterfile Royalty Free; p. 90: © Bloomimage/RF/Corbis; p. 93: Katsuo Yamagishi/SPORT/Jupiter Images.

Chapter 6

p. 100: Image Source/RF/Getty Images; p. 102: © Masterfile Royalty Free; p. 105: © Masterfile Royalty Free; p. 109: Skip Brown/National Geographic/RF/Getty Images.

Chapter 7

p. 111: David Madison/Photographer's Choice/RF/Getty Images; p. 121: Corbis/RF/Jupiter Images; p. 123: (Jesse Owens) © Bettmann/Corbis, (Eleanor Roosevelt) © Bettmann/Corbis, (Albert Einstein) Alan W. Richards/Princeton, (Nelson Mandela) © Paul Velasco/Gallo Images/Corbis, (Golda Meir) © Bettmann/Corbis, (Aung San Suu Kyi) Emmanuel Dunand/Getty Images; p. 125: Pixland/RF/Jupiter Images.

Chapter 8

p. 127: Stockbyte/RF/Getty Images; p. 131: (man) © Masterfile Royalty Free, (boy with romote) © Ron Chapple/Corbis, (airplane) © RF/Corbis; p. 134: Terry Vine/Blend Images/RF/Getty Images; p. 142: Goodshoot/RF/Jupiter Images.

Endnotes

Introduction

1. Robert Manning, "Hemingway in Cuba," *The Atlantic Monthly,* August 1965, 216, no. 2 (August 1965): 101–108, http://www. theatlantic.com/issues/65aug/6508manning.htm (accessed April 26, 2008).
2. Alex Osborn, *Applied Imagination: Principles and Procedures of Creative Thinking* (New York: Scribner, 1953).
3. Peter A. Facione, *Critical Thinking: What It Is and Why It Counts* (Millbrae, CA: California Academic Press, 2007), http:// www.insightassessment.com/pdf_files/what&why2006.pdf. Reprinted by permission of California Academic Press.

Chapter 1

1. David A. Kolb, *Experiential Learning: Experience as the Source of Learning and Development* (Englewood Cliffs, NJ: Prentice-Hall, 1984).
2. Neil Fleming, "VARK: A Guide to Learning Styles," 2006, http://www.vark-learn.com (accessed April 26, 2008).
3. Howard Gardner, *Frames of Mind: The Theory of Multiple Intelligences* (New York: Basic Books, 1993).
4. Arthur L. Costa and Bena Kallick, "Habit Is a Cable . . .: Quotations to Extend and Illuminate Habits of Mind," June 6, 2003, http://www.habits-of-mind.net/(accessed April 26, 2008).

Chapter 2

1. David Allen, *Getting Things Done: The Art of Stress-Free Productivity* (New York: Penguin, 2001).
2. Jane B. Burka and Lenora R. Yuen, *Procrastination: Why You Do It, What to Do About It* (Reading, MA: Addison-Wesley, 1983).
3. Michael Pollan, "Unhappy Meals," *New York Times,* January 28, 2007, http://www.nytimes.com/2007/01/28/magazine/ 28nutritionism.t.html (accessed April 26, 2008).
4. "A Snapshot of Annual High-Risk College Drinking Consequences," National Institute on Alcohol Abuse and Alcoholism, July 11, 2007, http://www.collegedrinkingprevention.gov/ StatsSummaries/snapshot.aspx (accessed April 26, 2008).
5. American Psychological Association, *Diagnostic and Statistical Manual of Psychoactive Substance Abuse Disorders* (Washington, D.C.: American Psychological Association, 1994).

Chapter 4

1. Walter Pauk and Ross J. Q. Owens, *How to Study in College,* Eighth Edition (Boston: Houghton Mifflin, 2005).
2. Joseph Novak and D. Bob Gowin, *Learning How to Learn* (New York: Cambridge University Press, 1984).

Chapter 5

1. Alzheimer's Association, "Brain Health," 2006, http://www.alz. org/brainhealth/overview.asp (accessed October 30, 2006.)
2. This article incorporates detailed suggestions from reviewer Frank Baker.

Chapter 6

1. Natalie Goldberg, *Writing Down the Bones: Freeing the Writer Within* (Boston, MA: Shambhala, 1992).
2. Quoted in Theodore Cheney, *Getting the Words Right: How to Revise, Edit and Rewrite* (Cincinnati, OH: Writer's Digest, 1983).
3. M. T. Motley, *Overcoming Your Fear of Public Speaking: A Proven Method* (New York: Houghton Mifflin, 1998).
4. Aristotle, *Rhetoric* (Amherst, NY: Prometheus Books, 1995).

Chapter 7

1. Maia Szalavitz, "Race and the Genome: The Howard University Human Genome Center," National Human Genome Center, 2001, http://www.genomecenter.howard.edu/article.htm (accessed April 26, 2008).
2. LaFasto and Larson refer to their book *When Teams Work Best* in their online article, written for the Center for Association Leadership: "The Zen of Brilliant Teams," July 1, 2002, http:// www.asaecenter.org/PublicationsResources/articledetail.cfm? ItemNumber=13295 (accessed April 26, 2008).

Chapter 8

1. National Center on Education and the Economy, *Tough Choices or Tough Times: The Report of the New Commission on the Skills of the American Workforce* (San Francisco: Jossey-Bass, 2007).
2. Frank Levy and Richard J. Murname, *The New Division of Labor: How Computers Are Creating the Next Job Market* (Princeton, NJ: Princeton University Press, 2004).
3. Richard N. Bolles, *What Color Is Your Parachute? A Practical Manual for Job-Hunters and Career-Changers* (Berkeley, CA: updated annually).
4. Adapted from "Plan for sophomore-year success," in *Becoming a Master Student Athlete* (Boston: Houghton Mifflin Company, 2006), p. 319.

Further Reading

Adler, Mortimer, and Charles Van Doren. *How to Read a Book: The Classic Guide to Intelligent Reading.* New York: Touchstone, 1972.

Allen, David. *Getting Things Done: The Art of Stress-Free Productivity.* New York: Penguin, 2001.

Allen, David. *Ready for Anything: 52 Productivity Principles for Work & Life.* New York: Viking, 2003.

Anthony, Jason, and Karl Cluck. *Debt-Free by 30.* New York: Plume, 2001.

Bandler, Richard, and John Grinder. *Frogs into Princes: Neuro-Linguistic Programming.* Moab, UT: Real People, 1979.

Becoming a Master Student Athlete. Boston, MA: Houghton Mifflin, 2006.

Bolles, Richard N. *What Color Is Your Parachute? A Practical Manual for Job-Hunters and Career-Changers.* Berkeley, CA: Ten Speed, updated annually.

Boston Women's Health Book Collective. *The New Our Bodies, Ourselves.* New York: Simon & Schuster, 1996.

Brown, Alan C. *Maximizing Memory Power.* New York: Wiley, 1986.

Buzan, Tony. *Make the Most of Your Mind.* New York: Simon & Schuster, 1977.

Corey, Gerald. *I Never Knew I Had a Choice.* Monterey, CA: Brooks Cole, 1982.

Covey, Stephen R. *First Things First.* New York: Simon & Schuster, 1994.

Covey, Stephen R. *The Seven Habits of Highly Effective People: Powerful Lessons in Personal Change.* New York: Simon & Schuster, 1989.

Davis, Deborah. *The Adult Learner's Companion.* Boston, MA: Houghton Mifflin: 2007.

Dominguez, Joe, and Vicki Robin. *Your Money or Your Life: Transforming Your Relationship with Money and Achieving Financial Independence.* New York: Viking, 1992.

Dumond, Val. *The Elements of Nonsexist Usage.* New York: Prentice-Hall, 1990.

Elgin, Duane. *Voluntary Simplicity.* New York: Morrow, 1993.

Ellis, Dave. *Falling Awake: Creating the Life of Your Dreams.* Rapid City, SD: Breakthrough Enterprises, 2000.

Ellis, Dave, Stan Lankowitz, Ed Stupka, and Doug Toft. *Career Planning.* Boston, MA: Houghton Mifflin, 2003.

Facione, Peter. *Critical Thinking: What It Is and Why It Counts.* Millbrae, CA: California Academic Press, 1996.

Fletcher, Anne. *Sober for Good.* Boston, MA: Houghton Mifflin, 2001.

From Master Student to Master Employee, Second Edition. Boston, MA: Houghton Mifflin, 2009.

Gawain, Shakti. *Creative Visualization.* New York: New World Library, 1998.

Gibaldi, Joseph. *MLA Handbook for Writers of Research Papers.* New York: Modern Language Association, 1999.

Glasser, William. *Take Effective Control of Your Life.* New York: HarperCollins, 1984.

Golas, Thaddeus. *The Lazy Man's Guide to Enlightenment.* New York: Bantam, 1993.

Greene, Susan D., and Melanie C. L. Martel. *The Ultimate Job Hunter's Guidebook,* Fourth Edition. Boston, MA: Houghton Mifflin, 2004.

Hallowell, Edward M. *CrazyBusy: Overstretched, Overbooked, and About to Snap!* New York: Ballantine, 2006.

Higbee, Kenneth L. *Your Memory: How It Works and How to Improve It.* Englewood Cliffs, NJ: Prentice-Hall, 1996.

James, William. *Talks to Teachers on Psychology and to Students on Some of Life's Ideals.* New York: Norton, 1983.

Keyes, Ken, Jr. *Handbook to Higher Consciousness.* Berkeley, CA: Living Love, 1974.

Keyes, Ralph. *Timelock: How Life Got So Hectic and What You Can Do About It.* New York: HarperCollins, 1991.

Kolb, David A. *Experiential Learning: Experience as the Source of Learning and Development.* Englewood Cliffs, NJ: Prentice-Hall, 1984.

Lathrop, Richard. *Who's Hiring Who?* Berkeley, CA: Ten Speed, 1989.

Levy, Frank, and Richard J. Murname. *The New Division of Labor: How Computers Are Creating the Next Job Market.* Princeton, NJ: Princeton University Press, 2004.

Lucas, Jerry, and Harry Lorayne. *The Memory Book.* New York: Ballantine Books, 1975.

Mallow, Jeffry V. *Science Anxiety: Fear of Science and How to Overcome It.* New York: Thomond, 1986.

Manning, Robert. *Credit Card Nation: The Consequences of America's Addiction to Credit.* New York: Basic Books, 2000.

McCarthy, Michael J. *Mastering the Information Age.* Los Angeles: J. P. Tarcher, 1991.

Nolting, Paul D. *Math Study Skills Workbook,* Third Edition. Boston, MA: Houghton Mifflin, 2008.

Pauk, Walter, and Ross J. Q. Owens. *How to Study in College,* Eighth Edition. Boston, MA: Houghton Mifflin, 2005.

Pennebaker, James W. *Opening Up: The Healing Power of Confiding in Others.* New York: Morrow, 1990.

Pirsig, Robert. *Zen and the Art of Motorcycle Maintenance.* New York: Perennial Classics, 2000.

Raimes, Anne. *Universal Keys for Writers.* Boston, MA: Houghton Mifflin, 2004.

Rajneesh, Bhagwan S. *Journey Toward the Heart.* New York: Harper and Row, 1980.

Robbins, John. *Diet for a New America: How Your Food Choices Affect Your Health, Happiness and the Future of Life on Earth.* New York: H J Kramer, 1998.

Robinson, Adam. *What Smart Students Know: Maximum Grades, Optimum Learning, Minimum Time.* New York: Crown, 1993.

Ruggiero, Vincent Ryan. *Becoming a Critical Thinker,* Fifth Edition. Boston, MA: Houghton Mifflin, 2006.

Schacter, Daniel L. *Searching for Memory: The Brain, the Mind, and the Past.* New York: HarperCollins, 1997.

Scharf-Hunt, Diana, and Pam Hait. *Studying Smart: Time Management for College Students.* New York: HarperPerennial, 1990.

Schlosser, Eric. *Fast Food Nation.* Boston, MA: Houghton Mifflin, 2001.

Strunk, William, Jr., and E. B. White. *The Elements of Style.* New York: Macmillan, 1979.

Tobias, Sheila. *Succeed with Math: Every Student's Guide to Conquering Math Anxiety.* New York: College Board, 1995.

Toft, Doug, ed. *Master Student Guide to Academic Success.* Boston, MA: Houghton Mifflin, 2005.

Trapani, Gina. *Lifehacker: 88 Tech Tricks to Turbocharge Your Day.* Indianapolis, IN: Wiley, 2007.

Ueland, Brenda. *If You Want to Write: A Book About Art, Independence and Spirit.* St. Paul, MN: Graywolf, 1987.

U.S. Department of Education. *Funding Education Beyond High School: The Guide to Federal Student Aid.* Published yearly. http://studentaid.ed.gov/students/publications/student_guide/index.html

Watkins, Ryan, and Michael Corry. *E-learning Companion: A Student's Guide to Online Success.* Boston, MA: Houghton Mifflin, 2005.

Weil, Andrew. *Health and Healing.* Boston, MA: Houghton Mifflin, 1998.

Weil, Andrew. *Natural Health, Natural Medicine.* Boston, MA: Houghton Mifflin, 2004.

Welch, David. *Decisions, Decisions: The Art of Effective Decision Making.* Amherst, NY: Prometheus, 2002.

Wurman, Saul Richard. *Information Anxiety 2.* Indianapolis, IN: QUE, 2001.

Index

Discover...
Commitment

The Master Student in you

You can use this book to attain mastery—a level of skill that goes well beyond technique. A master student is:

- Intentional—acting from a clearly defined life purpose, set of values, and list of goals.

- Courageous—taking action even in the face of fear.

- Focused—able to work and play with full attention.

- Open-minded—willing to experiment with ideas.

- Centered—calm in the midst of chaos and willing to see problems as opportunities to learn.

- Detached—remembering that we can take effective action in the world even when we do not control the outcomes.

- Contributing—using her presence to make a positive difference in the world.

- Articulate—using the power of his language to reshape his thinking and behavior.

- Responsible—willing to admit that her own thoughts and actions are the main factors in her failures and her successes.

- Thoughtful—testing ideas by looking for sound logic and solid evidence.

Three success essentials

Success is simply the process of setting and achieving goals. And this process includes just three essential steps:

- Discovery—telling the truth about your current thoughts, feelings, behaviors, and circumstances.

- Intention—committing to make specific changes in behavior.

- Action—using consistent behavior changes to produce new results in life.

Discover what you want

Once your goals are precisely defined, your brain begins to reorient your thinking and behavior. Remember that:

- Discovering what you want makes it more likely that you'll achieve it.

- Discovering what you want greatly enhances your odds of succeeding in higher education.

- Every day, you can do one thing—no matter how simple or small—that takes you one step closer to getting what you want.

Qualities of a Master Student

> " A master student is intentional. Her actions flow from a clearly defined life purpose and set of values. She translates these into a flexible list of goals.

Discover...
Your Style

Learning styles essentials

According to psychologist David Kolb, we learn best through four kinds of activity:

- Concrete experience—absorbing information through our five senses.

- Reflective observation—creating ideas that make sense of events.

- Abstract conceptualization—integrating our initial ideas into general models of how the world works.

- Active experimentation—using our models to create new behaviors and achieve new results.

There are other theories of learning styles to keep in mind, as well.

The VAK system focuses on preferences related to:

- Seeing, or *visual* learning

- Hearing, or *auditory* learning

- Movement, or *kinesthetic* learning

Howard Gardner believes that no single measure of intelligence can tell us how smart we are. In his theory of intelligences, Gardner describes:

- Verbal/linguistic intelligence

- Mathematical/logical intelligence

- Visual/spatial intelligence

- Bodily/kinesthetic intelligence

- Musical/rhythmic intelligence

- Intrapersonal intelligence

- Interpersonal intelligence

- Naturalistic intelligence

Make your learning styles work for you

To take yourself through the complete cycle of learning, ask:

- **Why?** to make a personal connection with a subject to be learned.

- **What?** to discover the main points, facts, and procedures related to that subject.

- **How?** to test ideas through action.

- **What if?** to apply ideas in new contexts.

Risk being a fool

We learn by taking appropriate risks. Be willing to appear the fool as you experiment with new learning styles. The rewards can include more creativity, more self-expression, and more joy. Remember that:

- We are all fallible human beings.

- Learning includes making mistakes.

- This is not a suggestion to be foolhardy or to "fool around."

Qualities of a Master Student

"A master student is courageous. He acts intentionally even in the face of fear. He is willing to take appropriate risks for the sake of learning something new.

Discover...
Your Resources

Take back your time

We cannot "manage" time, but we can manage our productivity by:

- **Completing** key tasks immediately, whenever that's appropriate.

- **Delegating** tasks that are better handled by other people.

- **Saying no** to low-priority projects.

- **Using a calendar** to schedule commitments that are tied to a specific date.

- **Writing reminders** about things to do in the future—and reviewing those reminders regularly.

- **Scheduling challenging tasks** for times when our energy peaks.

- **Looking beyond today** to get an overview of our commitments over the coming months.

More resources for success

Master students:

Manage money:

- Keep track of money that's going in and out.

- Increase income

- Decrease spending

- Start saving now

Maintain health:

- Eat for health and pleasure

- Stay active with exercises you enjoy

- Learn your best strategies for managing stress

- Get help for alcohol or drug abuse

- Make the right choices about sex and relationships

Use a variety of services available on your campus and in your community including:

- Career planning offices

- Libraries

- Athletic centers

- Student health clinics

Be here now

You can be more effective at any task when you give it your full attention. Remember to:

- Simply become aware of distractions instead of trying to resist them.

- Enter the present moment by tuning into sights, sounds, and other sensations.

- Keep returning your attention to the task at hand.

Qualities of a Master Student

" A master student can work and play with focused attention.

CHAPTER 3

Discover...
Your Reading

Essentials of effective reading

To get the most from books and other published material:

- **Question** your text by previewing it, outlining it, and listing what you want to discover.

- **Read** with focused attention, make multiple passes through the text, and find answers to your questions.

- **Review** by reflecting on those answers, reciting them, and returning to them at regular intervals in the future.

Taking your reading skills to a higher level

- When reading a difficult text, mark the places where you get confused and look for a pattern in your marks.

- Isolate key words—usually nouns and verbs—and define them.

- Read difficult passages out loud several times.

- Skip to the end of an article or chapter and look for a summary of the key points.

- Stop at least once during each chapter or section to summarize what you understand—and list questions about what you do not understand.

- Pose your questions to an instructor, tutor, or classmate.

- Take a break from reading and come back to the text with a fresh perspective.

- Focus on the sections of the text that directly answer your questions; skim or skip the rest.

- Adjust your reading pace, based on the difficulty of the text.

- Distinguish between texts that instruct by offering solutions to problems (nonfiction) and texts that instruct by narrating an experience (fiction).

- Create a reading plan for each term by estimating the number of hours needed to complete your assignments and scheduling appropriate blocks of time on your calendar.

Ideas are tools

- Notice your immediate response to new ideas.

- Instead of rejecting new ideas, look for their potential value.

- If an idea doesn't work for you today, then be willing to consider it again in the future.

Qualities of a Master Student

"A master student is open-minded and willing to experiment with ideas. When presented with a new concept, he looks first for its potential usefulness.

CHAPTER 4

Discover...
Your Notes

Note taking essentials

- Set the stage for note taking by completing your reading assignments on schedule.

- Arrive early to class and use the spare time to review previous notes.

- Label notebooks with your name, your phone number, the class name, and the date of the notes.

- Leave blank space in your notes so that you can add related information later.

- As you take notes in class, use the Power Process: "Be here now" to release distractions.

- Accurately record ideas even when you disagree with them.

- Focus on a speaker's content rather than appearance or presentation style.

- Place your own comments and questions in a separate section of your notes.

- Reduce a speaker's ideas to key words—essential nouns and verbs that are rich in associations.

- Write crucial points in complete sentences that use the instructor's exact words.

- Look for verbal and nonverbal clues from your instructor about which material is most important.

Create more value from your notes

- In your notes, flag possible test items.

- Experiment with various formats for note taking—the Cornell format, outlines, and concept maps.

- As you review your notes, revise them for clarity.

- "Rehearse" your notes by reciting key points in your own words.

- Create possible test items based on your notes, and practice answering them.

Love your problems

There are three possible responses to any problem:

- Deny it.
- Resist it.
- "Love" it—that is, accept it, admit it, and describe it in detail.

"Loving" a problem is most likely to uncover potential solutions.

Qualities of a Master Student

" A master student sees difficulties as opportunities to develop new skills. She can be centered even in the midst of chaos. She responds to people and circumstances based on how they are right now rather than what they "should" be.

CHAPTER 5

Discover...
Your Grades

Test prep essentials

- Remember that a grade is usually a measure of how you score on a test—not a measure of your intelligence or worth as a human being.

- To begin preparing for tests, create a checklist of the material that you intend to review.

- Create summary notes that integrate material from assignments, class meetings, lab sessions, and handouts.

- Create flash cards based on your notes.

- Create a mock test and "take" it before you take the real test.

- Do three levels of review—a daily review of new material in each course, a weekly review, and a major review before a scheduled test.

- To remember the content of your notes:
  - Relax when you study.
  - Reduce distractions in your study environment.
  - Reduce your notes to key points and supporting material.
  - Restructure material in meaningful ways.
  - Relate new material to things that you already know.
  - Recite key points.
  - Repeat your reviews until you know the material well.

Release test stress

- Prevent test-taking errors by reading test instructions carefully.

- If you get stuck on a question, reread it, come back to it later, and look for possible answers in other test items.

- Accept your feelings of stress about a test.

- Analyze your stress into thoughts and body sensations, and describe both in detail.

- Prepare for a test by eating well and sleeping well.

- Use stress management techniques, such as deep breathing, relaxation exercises, and aerobic exercise.

- If you feel consistently anxious about tests, see a counselor.

Detach

- Put a test into perspective by imagining how important the results will be in a month, a year, or a decade from today.

- Imagine the worst possible outcome of failing a test; it will be something that you can live with.

- Use the practice of mindful awareness to deal with test-related stress.

Qualities of a Master Student

" A master student remembers that his core identity and value as a person do not depend on his possessions, circumstances, or accomplishments. He notices signs of attachment—such as losing his sense of humor, believing that he is always right, and feeling fear—and reminds himself to detach.

CHAPTER 6

Discover...
Your Voice

Writing essentials

- Choose a topic that you can adequately cover in the assigned number of words for a paper—or the assigned length of a presentation.

- Write a thesis statement—a complete sentence that captures the main point you want to make about your topic.

- Choose a purpose for your paper or presentation: do you want to create a change in the way your audience members think, feel, or behave?

- Review and revise your thesis statement as you continue writing.

- Restate your thesis as a question and list related questions.

- Do research to answer your questions.

- Share your questions with librarians and topic experts.

- Write a first draft straight through without stopping to revise.

- Edit your draft for scope, structure, and style.

Essentials for effective presentations

- Organize your ideas for a presentation into three main sections: introduction, body, and conclusion.

- Grab your audience's attention with a compelling fact, quote, or story.

- State the main points early in your presentation.

- Practice your presentation several times—preferably in the place where you will deliver it.

- Deal with nervousness by accepting your feelings and focusing on the content of your presentation rather than your delivery.

Find a bigger problem

- Our responses to problems seem to follow the same law of physics that gases do: They expand to fill whatever space is available.

- To solve little problems in less time and with less energy, take on bigger problems as well.

- The goal of a master student is not to eliminate problems but to take on problems that are big enough to merit our time and energy.

Qualities of a Master Student

" A master student uses her voice to make a difference in the world. She offers her life as a contribution to others. She knows that solutions tend to generate more problems. Rather than trying to get rid of problems, she looks for problems that are worthy of her.

Discover...
Your Relationships

Essentials of effective listening

- During conversation, listen without interrupting—then pause for a few seconds before you begin to talk.

- Display openness through your facial expression and posture.

- Send messages that you are listening, such as "Umhum," "OK," "Yes," and head nods.

- While you listen, notice distracting thoughts and let them go.

- Listen without judging; you can share your own ideas later.

- Listen for the requests and intentions hidden in a complaint.

- Allow people to express emotion as they speak.

- Notice nonverbal messages.

- Keep questions to a minimum and avoid giving advice.

- When people stop speaking, ask: "Is there any more that you want to say?"

- Be willing to change your thinking and behavior as a result of listening.

Use your word to transform your relationships

- When you appreciate someone, say so.

- Speak more in terms of possibilities ("I could....") and promises ("I will....") rather than obligations ("I have to....").

- To prevent an overloaded schedule, say no to requests that are not high priorities for you.

- Use "I" messages to communicate you are upset without blaming other people.

- Before you say that you're upset with someone, see if you're holding a mental picture about how that person is "supposed" to behave; then be willing to release that picture.

- Before you speak, distinguish between your factual observations of another person's behavior and your interpretations of those behaviors.

- Be willing to admit when a problem is too big for you to handle alone, and ask for help.

- When speaking with people from other cultures, look for common ground and relate to them as individuals rather than group representatives.

- Reflect on your own experiences of prejudice—and privilege.

Choose your conversations

- Remember the power of conversations to shape our attitudes and behaviors from moment to moment.

- Focus on conversations that align with your values and intentions.

- When you find yourself in a negative, draining conversation, change the subject—or politely excuse yourself.

Qualities of a Master Student

A master student remembers the power of language, knowing that we can reshape our lives by taking charge of the way that we speak about ourselves and others.

Discover...
Your Future

Discover your skills

When planning your future major and career, take some time to inventory your skills. Find out what you do well and where you could stand to improve. Remember:

- Content skills involve a specialized body of knowledge that is applied in a specific context—for example, the ability to speak a second language, repair fiber-optic cables, or do brain surgery.

- Transferable skills involve knowledge that can be applied in several contexts—for example, listening, speaking, writing, and managing.

Also, remember to:

- Regularly make an inventory of your skills, including both content and transferable skills.

- Consider majors that call for the skills you want to use.

- Make a trial choice of major, and then test that choice through experiences such as internships.

Career planning essentials

Career planning involves continuous exploration. There are dozens of effective paths to take. Begin now with the following ideas.

- Begin career planning now.

- When creating a career plan, begin by ruling out the careers that you do not want.

- See career planning as a choice, rather than a discovery.

- Research the vast range of careers available in today's economy.

- In your career plan, name your preferred skills, your preferred job titles, your job contacts, your preferred employer or clients, and your preferred location.

- Test your choice of a career through internships and other work experiences.

- Revise your career plan frequently.

- To enhance your career prospects in a global economy, complete your education, create a long-term career plan, and develop skills in complex communication and expert thinking.

I create it all

There are two distinct positions in life: being a victim or being responsible.

- When you experience a problem, be willing to see if it results from any of your own beliefs or behaviors.

- Remember that you have choices about how to respond to any situation.

- Applying "I create it all" can prevent you from seeing yourself as a victim.

Qualities of a Master Student

"A master student takes responsibility for his attitudes and behaviors.

Master Student Essentials—
To Go

Your Commitments

- **Consider the possibility** that you can create the life of your dreams.
- **Apply the three essential elements of success**—discovery, intention, action.
- **Commit** to creative and critical thinking.

Your Style

- **You can learn anything** through four activities—concrete experience, reflective observation, abstract conceptualization, and active experimentation.
- **Your preferences** for combining those four activities is unique to you.
- When learning anything, you can expand your preferences by asking: **Why** is this important? **What** are the key ideas? **How** can I apply this? **What if** I could apply this in a new way?

Your Resources

- **Take charge of time** by translating your desires into specific goals and action plans.
- **Take charge of money** by aligning your expenses with your income.
- **Take charge of your health** by making informed choices about eating, exercise, stress management, chemical use, and sex.

Your Reading

- **Question** your text by previewing it, outlining it, and listing what you want to discover.
- **Read** with focused attention, make multiple passes through the text, and find answers to your questions.
- **Review** by reflecting on those answers, reciting them, and returning to them at regular intervals in the future.

Your Notes

- **Set the stage** for taking powerful notes by completing assignments on time, getting to class on time, and bringing essential materials.
- **Show up for class** by participating with full attention.
- **Reduce** ideas to their essence, record them in several formats, and review your notes regularly.

Your Grades

- **Detach** from grades by seeing them as measurements of test performance—not measurements of intelligence or self-worth.
- **Prepare for tests** by doing daily reviews, weekly reviews, and a major review before a scheduled exam.
- **Use stress management** techniques when taking tests.

Your Voice

- **Prepare to write** by defining your topic, writing a thesis statement, and listing questions to answer through research.
- **Write a draft** and revise it for scope, structure, and style.
- **Deliver effective presentations** through planning, practice, and focusing on your content rather than your delivery.

Your Future

- **Inventory your skills,** including content skills and transferable skills.
- **Declare your major** on a trial basis, and then test it through related experiences.
- **Begin career planning now** and revise your plan as you learn more about yourself and the work world.

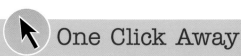

One Click Away

Visit the Website **www.cengage.com/ success/masterstudent/BAMSEssentials** to get access to more strategies for success.

INTRODUCTION: Discover... Commitment

Online version of the Discovery Wheel • Ten qualities of a Master Student • More suggestions for Discovery, Intention, and Action Statements • More information about the value of higher education • More strategies for critical and creative thinking • More sample purpose statements • More personal profiles in the Master Student Hall of Fame • Another look at the cash value of your classes—the "education by the hour" exercise • More ideas about discovering what you want

1 Discover... Your style

More information on Kolb's ideas, the VAK system, and multiple intelligences • Explore your learning styles • Using learning styles to succeed in school • More strategies for creative thinking • More learning styles strategies • More strategies for building effective relationships at work • More suggestions for creative foolhood

2 Discover... Your resources

Online goal setting exercise • Additional ways to become more productive • Discover where your time goes • Five more ways to get past procrastination • More strategies for taking charge of your health • 10 ways to pay for your education • More creative ways to think about money • More resources that can save you time and money • More ways to be here now

3 Discover... Your reading

More strategies for powerful previewing • More strategies for powerful reading • More strategies for powerful reviewing • More ways to think critically about your reading • More ways to master challenging reading material • More ways to finish your reading assignments on time • More strategies for reading across the curriculum • More strategies for avoiding misinformation on the Internet • More ways to experiment with active reading • More ways to see ideas as tools

4 Discover... Your notes

More perspectives on the power of note taking • More ways to set the stage for note taking • More strategies for "showing up" as you take notes • More ways to capture main points and supporting details • More strategies for reducing ideas to their essence • More ways to predict test questions • More formats for note taking • More ways to revise, review, and rehearse your notes • More ways to apply the cycle of

Discovery, Intention, and Action to note taking • More ways to love your problems

5 Discover... Your grades

Integrity in test taking • More strategies for test preparation • More memory strategies • More ways to avoid test-taking errors • More strategies for turning tests into feedback • More stress management strategies • Strategies for succeeding in science courses • Relate learning styles to mastering tests • More ways to detach

6 Discover... Your voice

More strategies for reducing confusion when you communicate • More strategies for preparing to write • More strategies that save research time • More ways to get started on your next writing assignment • More strategies for planning a writing project • More ways to make your writing sparkle • More problem solving strategies • More ways to master public speaking • Ways to apply learning styles to finding your voice • More ways to find a bigger problem

7 Discover... Your relationships

More strategies for succeeding in a diverse world • More strategies for deep listening • More ways to speak toward success • More ways to say no gracefully • More ways to resolve conflict • More ways to deliver an effective "I" message • More ways to benefit from releasing mental pictures • More examples of the differences between observations and interpretations • More strategies for getting help when you need it • More ways to cultivate an "attitude of gratitude" • More leadership strategies • More ways to choose your conversations

8 Discover... Your future

More suggestions about choosing what's next in your life • More information about the nature of skills • More information about identifying skills • More ways to choose your major • More career planning strategies • More suggestions for writing a career plan • More strategies for succeeding in a global economy • Strategies for successful job hunting • Online version of the Discovery Wheel • Creating a master timeline for completing your education • More ways to master self-responsibility

More Master Students
In Action

Casey Kiprakis

College: TriCounty Technical College

Major: Fashion Design

View of Success: The feeling of accomplishment and getting through hardships, and coming out on top for me is my ultimate feeling of success. I hope that while going to school full time, working full time, and paying my way through all by myself that I am always going to be happy and never regret a single moment. Happiness is the key to success.

Advice: Definitely take the time to make a study schedule. College is a huge transition from high school. You really need to buckle down and study for at LEAST three hours a day. Also another good thing to do is set due dates for yourself. Something may be due next week but set a date that it's due that Friday or something so you have the weekend to hang out. HAVE FUN because these are going to be the best years of your life. Make the most of it.

Photo courtesy of Casey Kiprakis.

Timothy Alley

College: American River College

Major: Theology

View of Success: Success is turning failure and lack into a tangible reality that rises up in the character of the individual who has learned that failure is no option. Success is knowing that every failure gives way to triumph.

Advice: Use all of the resources on campus, get to know your instructors and professors, attend every class, accept all new challenges, get a support group, have outside hobbies and passions, believe in yourself.

Photo courtesy of Timothy Alley/American River College

Alex Sithideth

College: Seminole Community College

Major: Pharmacy

View of Success: Achieving success means truly being happy and going beyond your comfort zone to do whatever it takes to achieve your goals…The road to success does not end, success is an attitude you carry with you to tackle all obstacles that may come your way.

Advice: Future college students should not view college as a "task," but rather a learning-filled journey. A journey filled with ups and downs and unlimited things to be learned. Always keep an open mind. Learning doesn't only exist inside the classroom. Students coming into college should not be afraid to challenge themselves. Give all tasks nothing less than 110 percent. You never know how great you truly are until you leave your comfort-zone and strive for the most out of life. Never settle for mediocrity, always strive for excellence, believe in yourself, think your dreams into being; nothing is impossible!

Photo courtesy of Alex Sithideth.